SPORT IN THE
AMERICAN WEST SERIES

Jorge Iber, Series Editor

LATINOS & LATINAS

in American Sport
Stories Beyond Peloteros

Edited by Jorge Iber

TEXAS TECH UNIVERSITY PRESS

Copyright © 2020 by Texas Tech University Press

This book is typeset in Athleas. The paper used in this book meets the minimum requirements of ansi/niso Z39.48-1992 (R1997). ∞

Designed by Hannah Gaskamp

Library of Congress Cataloging-in-Publication Data is on file.
ISBN: 978-1-68283-040-6

Printed in the United States of America
19 20 21 22 23 24 25 26 27 / 9 8 7 6 5 4 3 2 1

Texas Tech University Press
Box 41037
Lubbock, Texas 79409-1037 USA
800.832.4042
ttup@ttu.edu
www.ttupress.org

CONTENTS

CONTENTS

CONCLUSION

LATINOS & LATINAS
in American Sport

INTRODUCTION:

Broadening the Coverage of the History of Latino/a Participation in American Sport

Jorge Iber
Texas Tech University

IN EARLY NOVEMBER 2016, just days prior to the US presidential election pitting Donald J. Trump against Hillary Rodham Clinton for the highest office in the land, reporter Tim Rohan published an absorbing essay in the *Sports Illustrated* segment, "The Monday Morning Quarterback," entitled "Football in the Land of Bridges and Walls."[1] This article focused, in part, on the national debate concerning the US-Mexico border by highlighting the travails and experiences of a youth named Juan, who resides with his family in a poor section of the Mexican city of Matamoros (in Tamaulipas state). Although he lives south of the national divide, the individual in question was born in Brownsville, Texas, and is an American national. Each morning, Juan treks across the boundary to attend Gladys Porter High School in this southernmost Lone Star State community. Due to the 1982 Supreme Court ruling *Plyler v. Doe*, which stipulated that undocumented immigrant pupils had the right to be educated in American public schools, there are many other such individuals in the Brownsville Independent School District (BISD), and elsewhere along the Texas–Mexican perimeter, as of the time of this writing.

What makes Juan different from the majority of his classmates, in addition to his US citizenship, is his connection to one of the most significant of all "Texan" rituals: donning helmet and pads to play offensive line for the blue-and-white-clad Porter Cowboys on Friday nights in the fall. As Rohan notes, this scenario is a not infrequent occurrence in this corner of the state. Indeed, the motivations to participate in the action of the gridiron, for Juan and his cohorts, are as old as the game itself.

So the Porter and Lopez [another Brownsville high school] football teams are made up of mostly poor, Latino, first-generation football players. Some of them play football because they want to fit in. What's more American than Texas high school football...? Or they dream of football leading to a college scholarship and a way out. Or they simply need a distraction from the things going on in their lives.[2]

For Juan, the sport has become not only a way to enter into other facets of school life but also a vehicle to improve his academic performance. In Juan's first year on the team, his offensive-line coach dictated a "no Spanish" rule at practice and during film sessions. When Juan missed an assignment or was chastised for improper technique, teammates translated for the often befuddled youth. Juan made progress and, as his language abilities improved, colleagues called out more and more things for him in English. "After a year of this, Juan started making noticeable progress....His junior year, he became a starter and came out of his shell. He danced at pep rallies, cracked jokes with his teammates, and ribbed [Coach] Fortner whenever he could."[3] To make the story even more captivating, Juan helped his team make the playoffs (with a 6–4 record) for the first time in more than four decades.

Juan's senior year of 2016–2017, however, did not yield a fairy-tale ending, as the Cowboys finished winless and were close to achieving a victory only in their first game, a 14–7 loss to Brownsville Rivera. All subsequent contests resulted in double-digit defeats.[4] Still, the season held some positive occurrences for Rohan's protagonist. Juan got a job at a local fast-food joint in order to help his family in Matamoros. Additionally, his father managed to cross the border and watch him play. As Juan stated, "'With football in my life, I got more — I don't know how to say....I started to be more responsible, to be more disciplined — ah, right! More *disciplined*.'"[5]

On the negative side of the equation, Juan injured his hand and back and was near exhaustion from trying to maintain his grades and his level of play, as well as flipping burgers during the graveyard shift at the restaurant. As the end of his gridiron experiences neared, however, the young man looked forward to bigger and better things. "'I've got to keep moving,' he says. 'I don't want to stay in this corner of the United States....I need to leave from here. I want to make my parents proud of me. I can make it.'"[6]

A more academic perspective of stories such as the one detailed above comes from the recent work of Jorge E. Moraga, a PhD student in the Department of Critical Culture, Gender and Race Studies at Washington State University. In an informative online essay entitled "Remembering Super Bowl 50 through a Mestiz@ Sport Consciousness," Moraga articulates some of the key goals of this anthology — and indeed all efforts, both academic and popular, dedicated to bringing the historical role of sport in Latino/a life to light. First, given that the paradigm for analyzing sport in the United States has for so long focused on a black/white dichotomy, it has been easy to overlook stories of individuals such as Juan (at the local level), and even those of professional athletes and coaches, such as that of Ron Rivera (of both Puerto Rican and Mexican descent), at the highest echelons of sport in the United States. Consequently, as Moraga claims, "because Latino brownness often exists at the margins to these dominant racial reference points, its performativity, affects, and senses become overshadowed."[7]

Second, and even more significant, it is essential not only to seek out such stories but also to properly contextualize them. Moraga argues that the value of examining sport in the historical experience of persons of Spanish-surnamed backgrounds is not merely to praise their accomplishments on the baseball/softball diamond, field, court, gridiron, or elsewhere. Instead, it is to examine the deeper significance of "the browned sporting individual in relation to both family and community. In other words, we must go beyond seeing individual Latina/Latino as Hero, Star, and Superhero" and grasp what such men, women, teams, and *ligas* (leagues) have meant to fellow Spanish-surnamed people as well as to the broader (a way to challenge notions of inferiority?) American society.[8] The stories that follow are geared to move the discussion in that direction.

This volume is a follow-up to a similar 2014 compilation published by Texas Tech University Press. Therein were featured, among others, essays that spotlighted the importance of athletic activities to the lives of Spanish-surnamed peoples in locales as disparate as colonial San Antonio and early twentieth-century New York City (with connections back to Cuba) to life in the mid-century Arizona mining community of Miami and the significance of (mis)naming a professional sports franchise in early twenty-first-century Houston, Texas.[9] While the book was substantial in its coverage, there were some gaps noted by the editor and reviewers. This follow-up volume is an attempt to address some of those lacunae.

The genesis of this anthology comes from an issue of the *Journal of the West* (JOW) that appeared in fall 2015.[10] That project undertook to bring together two threads from previous JOW issues edited by Jorge Iber. One was an overview of the historical role of Latinos in the region; the other was an examination of the significance of sporting endeavors to the society and history of the American West.[11] Among those works was one article that served as the model for the Latinos and sport in the West issue, as well as for this collection: an offering by Maureen M. Smith of California State University, Sacramento on the Juan Marichal statue at AT&T Park, the home of the San Francisco Giants. Although Smith goes into greater detail than can be recounted in this brief introduction, the Giants' efforts not only were aimed at honoring the franchise's storied past through casting an all-time great in bronze but also were meant to serve a more practical purpose as "an effective means of reaching out to an increasing Latino fan population."[12]

As the issue of the JOW demonstrated, however, the intersection and significance of the Spanish-speaking population and sport in the West (and elsewhere) go well beyond an enticement to buy tickets to Major League Baseball games and other professional or collegiate sporting events. Indeed, sports, as this introduction and work argue directly, were and are a major part of the daily historical experience of Latinos/as and have been utilized for decades as effective tools for community organizing, ethnic pride, and as a counter to stereotypes embraced by many in the broader population. Therefore, the goal here is to demonstrate how athletic endeavors can be operationalized as yet another historical (and current-day) tool to be included in the arsenal of ordinary citizens' mechanisms for utilization at the forefront of efforts to improve daily lives amidst difficult circumstances both within, and outside of, barrios throughout the nation.

The Smith essay was an important contribution, as out of a total of fourteen articles in the 2006 and 2008 JOW issues there was but that one mention of how the experiences of Spanish speakers and some aspect of athletics intersected. This dearth provides convincing evidence of how little research had been conducted in regard to this subject matter, particularly when juxtaposed with how much research has appeared on the role of sport in the lives of African Americans, Native Americans, Jews, and other ethnic and racial groups. Fortunately, several scholars have stepped in to begin closing this gaping breach. Among some of the key publications concerned with the subject matter of Latinos/as and sport are the works of Samuel O. Regalado, José M. Alamillo, Ignacio García, and Adrian Burgos.[13]

Professor Regalado can be considered the intellectual "trailblazer" concerning research on the role of baseball among Latinos. Beginning in the late 1980s, in the JOW, Regalado published articles that dealt with the experiences of Latino ballplayers in the then minor league cities of San Diego, Phoenix, and elsewhere in the region. Subsequently, he provided the first examination of how the newly minted Los Angeles Dodgers purposefully pursued the Mexican American fan dollar (after helping chase out co-ethnics from Chavez Ravine to build their permanent home — but that is a story for another day) and hired the now legendary Jaime Jarrín (in 1959) to broadcast home games in Spanish. In addition to these essays, Regalado published various studies in the journal *Nine*; among these were endeavors that detailed the role of local *ligas* in East Los Angeles. As a culmination of these undertakings, the California State-Stanislaus historian generated the first full-length academic tome on Latino ballplayers, *Viva Baseball!: Latin Major Leaguers and Their Special Hunger*, which first appeared in 1988 and is now in its third edition.

José M. Alamillo has brought the role of sports (baseball and beyond) to a more localized level (building on Regalado's model in his East Los Angeles piece) and offered both an article, "Peloteros in Paradise: Mexican American Baseball and Oppositional Politics in Southern California, 1930–1950," which appeared in the *Western Historical Quarterly* in 2003, and his excellent book, *Making Lemonade Out of Lemons: Mexican American Labor and Leisure in a California Town, 1880–1960*, that covered the importance of sports in the lives of Mexican Americans in a California community. Here, Alamillo details how sport served not just a recreational purpose but was actually utilized for labor recruitment, occupational advancement, and the building of ethnic solidarity, among other issues.[14]

Another contributor to this project, Ignacio García, has published a wonderful study, *When Mexicans Could Play Ball: Basketball, Race, and Identity in San Antonio, 1928–1945*, on the role of on-court success to challenging stereotypes and notions of Mexican American inferiority in the state of Texas through the end of World War II. While Coach Nemo Herrera is a key historical actor in that book, the principal focus is on the team, players, and school setting. García's contributions here, however, shine the spotlight directly upon the experiences of this noteworthy teacher and athletic leader who is still, as of 2019, the only coach in the history of Texas to lead two different schools (Lanier in San Antonio and El Paso Bowie) to state titles in two sports (basketball at Lanier and baseball at Bowie).[15]

A final individual who has contributed to the development of the role of sport in the lives of Latinos is this humble editor, who in 2016 published a journal essay and full-length manuscript on the childhood and professional career of former Major League pitcher Mike Torrez: he of the famous/infamous (depending on one's perspective) pitch to Bucky "Bleeping" Dent in the one-game playoff between the New York Yankees and the Boston Red Sox on October 2, 1978. While many fans remember Torrez because of this single offering (similar to the fate that befell former Dodgers pitcher Ralph Branca after his haunting confrontation with Bobby Thomson in 1951), his life and career shed much light on the role of sport in the lives of Mexican Americans living in the barrios of the Midwest (in Torrez's case, Topeka, Kansas). By examining this player's story, it is possible to get a sense of the interconnections between teams (in baseball and other sports) in this region with Texas, California, and even into Mexico itself.

The other items featured in the 2015 volume of the JOW are included to provide coverage regarding various individual sports and local and racial issues tied to athletics. John Mckiernan-González's essay deals with the way US border officials "viewed" Mexicans — in particular, the members of the 1932 Olympic team (distance runners). These individuals were not afforded the same treatment as that of other international competitors, the author argues, because they looked "too working class" and did not resemble the lighter-skinned elites who mostly populated the Mexican nation's foreign service. Similar tensions about national identity are presented in a more current context in Luis Alvarez's essay on the intensity of the Mexican-US soccer (fútbol) rivalry.

Juan David Coronado's essay on the 1962 Hidalgo County (Texas) Colt League team that won that year's World Series shows the powerful impact sport can have on a Mexican American community when "their" boys make the entire city/town proud. If the Spanish-surnamed can "represent" an "entire" hometown, then why are people of this ethnic group not given a fair shake on a daily basis, one might ask. A further discussion of sports' power to build community and challenge assumptions of the broader society is demonstrated in Alberto Rodriguez's essay on baseball along the US-Mexico border in Texas.

The final three original contributions, by Arnoldo De León, Frederick Luis Aldama, and Aldama and Christopher González, shift the focus away from the local level and onto the experiences of Latinos in professional and collegiate sports. How were these individuals perceived by paying customers and fans of minor league baseball, for example? De León notes in his essay the many obstacles Wally Rodríguez overcame in his climb to baseball success, describes what he meant to his community, and details his decision to give up his Major League dreams in order to support his family. Aldama and González discuss how Latinos in the National Football League have been perceived, focusing on players such as Joe Kapp and Jim Plunkett and then shifting their focus to more current professional athletes in a variety of other sports. Finally, Aldama provides an in-depth interview about the key experiences of Hank Olguin, an athlete on the roster of the University of California at Berkeley Golden Bears, in the 1950s.

In addition to the items noted above, this anthology includes five new offerings. Two of these, specifically, are incorporated in order to provide coverage about the role and significance of Latina athletic participation and experiences tied thereto. To accomplish this task, it was necessary to range outside of the explicit parameters established by the Sport in the American West Series (with the subject matter focused on Siler City, North Carolina) for one of the essays. Although it went beyond the planned coverage region, the contribution is of great significance to the overall effort to document the historical record of Latina participation in sport in the US. An essay by Paul Cuadros (of the University of North Carolina, Chapel Hill), originally published in *Southeastern Geographer* in 2011, focuses on the development of female soccer leagues in a poultry-processing community. Cuadros's work examines how such endeavors have helped to reshape, in part, relationships between parents and daughters, husbands and wives, boyfriends and girlfriends, and employers and employees, all through the events taking place on the pitch. As one of the author's subjects noted, "I do feel empowered sometimes....I think you learn to express yourself better. All that I learned from fútbol is it helps me to defend myself at work."

A second chapter on female athletes is delivered by Greg Selber of the University of Texas, Rio Grande Valley (UTRGV), who spotlights the history and importance of basketball to young Spanish-surnamed women (at the high school and collegiate level) in the state of Texas (with the greatest emphasis being on the Rio Grande Valley, the same locale as discussed in Rohan's story at the start of this introduction). In a wide-ranging piece, Selber takes note of how, in the first half of the twentieth century, it was almost unheard of to see a Latina on the basketball court in most Valley schools. "In the heartland of the Valley, reaching from Mission and McAllen in the west to Weslaco, Donna, and Elsa in the Mid-Valley, and on to LaFeria, Harlingen, and areas in the eastern section, most seasons were played with all-Anglo basketball rosters and coaches." In the years after mid-century, as the number of Latinas staying in school and competing in athletics increased (slightly), these young women were still kept off of basketball teams as they were encouraged to play less popular sports (in terms of student and community engagement) such as softball and volleyball. As Selber delineates, the number of Latinas participating in basketball (and other sports) has increased dramatically since the 1980s for a variety of reasons.

A third new contribution is written by Ben Chappell and directs attention to the phenomenon of Mexican American softball tournaments, particularly two events of long standing: one based in Newton, Kansas, the other in Houston, Texas. The histories of these tournaments are in line with some of the issues noted by Alamillo in his 2003 article: the Latino athletes were often not allowed to play against whites, so they established their own teams, leagues, and events. For the final decades of the twentieth century, these clubs and endeavors were of great significance to communities throughout the Midwest and elsewhere, and the action on the diamond was pretty darn exciting as well. More recently, Chappell notes, an interesting trend has taken place among the leadership of such tournaments and has led to a discussion of how to deal both with individuals who are of "mixed" (not exclusively Latino) heritage and with "gringos" who simply wish to participate in top-notch competition. Should these athletes be allowed to participate, or should the tournaments be opened exclusively to Mexican Americans?

The fourth new addition to this work comes from a former graduate student in the Department of History at Texas Tech University named Andrew Harris. Mr. Harris is an aficionado of motor sports, and during class sessions he often regaled this editor with stories of his research concerning the ties between Mexican Americans and motor sports. Given the distinctiveness of the topic, I encouraged Andrew to generate an item for this project. His essay, "Adios, Amigos: Bean Bandits and Other Mexican Americans in the Golden Age of

Drag Racing," is, most likely, the first academic piece focusing on this subject. Not only does Harris's work provide a cursory introduction into the lives and careers of legendary individuals in the sport, such as "Flaming" Frank Pedregon (father of Cruz Pedregon) and others, it also details how participating in the sport often helped develop business opportunities for Spanish-surnamed youths.

The final addition to this manuscript comes from the work of Robert Sirvent of Hope International University. His essay is quite timely, given some of the goings-on (protests) at NFL games (and other sporting events), set off by the controversial conduct of Colin Kaepernick of the San Francisco 49ers. In this chapter, Sirvent details the actions of, and reactions to, a Latino ballplayer, Carlos Delgado (then with the Toronto Blue Jays), and his anti-war stance (against the invasion of Iraq and the use of Vieques Island near Puerto Rico for bombing practice) in 2004. Sirvent compares and contrasts Delgado's activities with those of another anti-war protester athlete: former NBA star Mahmoud Abdul-Rauf (formerly Chris Wayne Jackson).

An interesting way to summarize some of the trends developed in this anthology is to present how the "non-academic" audience is coming to accept/acknowledge the presence of Latinos at all levels of American sport. An item published by ESPN provides important evidence in this regard. An October 2014 piece on the development of the University of Texas–San Antonio football program clearly shows how the Roadrunners, coached until the end of the 2015 season by former University of Miami Head Coach Larry Coker, have directly tied their marketing endeavors to the city's mostly Mexican American population. From donning jerseys bearing the name "Los Roadrunners" (similar to the efforts by the NBA during their Noche Latina program) and broadcasting games in Spanish to purposely recruiting in heavily Latino South Texas, there is a concerted effort to embrace the culture of and give Spanish-surnamed athletes a chance to compete at the highest levels. As Athletic Director Lynn Hickey asserted, "That is who we are, and it is something to be very, very proud of. We're a minority-majority campus. We're very much that way as a city, and we're proud of that."[16]

As readers will note from the discussion above, the story of sport and Spanish speakers in the West (and elsewhere) is not really a new phenomenon but one whose time in the regional and national spotlight is only just coming into focus. This collection seeks to provide yet another conduit toward bringing this important topic to the attention of a broader cross-section of both an academic and a popular audience.

One final addition that has been made to this anthology was suggested by one of the outside reviewers: the inclusion of questions designed to stimulate discussion at the end of each essay. We hope that these queries will encourage dialogue among instructors and students. Sport is an integral part of Latino/a life in the US, and we need to talk about how this aspect of that history intersects with key historical issues such as race, gender, and class.

NOTES

1. Tim Rohan, "Football in the Land of Bridges and Walls," http://mmqb.si.com/mmqb/2016/11/01/high-school-football-brownsville-texas-matamoros-mexico-immigration.

2. Ibid.

3. Ibid.

4. http://www.maxpreps.com/high-schools/porter-cowboys-(browns-ville,tx)/football/schedule.htm

5. Rohan, "Football in the Land of Bridges and Walls."

6. Ibid.

7. Jorge E. Moraga, "Remembering Super Bowl 50 Through a Mestiz@ Sport Consciousness," https://ussporthistory.com/2016/02/22/remembering-super-bowl-50-through-a-mestiz-sport-consciousness/.

8. Ibid.

9. Jorge Iber, ed., *More Than Just Peloteros: Sport and* US *Latino Communities* (Lubbock: Texas Tech University Press, 2014). Specifically, see: Jesús F. de la Teja, "'Buena gana tenía de ir a jugar': The Recreational World of Early San Antonio, Texas, 1718–1845," 15–38; Enver M. Casimir, "A Variable of Unwavering Significance: Latinos, African Americans, and the Racial Identity of Kid Chocolate," 39–65; Christine Marin, "Courting Success and Realizing the American Dream: Arizona's Mighty Miami High School Championship Basketball Team, 1951," 150–83; and Ric Jensen and Jason Sosa, "Major League Soccer Scores an Own Goal in Houston: How Branding a Team Alienated Hispanic and Latino Fans," 256–80.

10. Jorge Iber, issue editor, "Latinos and Sport in the American West," *Journal of the West* 54, no. 4 (Fall 2015).

11. Jorge Iber, issue editor, "Hispanics in the West," *Journal of the West* 45, no. 4 (Fall 2006) and "Sport in American West," *Journal of the West* 47, no. 4 (Fall 2008).

12. The following are recent examples of such work by academics: Jorge Iber, *Mike Torrez: A Baseball Biography* (Jefferson, NC: McFarland and Company, 2016); Jorge Iber and Samuel O. Regalado, eds., *Mexican Americans and Sports: A Reader on Athletics and Barrio Life* (College Station: Texas A&M University Press, 2007); and Jorge Iber, Samuel O. Regalado, José M. Alamillo and Arnoldo De León, *Latinos in U.S. Sport: A History of Isolation, Cultural Identity and Acceptance* (Champaign, IL: Human Kinetics, 2011). See also: Maureen M. Smith, "Willie Mays Plaza, McCovey Point, and the Dominican Dandy in Bronze: (De)Constructing History at the AT&T Park in San Francisco," *Journal of the West* 47, no. 4 (Fall 2008): 60–69, quote on page 67.

13. José M. Alamillo, "American Latino Theme Study: Sports," https://www.nps.gov/heritageinitiatives/latino/latinothemestudy/sports.htm; Samuel O. Regalado, *Viva Baseball: Latin Major Leaguers and Their Special Hunger* (Champaign: University of Illinois Press, 2008); Adrian Burgos, *Playing America's Game: Baseball, Latinos and the Color Line* (Berkeley: University of California Press, 2007) and *Cuban Star: How One Negro-League Owner Changed the Face of Baseball* (New York City: Hill and Wang, 2011).

14. José M. Alamillo, "Peloteros in Paradise: Mexican American Baseball and Oppositional Politics in Southern California, 1930–1950," *Western Historical Quarterly* 34, no. 2 (Summer 2003): 191–211. See also: *Making Lemonade out of Lemons: Mexican American Labor and Leisure in a California Town, 1880–1960* (Champaign: University of Illinois Press, 2006).

15. Ignacio M. García, *When Mexicans Could Play Ball: Basketball, Race, and Identity in San Antonio, 1928–1945* (Austin: University of Texas Press, 2014).

16. Sam Khan Jr., "UTSA Builds Program, New Fan Base," October 15, 2014, http://www.espn.com/college-football/story/_/page/onenation-ncf101514/utsa-roadrunners-market-team-become-team-south-texas.

EVERYDAY DISTURBANCES:

Mexican "Indian Marathoners," the Los Angeles Olympics, and the El Paso Medical Border, 1932

John Mckiernan-González
Texas State University

ON FRIDAY NIGHT, JULY 21, 1932, members of the Mexican Olympic team navigated through the El Paso, Texas, Customs' procedures on their way to Los Angeles. As U.S. Customs officers interviewed Juan Morales and the other members of the track team on the train, the team's representative requested that they be recognized as official emissaries of the Mexican state and be allowed to pass freely. The officer did not acknowledge the claims of the trainer that the athletes in the train were representatives of the Mexican Olympic team.[1] Instead, the Customs officer recommended that the whole team pass through the United States Public Health Service (USPHS) medical office by the bridge and undergo medical inspections as would other Mexican sojourners to the United States.[2]

That night, Dr. Richard Allen vaccinated the members of the team, for whom he determined to be lacking satisfactory evidence of vaccination. He was comparing the athletes' appearance to that of the Mexican emissaries he met in the United States. Since Mexican consular officers tended to be younger and more credentialed members of the post-revolutionary Mexican elite, the group of athletes did not resemble his image of a Mexican diplomatic representative.[3] Dr. Allen resolved the ambiguity between the athletes' protected diplomatic status and their similarity to other working-class Mexican sojourners by vaccinating the sojourners in his office. The USPHS act revealed an ongoing inconsistency in the practice of vaccination on the Mexican border.

The team's trainer went to the Mexican Consulate in El Paso and reported that the United States Public Health Service employee refused to recognize the athletes' status as diplomatic representatives. The trainer reported that despite the documentation provided, the USPHS officer claimed medical authority over the Mexican athletes' bodies. Given that the team needed to cross into El Paso to get to Los Angeles, the consul encouraged the team members to accept the vaccinations and proceed to Los Angeles.[4]

At one level, this disjuncture between high diplomatic status and demeaning treatment is easy to explain. The US public health officer treated these world-class athletes — among them Juan Morales and Margarito Pomposo — like they treated working-class Mexicans. This conflict between diplomatic law and domestic medical law authority emerged because Dr. Allen refused to treat Olympic athletes possessing "Indian" phenotypic features with the official Mexican diplomatic status they earned on the track in Mexico. The appearance and local resolution of this tension exposed a racial logic in the working relationship between Mexican consular officials and United States Department of the Treasury employees. US officials learned to associate Mexican diplomatic status in the United States with a more Spanish and elite look.[5] The "Indio" look of these members of the Mexican Olympic track and field team exposed the informal association United States Customs officers made between "looking Spanish" and having protected diplomatic status.[6]

Dr. Richard Allen judged the team from his experience with the younger Mexican elite that usually comprised the Mexican consular class in the United States. The presence of six working-class Mexicans who claimed to be internationally respected athletes and therefore diplomatic emissaries of the Mexican state must have taken Dr. Allen aback. Members of the Mexican press shared this discomfort with indigenous bodies with Dr. Allen, headlining their coverage of the

Olympics and of long-distance-running events with the paternalistic term "Nuestros Indigenas."[7] This small incident, an everyday disturbance, revealed an unresolved ambiguity in the medical recognition of diplomatic authority in the practice of medical inspection.

The problem is that this facile explanation cuts off further inquiry into why the connection between American vaccination and border-crossing Mexican bodies could even constitute a source of diplomatic tension. The presence of "Indians" as Mexican diplomatic emissaries uncovered the exclusions in the compromise "on the ground" forged between the Mexican foreign office and the USPHS after 1920 and made them less tenable in 1932. That is, US and Mexican officials recognized — and then potentially denied — working-class Mexican indigenous claims on the Mexican nation.

This essay will use the journey to and from the Los Angeles marathon in 1932 to explore the labor that went into binding Indians into representatives of the *cosmic race* as Mexico sought a place on the international playing field.[8] The awkwardness that emerged underscores, in Renato Rosaldo's understanding, the importance of "the mundane disturbances that so often erupt during border crossings."[9] In this journey, the El Paso crossing disrupted a conventionally posited separation between Mexican- and US-based race and class hierarchies.[10] The "Indian" movement to the playing fields of Los Angeles brought Mexican racial common sense into an international focus, with awkward results.

This 1932 incident also matters to the history of medicine in the United States. The public outcry over the consequence of forced vaccination was part of a series of diplomatic conflicts sparked by forcible American vaccination practices and challenged by ethnic Mexicans on both sides of the Rio Grande. The relatively early and frequently extensive presence of the United States Marine Hospital Service (USMHS) and then the USPHS in municipal affairs on the border meant that Mexican citizens and nationals, after 1880, engaged federal medical authority on an everyday basis.[11] American medical attitudes toward Mexicans shaped federal policies toward Mexican residents, Mexican Americans, and Mexican migrants in the United States.[12]

The State Department created a special subject file for "complaints against quarantine." The claims filed across the US-Mexico border demonstrate the well-traveled connections Mexican and American immigrants made between citizenship and health care.[13] These diplomatic records highlight three significant themes in the legal culture of public health on the Mexican border. First, claimants demanded recognition of their individual rights due to their participation in a shared understanding of democratic and scientific progress (i.e., *I know what vaccination is; look at my vaccination scars*). Second, the claims placed great faith in expatriate nationality for the advocacy of common-law privileges in a foreign land (*I know my rights*). Third, they highlighted their membership in a larger community that shared their experience of legal abjection, previous vaccination, a shared modernity, and nationalist sentiment (*You don't like Mexicans, verdad?*)[14]

When ethnic Mexicans stepped into the medical gaze in the Customs office, they also confronted an American tension between common law and constitutional law. In *Jacobson v. Massachusetts*, the Supreme Court changed the legal reception for due process challenges to public health measures. If an adult endangered the wider community by refusing to allow his or her child to be vaccinated to attend public school, the legal advocates for the state of Massachusetts argued, a municipal authority had the obligation to fine, jail, or adopt other means to compel the adult to consent to the vaccination procedure. In *Jacobson*, the Court agreed that the state had a moral obligation to value collective safety over individual liberty, which, "[it] was the duty of the constituted authorities primarily to keep in view the welfare, comfort and safety of the many, and not permit the interests of the many to be subordinated to the wishes of convenience of the few. [The] rights of the individual in respect of his liberty may...under the pressure of great dangers, be subjected to such restraint...as the safety of the general public may demand."[15] The decision rested, as well, on the detentions written in the 1893 Immigration Act to justify a compelling state interest in collective safety over individual liberty.[16]

This constitutional principle had to wrestle with individual protections that were part of American common law. The various consular demands for the recognition of individual autonomy filed with the State Department asked that local courts recognize common-law principles that highlighted the importance of individual autonomy. Judge Benjamin Cardozo articulated this principle in the decision *Schloendorff v. Society of New York Hospital* when he stated, "Every human being of adult years and sound mind has a right to determine what shall be done with his body....[And] a surgeon who performs an operation without his patient's consent commits an assault."[17] In these cases, ethnic Mexicans used consular channels to oblige USPHS officers to recognize their consent to inspection and vaccination. The requests were frequently refused, but the presence of the claims speaks to the participation of most border residents in a shared legal culture.

The places on the Mexican border where United States federal vaccination practices met the most formal resistance adjoined the regions with the highest levels of vaccination coverage in Mexico. Mapping the complaints over the historical geography of Mexican revolutionary factions reveals something important about popular Mexican dissent with USPHS inspections. In the places where Pancho Villa's *División del Norte* was present or in control, people protested violently — like the three-day typhus bath riot in Ciudad Juarez — against public health measures.[18] In other places where either Venustiano Carranza or Álvaro Obregón took control, consular officials advocated against the intrusive nature and racist attitudes of the US medical border in the Rio Grande Valley. That is, people forced relatively conservative political authorities to challenge USPHS vaccination practices.

The people who filed the complaints knew vaccination, appreciated vaccination, and even embraced vaccination as a technology to prevent disease. They used their vaccination scars as clear evidence of their commitment to modern medicine. When federal health officers refused to recognize their vaccination scars, and especially when the USPHS adopted unreliable medical technology, these plaintiffs used recently arrived *Carrancista* consuls to challenge this insulting and demeaning practice. The tradition these Mexican nationals and Mexican Americans claimed was a commitment to modernity. The conflict over vaccination in the eastern railroad corridor on the Mexican border was between representatives of modern Mexico and the modern United States. The wide commitment to a Mexican version of modernity, in this case vaccination, led to a critique of American vaccination practices and an embrace of official diplomatic channels. As consuls moved to test cases that adequately challenged the "anti-Mexican feelings" among USPHS officers, they moved cases with border residents that reflected a pragmatic embrace of modernity.[19]

After 1923, Mexican consuls stopped using prior vaccination or obvious respectability to challenge American vaccination and inspection practices. Furthermore, the presence of forcible vaccination in USPHS border offices provided the working precedent to establish compulsory vaccination in municipalities across the state of Texas.[20] Justice Oliver Wendell Holmes Jr. used a perceived unanimity between state legislatures and the medical establishment to expand the legal authority provided to medical practitioners in public institutions.[21]

As he stated in *Buck v. Bell*, "The principle that sustains compulsory vaccination is broad enough to cover cutting the Fallopian tubes."[22] This decision justified involuntary sterilization of people without legal authority in the name of collective health. With this decision, the US Supreme Court undermined a large amount of the procedural autonomy of individual patients built into common-law practices.[23] Domestically, thus, Dr. Allen was well within recently established US constitutional doctrine when he vaccinated members of the Mexican Olympic team against their will — although they were probably the healthiest and fittest people in Mexico.

Vaccination was a constitutional right and a public requirement in Mexico. The Mexican Government adopted compulsory vaccination and a universal vaccination mandate in the 1917 constitution.[24] Federal institutions like the army initiated the practice of compulsory vaccination, a policy that branched out into cities and slowly made its way out to more rural areas.[25] This constitutional promise justified broad vaccination campaigns in urban areas and the army. Colonel Raymundo Izcoa, a member of the Mexican Olympic fencing team, was an officer in the Mexican army. Both the Obregón and Calles regimes had invested in the expansion of vaccine production in Mexico. As a consequence, it was very likely that these athletes had already been vaccinated in Mexico.

It did not matter whether Margarito Pomposo and Juan Morales had been vaccinated, however; their status as official diplomatic representatives of Mexico rendered their previous vaccination status irrelevant. International law gave them immunity from inspection and vaccination. Moreover, the US Congress passed bills to prevent Olympic athletes from being treated medically against their will upon entry into the United States. Both branches of Congress, in 1931, passed resolutions granting all Olympic athletes visiting the United States the same position as diplomatic representatives. They would be granted uninterrupted entry upon the display of official certificates. For the period of approximately forty-five days, Olympic athletes had the same status as consuls.[26]

With the diplomatic regalia and the Congressional sanction, the USPHS officer should have let the six long-distance runners on the Mexican track team pass through. The pertinent questions to ask, then, are: 1) Why did the USPHS officer object to their unfettered passage and 2) Why did Mexican consular representatives fail to follow up on their unofficial complaint?

I think the answers to both questions lies in the character of the knot that tied Mexican officials to the sporting labor the "Indian" athletes performed for the Mexican state. The runners were "Indians" and temporary diplomats. Dr. Allen and other USPHS officers probably learned the distinction in respectability that Mexican officials demanded between *gente de razón* (literally, "rational beings"; generally used to draw a contrast with women, native people, and enslaved people) and other allegedly more "Indian" compatriots.[27] The presence of urban Indians on the Olympic team troubled this sense of respectability. The popular upheavals of the Mexican Revolution shook the foundations of this racial order.

The *gente de razón*/Indio distinction broke down in Mexico City when some coaches transferred the distinction among day laborers who claimed Indios were faster and more resistant *jornaleros* and argued that this characteristic made Indios better suited to another sphere of performance: middle- and long-distance track events. Juan Morales and Margarito Pomposo "*Corren como el viento y tienen resistencia legendaria*" (ran like the wind and had legendary endurance).[28] Therefore, their performance in the marathon would demonstrate a deep Mexican capacity for long stretches of hard labor: "*La fuerza y resistencia para las carreras largas caracteristica de la raza Mexicana se pondra a prueba mañana en la maratón*" (the strength and endurance required for long distance races characteristic of the Mexican people will be proven tomorrow in the marathon).[29]

After the marathon, the Mexico City daily newspaper *Excélsior* led with the following line, "*El Indio Mexicano iba a la cabeza en las primeras etapas pero poco a poco perdio terreno*" (the Mexican Indian led in the first stages, but bit by bit lost terrain).[30] In its editorial, "*El desastre de las olimpiadas*" (the Olympic disaster), the paper emphasized the difference between Mexican athletes and those who allegedly received more rigorous training in other countries. First, "*Hasta los famosos indios, que corren como el viento y resisten largas jornadas, perdieron la carrera de la maratón*" (even our famous Indians, who run like the wind and are notorious for their ability to withstand long workdays, performed dismally in the marathon).[31] The editorial argued that despite this "Indian" affinity for arduous labor, the team could not surpass athletes trained from their childhood, with the advantage of accumulated years of expert coaching and special athletic diets.[32] Lamberto Alvarez Gayou made this assumption explicit in his review of the 10K and the marathon: "*Siendo México uno de los países más resistentes físicamente por contar con un ochenta por ciento de población india, su participación en esta clase de pruebas debería haber sido mucho más efectiva como lo demuestra la actuación de los aborígenes Juan Morales y Margarito Pomposo"* (given that Mexico has one of the highest capacities for endurance because 80 percent of the population is indigenous, the team should have been much more effective in distance events, as Juan Morales and Margarito Pomposo demonstrate).[33]

The Mexican coaches and USPHS officers probably shared a distinction between respectability and racialized manual labor, a distinction officers made every day when they selected who crossed the border without impediment and who underwent the de-lousing baths and the vaccination inspection. However, the context that maintained a shared notion of respectability broke down when "skilled and hardworking Indio" meant Olympic athlete and therefore diplomatic representative. The question of diplomatic immunity and Olympic representation prompted Henry Stimson's informal query into the situation in El Paso: "I should appreciate receiving a report as the number, if any, of these athletes were vaccinated or inoculated and for what diseases, in order that if there were none a denial of the above mentioned report may be made to Mexican authorities."[34] Stimson wanted to respond to the unrest in Mexico City around vaccination practices and Mexican failure in the Olympics.[35]

For Dr. Allen, the dissonance between an *Indian* appearance and the law became a situation where Mexican laborers were trying to avoid medical inspection. Thus, inspection and forced vaccination prevented deception. As mentioned in a US Treasury report: "During the month of July there entered at the port of El Paso three parties on different days totaling 75 persons credited to the Mexican Olympic contingent, of whom not all were athletes, some apparently being attendants of non-athletic members; that approximately 20 percent of the number were required to be vaccinated against smallpox only, due to their not having been successfully vaccinated against this disease within one year prior to entry."[36]

The team registered a complaint, but given their time and cost restrictions they took the vaccination and reported this to the consul.[37] In response, the consul confronted Dr. Allen. In the give and take of the conversation, Dr. Allen guaranteed that the revaccination would have no effect on the athletes' performance two weeks thereafter. The Mexican consul reported to the team and the Mexican press in El Paso that they would not file a complaint about the forced revaccination with the State Department or the International Olympic Committee.

The significance of this vaccination and this encounter shifted after the relative failure of the Mexican team in the distance events. As *El Gráfico Universal* reported, Dr. Allen's insistence that every person on the national team who had no acceptable proof of a successful vaccination had to submit to a vaccination or be barred from entry left a disagreeable impression. According to the editorial writer, "The above-mentioned procedure caused much feeling about the treatment — considered almost barbarous by the interested parties — employed by American health authorities, for they inoculated the majority of them against smallpox, tuberculosis, malaria, etc., the reactions to which brought on sickness and not a few ran high fevers for several days."[38]

The press transformed the tangled three-tiered relationship among consul, medical officer, and national athlete into a mutiny. The report never indicated a leader or a commanding party: "The protest made by the Mexicans on account of this procedure became actual mutiny, due to the unusually rigorous measures used against the athletes, as though it were intentionally sought to disable them by breaking down their physical powers."[39] As viewed by the *Universal* report, Margarito Pomposo and Juan Morales experienced weakness and dehydration because the USPHS vaccinated them against smallpox, malaria, tuberculosis, and cholera. To seek other relative causes ignored the lengths to which the United States would go to stay ahead, even in the Olympic Games.[40]

Excélsior's reporter, Don Gaspar, reported the medical indiscretion as part of the carnival of mistakes, calamities, and disasters that accompanied the Olympic caravan. In the *Excélsior* piece, the experience was framed around the aura of difference that accompanied the presence of Indios on the Mexican national team. Were there any effects? The two marathon runners reported that they felt weak and overheated in the marathon. The writers in *Excélsior* accounted for this problem in cultural and physiological terms: The runners weren't trained well, their legs were too short, and they trained for the shorter Mexican marathon.[41]

Observers at the time emphasized the relative backwardness of Mexican coaching. Lamberto Alvarez Gayou, the official observer from the Secretaría de Educación Pública, emphasized the unconventional coaching received by both Juan Morales and Margarito Pomposo. Juan Morales started slowly, basing himself on his track experience in

Mexico. Once he realized that his competitors would not slow down, "*decidió poner en juego sus mejores energías*" (he put everything in play), and passed a number of competitors but only arrived "*con un esfuer-zo sobrehumano*" (a superhuman effort), in eighth place. In contrast, Margarito Pomposo kept pace with Juan Carlos Zabala, even leading at the 18-mile mark.[42] Still, Pomposo arrived in last place, ahead of the others who collapsed trying to keep pace with Zabala and who did not finish the race.

Alvarez Gayou joked that Morales's and Pomposo's strategic instructions were switched somewhere in the journey. More crucially, he placed responsibility for the fate of the Mexican team on the global isolation of Mexican athletics: "*Me di cuenta de que en rama de pista y campo aún siguen en boga los mismos métodos de entrenamiento que se practicaban en la capital de México en este siglo. El entrenamiento de los Mexicanos en esta rama deportiva está en completo desacuerdo con los más elementales cánones modernos de este clase de actividades*" (the Mexican Olympic team still uses training techniques that were popular in Mexico City at the turn of the century. The training of the Mexicans is in complete disagreement with the current modern training canon for this class of activities).[43] Given his emphasis on institutional reform, Alvarez Gayou did not use "racial condition" or vaccination as the cause of the Mexican athletes' performance in Los Angeles.

Where did the medical inspection and vaccination in El Paso stand in the athletes' presentation of their experience as team representatives in the 1932 Los Angeles Olympics? In the press conference on their return to Mexico City, the long-distance runners summarized the hospitality offered by the United States in the following fashion: "*La comida buena, el trato bueno. El cruce de la frontera, con ciertas dificultades, pues los inyectaron antes.*" (The food was good; we were treated well. The border crossing presented some difficulties since they were injected before [entering the United States]).[44] The border crossing became a noteworthy aspect of the athletes' journey to the international stage of the Olympics.

The journey of the Mexican track and field team offered the best-case scenario for an inspection process by USPHS that would respect the legal autonomy of Mexican citizens arriving to El Paso from the interior of Mexico. That is, it demonstrated that fear of "Mexicans as a medical menace" trumped the internationally certified good health of Olympic athletes. Despite the Department of the Treasury circulars and the publicity associated with the Los Angeles Olympics, the medical officer in charge failed to recognize the Olympic credentials. He treated team members as if they were any other group of Mexican laborers from the interior crossing the border into the United States. This story illustrates the heavy weight of the visual inspection over the procedural requirements of diplomatic recognition. The medical officer in charge fell into the habit of vaccinating Mexican citizens who looked like *mestizo* laborers.

The appearance of these events in the historical record is fortuitous. The protected diplomatic status of the Mexican track and field team made the informal association of *mestizo* (i.e., Mexican) laborer and vaccination evident. The strong connection Don Gaspar and the editorial board of the *Excélsior* made between day laborer (*jornalero*) and "Indian" ethnicity highlighted the runners' place in the Mexican ethno-racial order. They never named the specific ethnicity of Margarito Pomposo and Juan Morales in the *Excélsior*. The social ambivalence that Mexico City chroniclers felt about the fact that "Indios" represented the Mexican nation in Los Angeles was highlighted in their continued association of these athletes with Indios and their special ability to endure the hardships of day labor (*las jornadas*). The position of Margarito Pomposo and Juan Morales as diplomatic representatives of Mexico became a clear case when "matter was out of place."[45] Their positions far above their expected social location highlighted the profile that triggered their collapse into the position of those the USPHS considered to be customary incoming arrivals from Mexico — laborers. Their position as Indios in Mexico City, working-class Mexicans on the border, and Mexican athletes in Los Angeles highlights fissures within regional ethno-racial orders.

Placing these modern interactions in the field of organized national leisure brings us to an obvious conclusion: interaction does not always imply proximity. Rather, the effort Pomposo and Morales applied to their position as athletes highlighted openings and closures within and across regional racial systems. For dissenters from shoemaker Homer Plessy to boxer Jack Johnson, railroads provided a key place to implement, enforce, and challenge Jim Crow racial orders in the United States.[46] This is clear for this period, for Pomposo and Morales rode the rails north, and *repatriados* took the same rail journey south to Mexico from Los Angeles.[47] This journey against racial currents in the United States enhanced the way Mexican runners represented "matter out of place" in urban Los Angeles.[48]

Perhaps Margarito Pomposo thought he earned his change in status as a diplomatic representative through his sporting labor; on the border, the perception of his status as a Mexican Indio overwhelmed his status as a temporary diplomat and placed him under the coercive regime of USPHS policy reserved for Mexican laborers. His arrival and performance in Los Angeles confirmed his status as an athletic representative of Mexico. The coverage of his team's return to Mexico highlighted his position as Olympic athlete and Indio in Mexico. Dr. Allen's decision made it clear that Jim Crow, West Texas style, had the power to shape Mexican experiences outside of Texas. The marathon journey Pomposo and Morales completed in 1932 challenged Jim Crow and the *mestizo* racial order. These runners exposed the politically awkward separation of "indianness" from reliability and respectability in Mexico and the United States.

This international playing field continually creates uncomfortable national dramas for audiences on both sides of the line separating Mexico from the United States. Soccer is another sporting realm that exposes inequalities on both sides of this border. For Mexican audiences, it was problematic that half of the Mexican women's national team were trained and educated in the United States.[49] For US athletes, the relatively weak commitment of United States fans relative to that of fans of the Mexican national team in Los Angeles prompted the famously awkward comment by Alexi Lalas, "I'm all for roots and understanding where you come from and having a respect for your homeland, but tomorrow morning all of those people are going to get up and work in the United States and live in the United States and have all the benefits of living in the United States."[50]

To retain its home-team advantage, the United States plays most of its games against Mexico in places far from regions with large numbers of ethnic Mexican residents. Finding non-Mexican places in the United States gets harder each year.[51] Moreover, President W. Bush's casual dismissal of President Vicente Fox's invitation to watch, in El Paso, the United States-Mexico game in the 2002 World Cup illustrates both the relative power and the divergent investments in international soccer by these two different countries. The Mexican loss in the subsequent game exposed the diverging investment in national sporting spectacles that shaped the "horizontal brotherhood" of Mexican fans in the US and Mexico and marked the boundaries of a nation's imagined community. Sadness and dismay spread across borders.

On August 7, 2012, Leo Manzano medaled for the United States in the 1500 meters. This silver marked the first time in forty-four years (since the Mexico City Olympics in 1968) that the United States placed in this event.[52] Much of the discussion revolved around his mechanical talents. Manzano consistently recalled, "They said I have the engine of a Ferrari in the body of a Pinto."[53] Manzano had once been an undocumented US immigrant but was amnestied and naturalized under the Simpson-Mazzoli Act; his decision to carry both the Mexican and United States flags after winning his silver medal scandalized columnist Ruben Navarrette. The ensuing debate and accompanying stigma again raised awkward questions about the return on the labor working-class Mexican migrants provide the United States and Mexico.[54] As Manzano put it, "I know the opportunities in Mexico are very scarce." But, "at the same time, when I was running, I mean I wanted to include people. I definitely didn't want to exclude anybody. I mean I'm very tied down to my roots. My roots are still in Mexico. The US is my home."[55] He faced difficulties landing sponsorships and achieving the adulation most medaling athletes receive. As he put it, "For me it's been a little bit frustrating because they judge the book by its cover."[56]

Given the recent political debate over the impact of migration to the United States, it is evident that a significant community of people in the US still find it difficult to believe that rural Mexicans have represented and will continue to represent the United States here and abroad.

QUESTIONS:

1. Why do people tend to use sports as a symbol for the country? What happens when athletes are then treated differently from others? Why are we surprised when this happens?

2. For many people on the margins of society, sports is one of the few arenas in which people consider that they have a fair chance. Do you think Margarito Pomposo and Juan Morales had a fair chance when they crossed into the United States and competed in their races?

3. Was the 1932 incident at the US-Mexico border a case in point? What about the track and field events at the Los Angeles Olympics?

NOTES

1. "Frijoles para los Indigenas," *Excélsior* 22 (July 1932): 4.

2. Alexandra Mina Stern, "Buildings, Boundaries, and Blood: Medicalization and Nation-Building on the U.S. Mexico Border, 1910–1930," *Hispanic American Historical Review* 79:1 (February 1999): 41–81.

3. Gilbert González emphasizes the class background of Mexican consuls in *Mexican Consuls and Labor Organizing: Imperial Politics in the American Southwest* (Austin: University of Texas Press, 1999), 10–13.

4. Mexican Embassy, "Complaints regarding inoculation of Mexican Olympic team in El Paso, 1932," Records of the State Department. Record Group 59. Decimal Subject Files, entry 158.1208 NARA II, Hyattsville, Maryland.

5. González, *Mexican Consuls and Labor Organizing*, 10–13.

6. "Nuestros Indigenas," *Excélsior* 22 (July 1932): 4.

7. Ibid.

8. Benedict Anderson, *Imagined Communities: Reflections on the Origin and Spread of Nationalism* (New York: Verso, 1982).

9. Renato Rosaldo, *Culture and Truth: The Remaking of Social Analysis* (Boston: Beacon Press, 1989), 28–29.

10. Ibid.

11. John Mckiernan-González, *Fevered Measures: Race and Public Health at the Texas–Mexico Border, 1848–1942* (Durham, NC: Duke University Press, 2012).

12. Natalia Molina, "Fear and Loathing in the U.S.-Mexico Borderlands: The History of Mexicans as Medical Menaces, 1848 to the Present," *Aztlán* 41:2 (Fall 2016): 87–116.

13. Mckiernan-González, *Fevered Measures*, 198–235.

14. The Mexican foreign office registered the largest number of complaints by de facto and official state authorities against compulsory vaccination between 1910 and 1940. See the file Records of the State Department. Record Group 59. Decimal Subject Files, "Complaints against quarantine." Entry 158.1208, NARA II, Hyattsville, Maryland.

15. Henning Jacobson v. the Commonwealth of Massachusetts, 197 U.S. 11 (1905).

16. Michael Willrich, *Pox: An American History* (NY: Penguin, 2012), 286–318.

17. This decision did not mandate vaccination or any other medical procedure over individual consent. Martin S. Pernick, "Eugenics and Public Health in American History," *American Journal of Public Health* 87:11 (1997): 1770.

18. Mckiernan-González, *Fevered Measures*, 78–122, 165–235.

19. Ibid., 198–235.

20. Texas State Medical Association, "El Paso Solves the Vaccination Question," *Texas State Journal of Medicine* 19:2 (1923): 318.

21. William J. Novak, *The People's Welfare: Law and Regulation in Nineteenth-Century America* (Chapel Hill: University of North Carolina Press, 1996) and Morton Keller, *Regulating a New Society: Public Policy and Social Change in America, 1900–1933* (Cambridge, MA: Harvard University Press, 1994).

22. See Susan E. Lederer, *Subjected to Science: Human Experimentation in America before the Second World War* (Baltimore: Johns Hopkins University Press, 1995), 1616. For patient consent in nineteenth- and twentieth-century medical theory and practice, see Martin S. Pernick, "The Patient's Role in Medical Decisionmaking: A Social History of Informed Consent in Medical Therapy," in Morris Abram, ed., *Making Health Care Decisions: The Ethical and Legal Obligations of Informed Consent in the Patient-Practitioner Relationship, Volume Three: Appendices, Studies on the Foundation of Informed Consent* (Washington, DC: Government Printing Office, 1982), 1–31. See also Jay Katz, *Experimentation with Human Beings* (New York: Russell Sage Foundation, 1972), 526–29.

23. Michael Hillrich, *Pox: An American History* (New York: Penguin Random House, 2012).

24. Mckiernan-González, *Fevered Measures*, 198–235.

25. Ibid. See also Miguel E. Bustamante, "Vegisimoquinto aniversario de la erradicación de la viruela en México," *Gaceta Médica de México* 113:12 (December 1977): 556.

26. "In view of the international character and purposes of these games, the privilege of free entry and usual customs courtesies and facilities accorded distinguished foreign visitors will be accorded to the entire personnel of delegations duly accredited by the Olympic games committee of foreign nations participating in either or both of above mentioned series of games." Bureau letter no. 91004, dated August 3, 1931, addressed to the collector of customs, New York, NY. By Acting Secretary of the Treasury Seymour Lowman, to the extension of free entry privilege to foreign participants in Olympic Games, has been received through the office of the Deputy Commissioner, Divisions of Customs Agents. Treasury Department, Washington, D.C. Los Angeles Olympic Committee, *The games of the Xth Olympiade, Los Angeles, 1932; official report* (Los Angeles: The Xth Olympiade Committee of the Games of Los Angeles, USA), 225.

27. Ramón Gutiérrez, *When Jesus Came, The Corn Mothers Went Away: Marriage, Sexuality and Power in New Mexico, 1500–1846* (Stanford:

Stanford University Press, 1992), 143–298. See also: Ana Maria Alonso, *A Thread of Blood: Colonialism, Gender and Revolution on Chihuahua's Northern Frontier, 1800–1920,* 115–231; Ramón Gutiérrez, "Hispanic Identities in the Southwestern United States," *Race and Classification in Mexican America,* Ilona Katzew, ed. (Stanford: Stanford University Press, 2009).

28. "Los Mexicanos en la carrera de maratón," *Excélsior* 7 (August 1932): 4.

29. Ibid.

30. "Zabala dio triunfo en la Maratón," *Excélsior* 8 (August 1932): 4

31. "Editoriales Breves: El Desastre de las Olimpiadas," *Excélsior* 13 (August 1932): 5.

32. Ibid.

33. Lamberto Alvarez Gayou, *La Influencia de la Décima Olimpiada en la Nueva Educación Física de México,* Archivo de la Secretaria de Educación Pública SEP. Sección subsecretaria de educación pública, Caja I, expediente 21. Subserie Lamberto Alvarez Gayou, 1931–1932, folio 22–27, Mexico City.

34. Henry Stimson, "Alleged Inoculation, 08/18/2932," RG 59. Decimal Files. 811.4063 olympic games/372, Record Group 59, *State Department,* National Archives and Record Administration, Hyattsville, MD.

35. "Complaints regarding inoculation of Mexican Olympic team in El Paso. 1932," entry 158.1208. Decimal Subject Files. Mexican Embassy. Records of the State Department. Record Group 59, NARA II.

36. Ibid.

37. Reuben Clark, "Alleged inoculation of members of Mexican Olympic teams," RG 59, Records of the state department. Decimal files. 811.4063-olympic games/367.

38. Translation, *El Gráfico Universal,* 08/08/1932, RG 59, Records of the State Department. Decimal files. 811.4063-olympic games/367.

39. Ibid.

40. Ibid.

41. "Han vuelto los Mexicanos, pero vuelven alegres," *Excélsior* 13 (August 1932): 3.

42. Lamberto Alvarez Gayou, *La Influencia de la Décima Olimpiada en la Nueva Educación Física de México,* folio 22–27.

43. Ibid.

44. "Han vuelto los Mexicanos, pero vuelven alegres."

45. Mary Douglas, *Purity and Danger: An Analysis of Concepts of Pollution and Taboo* (London: Routledge and Kegan Paul, 1969), 2.

46. Barbara Y. Welke, *Recasting American Liberty: Gender, Race, Law,*

and the Railroad Revolution, 1865–1920 (New York: Cambridge, 2001).

47. George J. Sanchez, *Becoming Mexican American: Ethnicity, Culture, and Identity in Chicano Los Angeles, 1900–1945* (NY: Oxford University Press, 1994), 209–252.

48. Douglas, *Purity and Danger*, 2.

49. Benjamin de Bueno Kalman, "La mitad que también juega: una población, la femenina, que reclama sus derechos," *La Opinión,* Mexico City, September 2002.

50. Grahame L. Jones, "Mexico Is Right at Home in Win," *Los Angeles Times*, February 16, 1998, C1. David G. Gutiérrez contextualizes this statement in "Migration, Emergent Ethnicity, and the 'Third Space': The Shifting Politics of Nationalism in Greater Mexico," *Journal of American History* 86:2 (Summer 1999): 481–517.

51. Brian Strauss, "The Dos a Cero Foundation: Josh Wolff and the Goal that Kickstarted It All," *Planet Fútbol: Sports Illustrated*, November 7, 2016, https://www.si.com/planet-futbol/2016/11/07/USA-mexico-2001-columbus-josh-wolff-dos-cero-world-cup-qualifying.

52. Alfie Crow, "Leo Manzano Takes Home Silver in 1500," SB *Nation*, 08/07/2012, http://www.sbnation.com/london-oiympics-2Q 12/2012/8/ 7/3 2269? 5/summer-olympics-2012-mens-1500m-leo-manzano.

53. Aimee Berg, "A Small Runner with a Capacity for Big Things," *New York Times*, September 24, 2010, http://www.nytimes.com/2010/Q9/25/sports/25runner.html.

54. Ruben Navarrette, "One Athlete, Two Flags," CNN, 08/10/2012, http://www.cnn.com/2012/08/10/opinion/navarrette-olympics-flags/.

55. Michel Martin, "U.S. Medalist Makes No Apologies for Mexican Flag," NPR, 09/18/2012, http://www.npr.orR/2Q12/09/18/161346427/us-medalist-makes-no-apologies-for-mexican-flag.

56. Michael Madison, "Leo Manzano Embodies the American Dream," *Austin Fit Magazine*, April 9, 2013, http://www.austinfitmagazine.com/April-2013/Track-Star-Leo-Manzano-Embodies-the-American-Dream/.

WILLIAM CARSON "NEMO" HERRERA:

Constructing a Mexican American Powerhouse while Remaining Colorblind

Ignacio M. García
Brigham Young University

AS THE POLICE CARS CLEARED the way for the bus carrying his players home, William Carson "Nemo" Herrera must have thought hard about what had just happened inside the gym, where players and fans engaged in an all-out racial brawl. It surely dawned on him that the fans of two of the institutions dearest to him — G.W. Brackenridge and Sidney Lanier high schools — had gone after each other with a ferocity theretofore unseen in a sports competition in his beloved San Antonio.

The fight began when a fan jumped out to punch Herrera's team leader and top scorer after he made the basket to win the game. The moment of celebration ended quickly, however, and the scene turned into one of fists, pushing, kicks, and even hurled rocks that took police almost an hour to control. It was the 1939 city championship, and the victory had come in a place so familiar to Herrera. Yet, his moment of triumph ended ugly, and what most people would talk about was the final shot and ensuing fight. Gone from memory would be this rubber match between two teams that had split their first two games and entered the final game having scored the same number of points against each other, or the brilliant play and the last-minute heroics to tie the game and then the overtime win.

No one — except the most committed fans — would remember the massive brown body of Joe Trevifio, the largest Mexican anyone had seen play this sport, fly high in the air to snatch that rebound in overtime, fire it to Billy Saldana, who passed it on the run to little Tony Cardona who zigzagged past taller players to score the winning shot. The euphoria from the Mexican American fans erupted as the ball went into the basket and the players rushed the court. Herrera remembered himself looking around for someone to hug; he who was always calm and reserved during the game wanted to scream out but he nonetheless remained composed. In the stands the fans were jumping up and down and hugging each other. But all had ended as that "fellow," nobody remembers who it was exactly, came dashing from the stands to punch Tony in back of the head. When his teammates sought to restrain the "fellow," the opposing team had flung themselves in full fury, punching and pushing them to relieve the profound disappointment at letting the championship slip away at home and to a team of short — with the exception of the center — players from the west side, the Latin Quarter, the Mexican side of town.

On the ride home, Herrera felt a great sense of disappointment at the moment of his greatest triumph. It was his first championship and against a talented team. More important, the team had qualified for the state playoffs, and while few sports writers gave them a chance, he felt they had what it took to go far, possibly all the way. But perhaps even more disappointing was where the fight had occurred and between which teams.

Herrera had played at this gymnasium several times while in high school, scored numerous points and claimed many victories, proudly donning the Brackenridge High School purple-and-white shorts and jersey. His high-school years had been full of wins, district and city titles, and other memorable moments, and well-earned respect even though he was different from most of his teammates and "his" fans. The sports headlines had been plentiful when this "midget" — all 5-something of him — had been known for scoring, hustling, and fast dribbling. But the last four years had seen him coach the Sidney Lanier

Voks to prominence and now a city championship. He was known as the coach with the squads that scored in bunches, hustled for every ball, and had outstanding dribblers who knew how to run a fast pace, make quick passes, and "burn out" opposing teams.

For Herrera, basketball had always been about fun, character, good sportsmanship, and young men coming together to entertain the fans and win the contest. But the Brackenridge-Lanier brawl reminded him that coaching basketball in the state of Texas complicated the life he had set out to construct for himself as a coach. It would not be just about intense practices, well-planned strategies, and good relationships with the newspaper guys. It was about navigating hostile gymnasiums, overcoming limitations caused by poverty and segregation, and keeping dreams alive in places where dreams usually went unfulfilled, all while maintaining himself above racial conflicts. He couldn't just coach. But somewhere before the ride back home ended, Herrera probably remembered that he had made up his mind early on that he would take things in stride, never complain, and most of all never engage in the dialogue or the thinking about the divisive things that often went on in such a racially divided city as San Antonio.

This perspective did not reflect an indifference to what was happening around him. His players remembered that he often prepared them for the hostile places in which they played by reminding them — no, drilling into their heads — that they came to play basketball and that the best way to respond to hostility, racial or athletic, was "to win." Winning did not itself change people's racial views or make them unmitigated admirers, but it did disarm them and challenged them to evolve their views of Mexicans, if not as neighbors and fellow citizens, at least as athletes. It made the Mexican American players a part of the more obvious "athletic scene," which in Herrera's mind was a way to have them be accepted as young men playing an American game.

Herrera knew that his players also understood that basketball in Texas shortly before and surely during World War II was not simply a game in which two teams met on the court and played to see who was the best. Many years after the contentious 1939 game, Joe Bernal, a member of the very talented 1944 team and then a well-known civil rights advocate, remembers receiving an e-mail from a friend and former president of the Southwest Basketball Officials Association telling him that the Lanier Voks always played five against seven. "The opposition," wrote his friend, "was five high-school opponents and two refs."

For Herrera, who probably struggled with his own identity, winning meant that sports-page discussions of the Sidney Lanier Voks would not be about their being "Mexican" but about their being good basketball players. This was the case when they went to play the Kerrville Antlers two years later, whose coach was quoted in the local papers as telling the hometown fans that they were in for a "revelation... insofar as the visitors' ability to play the game as it should be played." The *Kerrville Mountain Sun* added that "The name of Lanier in basketball circles is akin to the reputation of the Amarillo Sandies in football." The Sandies were a famed high school team that had dominated Texas football for several years. Hall of Fame Coach Milburn "Catfish" Smith would be just as laudatory when he described the Lanier Voks as the "best team in the state" during the 1943 state tournament. For Mexican American athletes, this was as good as it got. They would rather be known for their athletic abilities and tenacious play than for their ethnicity, because the former brought accolades and respect, whereas the latter generated only derision or at best sympathy.

Of course, the fact that they were Mexican never really disappeared from the discussion of their basketball abilities. Sometimes they were described as being like "mosquitoes" that ran around the taller white players, or were lauded for knowing their X's and O's "even better than their tortillas and frijoles." Most sports stories were incomplete if they failed to mention that the Voks were "short," "skinny," or "surprisingly quick" and a host of other coded terms that underscored that they were playing at a level that would normally not be a part of their game. Many sports writers would come to admire them and even cheer for them, but they never stopped being "surprised" at Lanier's audacity to dominate Texas basketball for most of the Second World War years.

From 1939 to 1945, no Texas boys' basketball team went to the playoffs and won as many games as did the Sidney Lanier Voks. Their two state titles (in 1943 and 1945), their one second-place and two third-place finishes, and their six consecutive regional titles were unprecedented in that era. Placing seven players in the all-state team, with two of them making it twice, and having three players at once on the all-star team (and by the way, all three were named Rodriguez), has never been equaled by any high school team in Texas, and possibly any other in the Southwest. These Mexicans could play ball and, more important, they could win and win consistently.

Nemo Herrera's ability to create, for the most part, a "friendly" environment for his players was possible only because he had learned to create his own space while a young athlete. Born in the Rio Grande Valley of Texas, he moved with his family to San Antonio before entering public school. For whatever reason, his Mexican American working-class family did not move to the barrios of the west side of San Antonio, where most of the Mexicans and Mexican Americans lived. They instead chose the south side, a white lower-middle and working-class section of town where Herrera ultimately attended Brackenridge High School.

Nemo's mother was part-white, but she also descended from one of the Mexican heroes of the early Texas Republic which made her, at least in her mind, a double-elite within her own community. Some may have perceived her as too acculturated into white society — his father was born in Mexico — but probably not enough to have a better relationship with Nemo's eventual wife, a Cajun from Louisiana. This genealogy placed Nemo at the crossroad of Texas racial boundaries. Mexican Americans who were considered of "finer ways" were always able to navigate Texas racial waters better than those who were seen as too brown, too poor, and too Mexican. Although Herrera's family was rather poor, his genealogy allowed him and his family to see themselves as part of the larger society and not of its fringes.

Like other Mexican Americans who flourished during this period, Herrera brought with him some rather special skills. Before discussing those, however, it would be appropriate to understand the generation of Mexican Americans who like Herrera transcended the barrios during those early years of the twentieth century. While mostly apolitical, he shared some of their life experiences and perceptions of American society. Historian Mario T. García defines this group of individuals as a "generation" or "a group of human beings who underwent the same basic historical experiences during their formative years." It was a generation that reacted to the "historical dramas" of their time in a collective fashion and responded to them in a way that defined them differently from those before them.

While García considers World War I, the Depression, massive immigration, and rising expectations as helping construct this generational view, it is important to point out that some aspects of that construction were individual or familial and came from personal decisions. For Herrera, part of his world view might well have come from his mixed parentage (not only white and brown but also a Mexican national father and a native-born Mexican American mother), his having gone from the Rio Grande Valley and its total Mexican American reality to San Antonio and its conflicting racial culture, and his attending a working-class Anglo school.

Too often those like Herrera who went to predominantly white working-class schools found themselves without the luxury of numbers, and so their "survival" strategies were based on ingratiating themselves with their white classmates, or avoiding as much as they could any interaction that placed them at odds with the majority. Their actions were more similar to the life patterns of most Mexican Americans who participated in a "white world" than were the actions of activists, founders of organizations, or intellectuals who sought to make collective change in their communities in order to live up to American ideals.

Those who were not engaged in activism were not necessarily unconcerned about their relationship to this land, at least within themselves. Nemo, for instance, was committed to American "ideals" from an early age. On the inside cover of a scrapbook that he kept of his playing and coaching years, he pasted William Tyler Page's "American's Creed," which was adopted by an act of Congress on April 1918, the same year Herrera graduated from high school. Below it, he copied the creed — he made some errors in transcribing it — that read:

> I believe in the United States of America, as a government of the people, by the people...for the people, who[se] just powers are derived from the consent of the government ["governed" in original], a democracy and ["in a" in original] republic; a sovereign Nation of many sovereign States; a perfect union....I therefore believe it is my duty to my country to love it, to support its Constitution, to obey its laws, to respect its flag, and to defend it against all enemies.

Herrera, like many other successful individuals of his generation, found his bearings in the larger society by exercising a particular skill or talent. His was his incredible athletic ability. By the age of around twelve he was already a champion as a member of the San Antonio Comanches basketball team. As soon as he entered high school he joined sports and excelled in baseball, football...and of course basketball. From his recollections and the pictures in his albums, it is obvious that he felt secure in that "sports environment" and that race seemed not to be an insidious intruder in his life. More likely, he was the beloved "different kid." The fact that he adapted well and seemed to take things in stride no doubt made it easier for him to integrate into this racially conscious environment.

The story of how he got his nickname illustrates a point about the complicated world that he navigated. At home he was Guillermo — the Spanish equivalent of William — and thus his nickname among family members was "Memo." Although he went by William Carson Herrera for most of his life, the fact that his nickname was "Memo" indicates that his youthful life was not one of complete assimilation. In fact, many years later, his son William would discover cousins and relatives who were quite Mexican, as he put it, during one of a number of celebrations honoring his father. And while Herrera's players don't remember his using much Spanish — and some even believed he could not speak it — he spent many summers in Mexico umpiring in the Mexican baseball leagues.

But back to his nickname. At the age of twelve he was a bat boy for the San Antonio Bronchos, a Minor League Baseball team; he recalled years later that several white players had trouble repeating his Mexican nickname. In an interview he nonchalantly mentioned that one of the baseball players simply changed the nickname to "Nemo." By one quick verbal stroke Herrera joined the millions of ethnic Americans whose names or nicknames were changed on a whim by those who were unwilling to invest the time to learn non-English pronunciations.

For people like Herrera, it was the price to be paid to be part of a team. Nemo, a minority in this world, simply went along. Too young to understand the implications to his identity and his connection to his own community, he accepted the name change and it became part of his identity. His language became predominantly English and so did his world, so much so that his youngest son would admit to being quite emotional when he met his Mexican side of the family, setting him off on a search for his roots.

Because of his athletic prowess, Herrera was one of eighteen young men from San Antonio (all but he were white) to get a scholarship at Southwestern University near Austin. If high school could be inhospitable to Mexican Americans, colleges were sometimes worse because unlike the public schools, colleges in the 1920s were not necessarily intended for the masses of American society. While working-class youth did attend college in the earlier part of the twentieth century, the overwhelming majority of college students were middle- and upper-middle-class individuals. Those who were not were usually those who had strong ambitions and skills or talents beyond their class. At the time, colleges were conservative and very conscious of the status quo. Herrera responded to this new environment the same way he did in high school: he excelled in sports and did everything he could to fit in, including joining a fraternity.

After four years, or at least four seasons, at Southwestern University, Herrera left to find a job. It is unclear why he did not graduate, although it is possible that once his eligibility ran out he had no more funding to continue his schooling. Devoid of eligibility, he returned to his actual status as a Mexican boy in a white space. Although his exploits could not garner him the rest of his education, they got him his first job in Beaumont High School in 1923. Not much is known about his one-year stay at the East Texas school, but we do know that his team lost only one game that year. We also know he made a profound impression on one of his players, Holly Brock, who went on to become one of the "all-time basketball greats" at the University of Texas and the head of the Houston Junior Chamber of Commerce Invitation Basketball Tournaments, to which Herrera took his Voks for several years. Said the successful insurance businessman of Herrera, "[He taught me] more basketball than any coach under whom [I] played."

Herrera himself was impressed by the man who hired him. We don't know why he left Beaumont except that maybe he wanted to play baseball. While he had done this while in high school, it was more likely that the time spent on the diamond would best be enhanced if he played for a large company team. While he made his fame as a basketball player in college and initially as a basketball coach, it seems obvious from his scrapbook that baseball was his first love as an athlete and eventually as a coach. Herrera left Beaumont to play for the Gulf Oil Company (later to become Chevron) in Mexico, and it was there that he met his wife, Mary Leona Hatch, a Louisiana orphan who had gone to Mexico as a nurse. Mary Leona, lifelong companion and supporter of Herrera's coaching ambition, proved to be the final breach to his Mexican past. Her relationship with his family and her strong character in teaching her boys to be good Americans maintained the gap until they entered their 70s.

After marriage, Herrera returned to San Antonio and got his first job at a utility company, also playing ball for them, but by this time he was playing basketball, now avoiding the baseball cleats that had led to the injury that took him to the hospital where he met Mary Leona. He gave up Minor League Baseball, which had him playing with future Major League Baseball Hall of Famers. Within a year, the job at Lanier opened up and he became a coach, although the promised head coaching job would take almost five years to become a reality.

So here, the young man and now married father who had navigated the ethnic landscape seeking his own American sports dream ended up in a Mexican American vocational high school. Interestingly, this American voyage had taken a Mexico detour and landed him in a high school only a few miles from where he had lived and played. The job brought him back to his roots, but he managed to maintain his distance even while embracing the Mexican American world in which he found himself for seventeen years. In ways that he might not have admitted to himself, he accepted the reality that he was not likely to get a job in one of the city's major high schools, and that he was getting his first major coaching job — given what a jump it was from a Beaumont high school to one in San Antonio — exactly because he was a Mexican American. Even back in the 1940s, an educated Mexican American was a prize for a school in the middle of the west side of town.

If Herrera ever had qualms about teaching or coaching in the "Latin quarter," there is no evidence of it. The players remembered him as a sober leader during the games. He was not a screamer, nor did he become animated with the flow of the game, but during practice and at other times he was a different person. Herrera liked to joke around with his players and to share their thoughts and dreams. He became a lifelong friend to many and a permanent mentor to others. He not only coached them, he educated them and made them aware of what awaited them after high school. Several players would say later that he was the reason for their getting a college education or a job with the city, state, or federal government. He bailed some out of jail, lectured them on their dating habits, and visited others at the hospital when they were injured in the war. He often brought his sons to practice to be with the players, and Mary became the Voks' most tenacious advocate, sometimes offering advice to the players on their play — to Herrera's displeasure.

Herrera occasionally popped in at the neighborhood drugstore where the players congregated and would say to them, "You probably say, 'Hay viene el Viejo' ('Here comes the Old Man')." Although he didn't know it they probably also said, "Here comes Chato," a nickname they had for him since most of them had nicknames of their own, a common ritual among Latinos and many working-class people. In fact, years later, after he had been gone for a number of years from San Antonio, he came back for a conference and asked a couple of his former students to get as many of the former players together as they could. They did, as hundreds of people showed up to a banquet organized in just a few days. But the humor of the event was that Nemo couldn't remember many of their names, although he hadn't forgotten their nicknames.

A sports columnist for the *San Antonio Express*, Dan Cook, put it this way:

> Herrera is worried. You see, when he was building champions and putting Lanier into the record books every Latin athlete with a pound of desire or an ounce of talent had a nickname.... The old man well remembers his boys but he remembers most by nicknames that have long since been dropped....Oscar Flores, for instance, isn't too willing to admit that for many years he was known simply as "Dracula." But Drac will be there Monday night. Along with Chivo, La Chispa, Goofus, King Kong, El Pelón, La Rata, The Tooth and many others.[1]

Cook added that it sounded like a roll call at San Quentin, but most of the players were now "highly respected" men in San Antonio.

This kind of camaraderie was the counterbalance to the brutal workouts that had the players dragging not only their feet but their tongues. Herrera believed that his Mexican boys were not going to be winners until they could win the battle against fatigue and the limitations of their small stature. And until they believed that they could win and that nothing — poverty, less than optimal facilities, and surely not their racial makeup — was an excuse not to be the best they could be. He pounded that notion into their minds and reminded them that he was shorter than even they when he played and he also had "nothing" growing up.

He taught them to play big and to play fast. His basketball system at times seemed like organized chaos, but it was meant to take advantage of each young man's skill and talents and to put each of them in position to score, rebound, steal a pass, or effectively receive or pass the ball. This was the way Herrera built his success: hard work, total dedication to the process, full-court pressure, quick ball movement, and each player doing what he did best. They were to be always looking past the obstacles and pitfalls so as not to give them more weight than they already had. It was a system that also taught the young men how to live life. For Herrera, it was the way disadvantaged young men from all walks of life found success in a nation that offered many opportunities even to those who were "different." It was the American way.

Herrera's style and approach were no different from those of other educators and social advocates of the early to mid-century. Like Jane Addams's settlement movement (in which houses were established to offer community services, largely to immigrant populations, to address problems such as poverty and poor education), Herrera's approach sought to make ethnic-youth Americans not to be removing all the obstacles they faced but by providing them the skills and the motivation to overcome them. While Herrera might have avoided a discussion of the racial conflicts these young men faced, he nonetheless provided them a way to respond. Part of that response revolved around developing a non-offensive persona and being respectful winners and gracious losers. He understood that the larger society could "stomach" his boys winning championships if they saw them as players who accepted defeat without questioning the fairness of the outcome. The gracious attitude affirmed to the outsider that the players believed the "system" did not provide anyone unfair advantage, nor did it place undue burdens on others.

Herrera was not so much naive as he was both hopeful and cautiously optimistic that his "boys" could discover the space to find a good life in American society. In his early years in the Rio Grande Valley, at Brackenridge High School, and then at Lanier, he knew that many if not most Mexican American youth were going to struggle and very likely not receive the benefits he believed were possible in American society. One of his players died from gang violence, and one of his potential stars dropped out to work to help his family even before he played his first game. Herrera understood what obstacles they faced and would face after high school. If they focused on the limitations and the hardships, they might simply choose the path of others before them who remained in the barrio and stuck to what they knew. He wanted so much more for these young men.

Yet, his unwillingness to discuss the problems or to become involved in greater efforts to improve the Lanier students' educational experience revealed his limitations as an educator and as an advocate for his players. Many years later, some of his players continued to reveal ambivalence about their public identity, if not their private one. Many stayed close to the west side and loyal to Lanier, but few of them ever engaged in questioning the educational system that had many Mexican American youths dropping out of school and that provided limited college preparation. Still others continued to avoid using the word "Mexican" and sometimes even "Mexican American," although they engaged in all the cultural activities the barrios provided and often complained about why "their own" were treated unfairly. Herrera provided many of his players the skills to move forward, but he failed to help them "crack" the barrio "bubble" that resulted from segregation, limited educational opportunities, and external racial and ethnic biases.

In the end, Coach Nemo Herrera's greatest contribution to his players was the space that he occupied between his barrio boys and the mainstream of American society. He served as bridge, and while often his players only understood the "experience" through him, it did provide them a glimpse of what awaited them once out of high school. They came to appreciate that hard work, a strong belief in themselves, and disregarding the racial hostility they would confront was the way to not only survive but to find a place in American society. In essence, Herrera helped each boy to construct a bubble around them when on the outside and to focus on life skills when they worked or lived within their own community. More important for them as sportsmen, he helped them create an athletic legacy that empowered them as individuals and provided the school a history that its students and alumni periodically endorsed to push back against a sometimes insensitive society that rarely believed that Mexicans could play ball.

When he left the school in 1945 after 17 very successful years to go coach in another all Mexican American high school in El Paso, Herrera left behind a legacy that would be remembered for many years after, particularly by his players who learned what it meant to win in the game of life while maintaining a strong sense of self-worth and dignity.

QUESTIONS:

1. What were some of the issues that Coach Herrera faced as he took his Voks to play in gyms in various parts of Texas?

2. What impact did the Voks' successes have on how they were perceived by the majority population of the state? Why was this perception significant?

3.   How did being a skilled athlete help Coach Herrera navigate the Jim Crow-type atmosphere that existed during his youth? Do you see any similarities between his experiences and those of some contemporary athletes?

NOTES

1. Dan Cook, "West Side's Little Giant," *San Antonio Express*, August 6, 1967, 2S.

For a description of the high-school game riot and the complete story of the Sidney Lanier High School Voks during their successful years, see the author's *When Mexicans Could Play Ball: Basketball, Race, and Identity in San Antonio, 1928–1945* (Austin: University of Texas Press, 2014). For a discussion of racial conflicts in San Antonio during some of Herrera's tenure as coach see Richard A. García's *Rise of the Mexican American Middle Class, San Antonio, 1929–1941* (College Station: Texas A&M University Press, 2000). See also Laura Hernández-Ehrisman's *Inventing the Fiesta City: Heritage and Carnival in San Antonio* (Albuquerque: University of New Mexico Press, 2008) for a discussion of how city and social leaders of San Antonio sought to create an image of a city with no racial conflicts or social divides. Another work of a more recent era that analyzes the "accommodation and conflict in this asymmetric relationship" is Roberto Rosales's *The Illusion of Inclusion: The Untold Story of San Antonio, Texas* (Austin: History, Culture, and Society Series, University of Texas Press, 2000).

Mario T. García's *Mexican Americans: Leadership, Ideology, and Identity, 1930–1960* (New Haven: Yale University Press, 1989) provides a lengthy discussion of the "Mexican American generation." See Marvin Rintala's *The Constitution of Silence: Essays on Generational Themes* (Westport, Conn., 1979) for a discussion of what constitutes a political generation. Another work that discusses political generations is Karl Mannheim's "The Problem of Generations," in *Essays on the Sociology of Knowledge* (New York, 1952). For a further discussion of sports among Mexican Americans and Latinos see Jorge Iber, Samuel O. Regalado, José M. Alamillo, and Arnoldo De León's *Latinos in U.S. Sport: A History of Isolation, Cultural Identity, and Acceptance* (Champaign, IL: Human Kinetics, 2011); Jorge Iber and Samuel O. Regalado, *Mexican Americans and Sports: A Reader on Athletics and Barrio Life* (College Station: Texas

A&M University Press, 2006); also see Christine Marin's "Courting Success and Realizing the American Dream: Arizona's Mighty Miami High School Championship Basketball Team, 1951," *International Journal of the History of Sport* 26, no. 7 (June 2009): 924–946 for a discussion of basketball among Arizona's Mexican Americans.

A PELOTERO FROM THE CHAPARRAL:

The Baseball Career of "Wallopin'" Wally Rodríguez

Arnoldo De León
Professor Emeritus, Angelo State University

HISTORY HAS NOT BEEN GENEROUS in acknowledging the agency of ordinary people. Until the late twentieth century, regrettably, historians neglected writing about the actions of Hispanic men and women from farm or ranch areas, or from small-town sites, who against the odds made contributions worthy of integration into the larger US narrative. In contrast, family, friends, and neighbors considered these individuals of remarkable accomplishment as luminaries. Community members regarded local notables as heroic not solely because they excelled at their craft but also because of the character they personified. Standouts brushed aside immense obstacles on their way to stardom, succeeded by practicing perseverance and taking pride in their determination at the moment of competition, and, finally, acquitted themselves well in shouldering the responsibility cast upon them. Wally Rodríguez, who earned distinction as a Minor

League player from 1949 to 1951, embodied the attributes of such a persona.

THE CHAPARRAL

Benavides, Texas, where Guadalupe ("Wally") Rodríguez grew up and attended public schools, is located in the South Texas county of Duval. This section of Texas may be associated with brush thicket, or *chaparral*. Thorny shrubs, burr-bearing bushes, prickly pear cacti, mesquite trees, small oak, a variety of grasses, and other wild vegetation take up much space in the area. Despite problems of nature, Duval County — with annual rainfall of about 22 inches — contains portions of productive ranch and farmland. In fact, the prospect of making a respectable living raising cattle, sheep, and goats initially brought settlers to the county in the years following the removal of the indigenous Indian peoples from South Texas after the Civil War. A railroad line linking Corpus Christi to Laredo in 1881 and traversing Duval County bolstered the county's commercial development. By that time, ranchers had turned to clearing up part of their land and converting it to use as cotton fields (in subsequent decades, Duval farmers would also plant crops such as corn and grain sorghums). As of the 1930s, Duval County, according to data accumulated by the *Texas Almanac and State Industrial Guide*, rated as "ranch-farm" country.[1]

The county continues to be primarily rural and not heavily settled. In 1930, the federal census enumerated 12,191 inhabitants; the population increased to 20,565 in 1940, but it then dropped to 15,643 by 1950. Today, towns are few and none can be considered as deserving "city" status. San Diego has been the county seat since 1876; northwest of it is Freer, and south of it are Benavides, Realitos, and Concepción. Other rural hamlets in the county during the 1930s–1940s included Sejita, Ramírez, Sweden, and Guajillo, all of them with fewer than 50 inhabitants, but maps today do not even include some of these villages.[2]

Manufacturing has never been a striking characteristic of the county, although the oil industry has. In the late 1920s and into the 1930s, wildcatters discovered an abundance of oil deposits in parts of Duval County. Oil drillers struck a bonanza near Freer in 1928 and the local economy flourished. During the middle of the Depression, Benavides also became the center of oil production. Smaller oil fields cropped up here and there throughout the thirties. Although the boom dissipated by the 1940s, petrochemical plants remain active in parts of the county today.[3]

A HISPANIC ZONE

Duval County, like neighboring counties in South Texas, has historically been "Hispanic." Actually, identity is bicultural. Certainly, people developed bilingual abilities through the years and, while they absorbed American values and traditions, they retained many Mexican customs and habits. Several forces nurtured such a bicultural identity. Demography fueled it. During the pre-WWII era, there lived in the county a small Anglo American element made up mainly of large landowners, sulfur mine owners, oil company officials, and teachers. But a high percentage of the population in Duval County — anywhere from 50 percent to 70 percent between 1930 and 1950 — has always been of Hispanic origin. Further, the educational system in the county failed to reach a good many children. Illiteracy stood at 35 percent for Mexicans in 1930, and as late as 1950 only 7.6 percent of those over age twenty-five had graduated from high school. Then, most people lived in poverty; the majority of men worked as manual laborers around the various ranch and farm settlements.[4]

On the other hand, there persisted, as had since the county's founding, the presence of a small but vibrant middle class of Hispanic ranchers, farmers, merchants, and civil officials that shared control with the Anglo minority presiding over county affairs.[5] The ease and comfort with which this cohort interacted and communicated with ordinary citizens legitimized a bicultural lifestyle prevalent in the region. Despite the school system's failure to successfully educate a larger percentage of youngsters, several children did attend school, learn English, gain ideas as to the democratic promise, and come under Americanization influences. The school as a medium of acculturation naturally bolstered individual instincts for engaging in the regimens of American life, including athletics.

This ambience prevailed in Benavides in the early 1930s. During this time, the town's population rose from about 1,200 inhabitants to some 3,081 as of the 1940s (but its population has declined ever since).[6] Mexicans thus experienced small-town life, one culturally familiar to them and nourished daily through interaction with family members, neighbors, and mainstream institutions. The fact that the city contained Hispanic officials (on occasion as justice of the peace or as mayor) further fostered and sustained "*lo mexicano.*" Several of the downtown businesses were Mexican owned, including the local pharmacy, the Piggly Wiggly, the filling station, the theater, a department store, and other mercantile enterprises. The Catholic Church had all-Mexican parishioners. Entertainment activities included forms that residents' forebears had imported from Mexico. At the local plaza, they came together to commemorate the *Diez y Seis de Septiembre* or the *Cinco de Mayo*, to observe special occasions, or to host family functions. People could easily walk to the plaza (or to wherever a fiesta might be celebrated) and enjoy music, dancing, the many *puestos* (food booths) traditionally set up at these events, and the popular *lotería.*[7]

Long-entrenched racial practices and attitudes, on the other hand, deepened people's ethnic consciousness. Racial separation did not exist in the city's schools (established in the 1920s) since all students would have been Mexican, but the teachers were always Anglo — a constant reminder to young hearts of their second-class status. The earliest football teams (1920s) must have had Mexican American athletes (in order to assemble the necessary number of players!) however, an Anglo member of the first squad mustered in the city mentioned none. He listed only Anglos in the first-string lineup.[8] Then, there prevailed in the city, as common throughout South Texas, the rule that white females were off limits to Mexican boys. In one case in the 1940s, the local political machine ordered a teenage Benavides cotton picker to relocate from Duval County after he had fallen in love with a white girl.[9]

GROWING UP IN CHAPARRAL COUNTRY

Wally Rodríguez's roots lay deep in the South Texas chaparral and its cultural milieu. He was born on November 22, 1925, in Concepción (*La Chona*, as South Texas Tejanos called it in Spanish), a village of a few hundred (apparently less than 500) located in southeastern Duval County. His parents were Texas–born, his father Emiliano in La Chona and his mother Eleuteria in Roma (Starr County). As did other families residing in the brush country in that part of the state, his father worked as a *vaquero* doing range work and his mother took care of the children at home. In total, Wally had five sisters and two brothers. He was the youngest.[10]

His childhood experience mirrored that of many others living in early twentieth-century South Texas. The Rodríguez clan faced trying times, especially after Emiliano's tragic death at the Salas Ranch (in Concepción) due to a horse accident. Wally grew up not knowing his father; the boy was younger than three when Emiliano died. When still children, Wally and his brother Armando left for Benavides (located some fourteen miles from La Chona) with their mother. By then the rest of the siblings had married and left the household. In Benavides, Eleuteria made do as a domestic worker by taking in laundry, ironing, and cleaning — any work that allowed her to feed her boys. Growing up in Benavides during the time of the Depression, Wally and his brother helped out by shining shoes, picking cotton and watermelons, ranching, and turning to oil-field work.[11] Wally copied the examples of relatives and friends from Benavides who adhered to a hard-work ethic, accepting its value as a means for life improvement.

From what can be reconstructed of his growing-up years, Wally received his entire education in the Benavides schools. For a time he lived with his sister Eliza's family at a ranch some four miles from Benavides where her husband Epigmenio worked, but he then moved back in with his mother Eleuteria on entering high school.[12]

THE HIGH-SCHOOL STANDOUT

It was in high school — the time when the nation was subsumed in World War II (indeed, his brother Armando saw military service) — where Wally began establishing a record as a superior athlete. He had innate physical qualities that his competitors envied. School annuals of these years show him towering over his teammates, all of them under 6 feet. According to the 1941–1942 *El Cenizo*, the school's annual, Wally — or "Lupe" (for Guadalupe) as some of the Spanish speakers called him — was already 6 feet 1 inch and weighed a trim 150 pounds. Contemporaries, acquaintances, friends, and family members testify to Wally's possessing an athletic frame, natural playing acumen, and exceptional agility. He enjoyed, recalled a Benavides teammate, "good eye-to-hand coordination to hit baseballs, soft hands to catch footballs, and speed to outrun anybody or chase a deep fly ball to center field." He was "a coach's dream."[13]

Mexican Americans made up approximately 90 to 95 percent of the Benavides school population; therefore, Wally's teams were predominantly Mexican and poor. Opposing schools and players presumably had no material edge on Benavides. In football, Benavides High played Laredo Martin, Premont, San Diego, Sinton, Freer, Falfurrias,

Alice, Mission, and Eagle Pass, all of them primarily Mexican American towns and probably with meager athletic budgets. Against all competition, Wally excelled. He was fortunate to be mentored by E. C. Lerma, a South Texas coach who would go on to earn legendary status in Texas sports. Playing end in football, Rodríguez earned the label of the "two-fisted cyclone" for his reckless type of play. At a triangular meet with Freer and San Diego during the 1941–1942 school year, Wally won the 880-yard run. On the school's basketball team, Rodríguez played forward.[14]

The year 1943, under Coach Lerma, brought the greatest of triumphs to Benavides, the little town in the chaparral. That fall season, Wally played on a football team that gained Benavides High School a perfect 12–0 record. The performance included a defeat (at home, in Benavides stadium) of the Eagle Pass Eagles to win the regional championship. Individually, Wally (the receiver) attained selection as All-District Player of District 39-A.[15]

In other sports, Wally's feats in 1943–1944 matched his achievements in football. He played on the Benavides basketball team that won the Regional 1944 championship against South Texas teams from Premont, Mirando, Hebbronville, Brownsville, Lyford, Mission, La Feria, Donna, Mercedes, San Benito, Kingsville, Laredo, Ingleside, Aransas Pass, San Diego, and Taft. The 1944 *El Cenizo* shows Wally standing proudly next to Coach Lerma. In track, Wally was equally successful at competing in the 100-yard dash, the 880-yard run, and the 440 relay.[16] Applying the same dedication to sports training and execution as he had in friendly competition against fellow workers in the cotton and watermelon patches, Wally held account of himself on the playing field just as he had doing manual labor.

Wally (and presumably other athletes) received enthusiastic support from the town's citizens — Benavides in those days of winning seasons was very much sports-minded. Success nurtured community pride. Coach Lerma would approach the town's businesses soliciting donations of money and sports equipment. Parents and community folk sponsored fundraisers to provide the players with athletic gear, such as socks and tennis shoes, and to pay for lunches when the team traveled. For out-of-town trips, the community would sacrifice (the WWII years were ones of gas rationing) by arranging carpools to ferry the boys to their next contest.[17]

Because baseball did not become part of the Benavides schools' athletic program until the 1960s, Wally did not see action in that game as a high schooler. But there was enough baseball to be played around Duval County (and in fact throughout South Texas) for Wally to hone his skills on the diamond. Benavides during his growing-up years, in fact, earned a reputation as a hub of baseball activity, and the prevailing enthusiasm there kindled a small league of semi-pro teams. Even Coach Lerma played on these squads in his free time.[18]

Wally's reputation as a consummate athlete continued into his senior year. He was by then a 185-pounder and a four-year football letterman (receiver). Sadly, disaster struck him that season on the football field. A blow from a rival player rendered him prostrate; his manager and teammates helped him off the ground. He recovered slowly, but the injury ended any hope Wally entertained about furthering his career in football or basketball. Still, his legacy at Benavides High remained intact. *El Cenizo* bid him goodbye with the promise, "Your name will always live in BHS!"[19]

His record in football, basketball, and track by then had attracted at least some college schools, among them Trinity (San Antonio) and Rice University (Houston). Home life, the bicultural environment pervasive in South Texas, and the Benavides schools had prepared him well enough that he could adapt to a larger urban setting. He trusted and placed faith in institutions to be encountered in a broader context — his involvement in sports and the satisfaction he drew from playing inflated his esteem as an American. Simultaneously, Wally evaluated his prospects in college given his injury. He understood further that he did not possess the natural endowment essential for success at a higher academic level; he worried that he would not receive the proper tutoring and mentoring that he would need. Thus, he declined invitations from these two schools. In any case, colleges in the post-WWII years and into the 1950s did not easily grant scholarships to those of Hispanic descent.[20]

EL PELOTERO

Minding his obligation to military service, Wally left the chaparral of South Texas and enlisted in the United States Army. After basic training at Fort Hood, in Killeen, Texas, he received orders for overseas duty in Germany. His contingent was to replace the men from Allied forces who had seen front-line action. But his reputation as an athlete in Benavides had accompanied him overseas. An officer one day called Wally into his office and suggested he try out for a baseball team to compete against other military squads in an Army league formed in Germany. Baseball had not been Wally's strongest sport. As indicated earlier, Benavides High did not have a baseball program during the 1940s (although Wally had played the game informally in sandlots and probably with local baseball organizations). His inability to continue pursuing a dream in football or basketball after suffering his injury, however, had left him little choice of sports other than baseball. But inherent athletic dexterity permitted him to adjust easily to the game. Wally's playing days with the Army involved competition with units from Frankfurt and various other German cities recovering from Allied bombing.[21]

Recognizing his athletic versatility, the Army picked Wally for a track team. In 1946, he competed in what organizers called the Army Olympics, staged in Berlin Stadium, one of the largest sports arenas in the world. That was the same track on which US marvel Jesse Owens had set several records in 1936. Representing the United States, Wally ran as second leg in a track team competing in the 1,600-meter relay against France, Czechoslovakia, and other Allied nations.[22] Learning of the Benavides wonder's feats, *La Prensa* of San Antonio headlined the news with *"México-Texano que Triunfa: Nos informan del brillante papel que hizo en dichos juegos Wally Rodríguez, un soldado de origen mexicano, nacido en Texas, formando parte del tim que corrió la prueba de 1,600 metros de relevos."* ("A Texas–Mexican who triumphs! We are informed of the brilliant role played in these [aforementioned] games by Wally Rodríguez, a soldier of Mexican origin, born in Texas, who formed part of the team that competed in the 1,600-meter relays.")[23]

Rodríguez finished his tour of duty in 1948 and returned home to Benavides. His time in the military had been enlightening and satisfying. He had traveled far from the chaparral, earned promotions almost effortlessly, and made good in his favorite pastime: sports. His athletic ability no doubt contributed to his successes — he received promotion from private to sergeant three months after arriving in Berlin. He recalled later that Army men extended the utmost respect to those in military sports teams. His fellow soldiers had accepted him as equal (he encountered no prejudice in the military) in part because of his athletic capabilities. But Wally possessed assets even then (they would be salient throughout his adult life) that opened doors. A magnetic personality, an amiable demeanor, an unassuming character, and a fair complexion complemented his sports prowess.[24]

In Benavides, a scout representing the St. Louis Cardinals contacted him about possibly playing pro ball. The scout, from Corpus Christi, invited Wally to meet with him at the Oasis Hotel on the Corpus Christi bay front. The scout explained the Cardinals' interest in Rodríguez; they were looking for young players from South Texas and they had become aware of the military veteran's playing record while he was stationed in Germany. Rodríguez received instructions to report to the Houston Buffaloes team where training would start at Buffalo Stadium. But the terms of the contract were hardly appealing: only $200 a month, too little for Wally to support his family. Unable to agree on terms, he returned to Benavides.[25]

But Wally's drive to play baseball landed him in a semi-pro team in Robstown, Texas, named the Sun Spot Bottlers. Despite prevailing Jim Crow customs, the owner of the Sun Spot Bottling Co. apparently accepted integration as a necessary means to having a contending team, for aside from Wally the Bottlers had several other Hispanic players. As was the case with similar baseball outfits in South Texas, the Sun Spot Bottlers played teams from border towns in Mexico as well as clubs from other parts of Texas.[26]

There in Robstown, George Schepps recruited Wally for the Corpus Christi Aces, a Class D (the lowest designation for a minor-league team) outfit in the Rio Grande Valley League then affiliated with the St. Louis Cardinals. In the post-World War II era, baseball-team owners searched vigorously for Spanish-speaking players, recognizing the value of their appeal to Mexican American spectators. Corpus Christi, and much of South Texas for that matter, was home to large numbers of Hispanics; in many towns they constituted a majority of the population. The Rio Grande Valley League in fact played before largely Mexican-origin crowds, as the league had teams in Brownsville, McAllen, Laredo, Del Rio, Victoria, and of course, Corpus.[27] Spectators — probably common laborers who not long before had faced difficult struggles — watched men like themselves display manly skills, bring credit and recognition to *la raza*, and level race status by equaling or excelling the play of Anglo teammates.

Wally began as a rookie outfielder for the Corpus Christi Aces in the spring of 1949 immediately after being recruited from the Robstown Sun Spot Bottlers. In the team's inaugural game, he lived up to prospects, hitting a home run at his first turn at bat, then another on his last appearance at the plate. In 1976, he recalled the evening to a reporter. "It [the first homer] was against Del Rio and it went about

440 feet into dead center-field. Then on my last time up that night, I hit another one. This time over the left-field fence, 320 feet away." For his sensational feats with the Aces, he soon earned the moniker of "Wallopin'" Wally. Throughout his career in baseball, Wally would receive positive tribute and encouraging commentary from the media, as this example shows.[28] Sports writers have historically been complimentary of sports superstars, often associating superior play with masculinity. Certainly the tag "Wallopin'" Wally connoted as much.

Obviously, Rodríguez's Army years had not affected his playing form. By August, he had raised his batting average (BA) with the Aces to above .370. It was good enough to gain an assignment to the Lubbock Hubbers of the West Texas–New Mexico League, although the Aces may have seen the transfer as necessary because the club had a surplus of experienced outfielders already and perhaps wanted him to get more playing time with another team. Accompanied by his wife Delia, Wally made the long trek to the Panhandle, going on options (i.e., to be moved freely between clubs) from Class B (a mid-level minor league) Greenville of the Big State League.[29] The stay in Lubbock had no discernible effect on his hitting, for when he returned to Corpus in early September, he continued to batter Rio Grande Valley League pitchers. Toward the end of the 1949 season, the Aces played in the Little Dixie Series against Big Spring for the Class D Championship of Texas. Wally's team won the series.[30]

The next year found Wally playing in East Texas, appointed by the Corpus Christi Aces to the Longview Texans on options. The assignment in Longview, where he batted .304, proved brief.[31] For the remainder of the 1950 season, Wally played for the Lake Charles Lakers (Louisiana) of the Class C (an advancement made from Class D leagues) Gulf Coast League. He had a solid showing in a series against the rival Galveston White Caps, hitting one double and two singles in a May 20 game. However, the long ball soon became his signature, according to newspaper reports, but also by Wally's own appraisal. In a radio interview on May 29, 1950, the self-assured Wally predicted hitting a home run sometime during the next ball game. He did so at the first time up to bat, driving a 420-footer to help the Lakers defeat the rival Port Arthur Seahawks.[32]

Wally's success with the Lakers during the 1950 season could not but help scouts regard him as a budding prospect for the big leagues. After two weeks with the Lakers, the Benavides outfielder — "a tremendous figure of a man," as one columnist described him — had taken over the Gulf Coast League batting leadership with a .387 BA, while hitting four home runs.[33] Some newspaper reporters continued referring to him as "Wallopin'" Wally (in the protocol of the age, they denominated him as "Latin American").[34] In July, the Gulf Coast Press-Radio Association (composed of radio announcers) chose Rodríguez, still hot with a .341 BA, as an all-star outfielder (right field) to play in the first annual Gulf Coast League All-Star game in Port Arthur. Wally fell one point short of getting a perfect score from the voters. Apparently, his hitting success declined for the rest of the season. Statistics show that in the eighty-two games he played with the Lakers, he recorded a .302 batting average and blasted five home runs.[35]

Rodríguez's service in professional baseball started coming to an end around 1951. He had not always been satisfied with the treatment given him. In training, he felt slighted when coaches or managers did not offer him the attention necessary to improve upon his natural skills. They appeared not to care as long as he kept hitting over .300. Wally sensed, further, that management did not promote Latinos. The possibility of racial discrimination lingered always. Of fair complexion, he seldom encountered it on his travels, but he witnessed discrimination constantly being practiced against fellow teammates of Cuban descent. He had seen segregation against Mexicans in South Texas firsthand, so fears that it would be applied to him on the road caused him continual concern. Then, family commitments, low pay, and the unpredictability that is part of minor-league play had to be considered. In January 1951, the Class B Corpus Christi Aces sold him outright to the far West Texas Class C Odessa Oilers, then the defending champions of the Longhorn League. Although still regarded as a "heavy hitter," he went there on "limited service," having to vie with five other players for two spots in the outfield.[36]

According to newspaper accounts, Wally started playing in April with the Clovis Pioneers (of the West Texas–New Mexico League), whose opponents included Wally's old team, the Lubbock Hubbers. He competed with the same commitment as ever; in one game against Lubbock in May 1951, he led the Pioneers' assault on the Hubbers with three hits, according to the Pampa *Daily-News*. Still, Wally had to struggle to keep active with the Pioneers. As of June, the team was to reduce the number of outfielders by one, and Wally hoped to remain playing for the remainder of the season. At Clovis, in 50 games and 174 at bats, Wally finished with a .299 average.[37]

At age 25, Wally decided to end his dream of a Major League career. He had been sold to the Chicago Cubs organization for the 1952 season but declined the promotion. The contract terms hardly met the bare essentials (apparently the same low pay as with the St. Louis Cardinals in 1948) he needed for supporting his young family. Consequently, he did not report for spring training in Chicago.[38]

RETIREMENT

By 1952, Wally had gotten a job with Reynolds Metals Company in Corpus. He recalled many years later that the company was recruiting "Latin boys" able to communicate with the mostly Spanish-speaking workers. It made him a handsome offer as a supervisor, a position that carried good pay. He liked the job but the work environment proved hazardous, as inhaling aluminum vapors caused stress on lung functions. He took his wife Delia's advice and left Reynolds after nine years.

He opted to open a filling station (a popular route taken by many Mexican American businessmen in that era) in Corpus and earned a fair living. Self-employment was satisfying but it demanded long hours and neglect of family. Then opportunity called.

By happenstance, a customer friend of Wally's who worked for the Sheriff's Department stopped by the filling station to gas up one day. The detective wondered if Wally would be interested in a career in law enforcement. Specifically, the Corpus Christi force needed Spanish-speaking officers. The position did not pay well, but extra duty made up for a low salary, Wally was told. Following initial training, "the *pelotero* from the chaparral" became a permanent fixture in the Corpus Christi Sheriff's Department. He worked in the department for almost 30 years, retiring in 1989.[39]

Rodríguez's love of the game of baseball never ceased. One newspaper account in 1952 reports his playing with the Robstown Merchants (probably a local, Sunday afternoon semi-pro type team like many popular then).[40] Regularly during his lengthy career as a peace officer, he would attend local Corpus Christi games, often being recognized as the "Wallopin'" Wally who had played with the Aces once upon a time and who had hit the first home run out of Schepps Palm Field. On June 3, 1976, he was present at Cabaniss Field, when the Corpus Christi Seagulls opened their season as part of the new Gulf States League. At some games, he would even throw out the first ball.[41]

CONCLUSION

Wally Rodríguez passed away on January 17, 2014. His origins in Concepción, his struggle with poverty, and his play for a small South Texas high school did not seem to augur well for an auspicious future. But gifted with natural skills, the support of family, and encouragement from community boosters, Rodríguez went on to achieve marked success, falling one decision short of joining the Chicago Cubs. His story offers lessons of individual exploits and of the function of sports, topics once thought (as noted at the beginning of this essay) insignificant for the history books. In Rodríguez's advance toward the major leagues, we observe that survival strategies formed while growing up become useful in adulthood, that a work ethic developed during youth finds relevance throughout all phases of life, that success may be attainable notwithstanding the disadvantages one inherits at birth, and that competitors may be bested despite the prevailing wisdom that the adversary is superior. His role in history also speaks to another largely ignored element: that of the place of sports in communities. Sports stand as an integral activity in Hispanic barrio life. Sports give vibrancy to communities. Sports bring solidarity and unity to *la colonia Hispana*. Sports can make a hero of someone from an unlikely community. Certainly, small towns as well as ranches and farms have produced other "Wallopin'" Wallys — their stories yet to be rescued.

QUESTIONS:

1. What circumstances in Wally's background and upbringing enabled him to achieve a successful athletic career?

2. What cultural and personal traits may be identified as facilitating Wally's life achievements?

3. What several causes led him, and other Mexican Americans of that generation, to leave behind their careers as professional baseball players?

NOTES

1. Terry Jordan, *Texas: A Geography* (Boulder: Westview Press, 1984), 33, 37, 155; *The Texas Almanac and State Industrial Guide*, 1945–1946 (Dallas: H. Belo Corporation, 1945), 441; Daniel D. Arreola, *Tejano South Texas:*

A Mexican American Cultural Province (Austin: University of Texas Press, 2002), 111–112; Evan Anders, *Boss Rule in South Texas: The Progressive Era* (Austin: University of Texas Press, 1982), 171; David Montejano, *Anglos and Mexicans in the Making of Texas, 1836–1986* (Austin: University of Texas Press, 1987), 246–247.

2. Arreola, *Tejano South Texas*, 110; *The Texas Almanac and State Industrial Guide, 1945–1946*, 441–442; *The Texas Almanac and State Industrial Guide, 1952–1953* (Dallas: H. Belo Corporation, 1951), 70; Ron Tyler, et al. (eds.), "Duval County," in *The New Handbook of Texas* (6 vols.: Austin: Texas State Historical Association, 1996), II, 742–744, "Sejita," V, 967–968, "Ramírez," V, 424, "Sweden," VI, 169, "Guajillo," III, 367.

3. Diana Davids Olien and Roger M. Olien, *Oil in Texas: The Gusher Age, 1895–1945* (Austin: University of Texas Press, 2002), 209–210; Tyler, et al. (eds.), "Duval County," in *The New Handbook of Texas*, II, 742–744; and ibid., "Freer," II, 1170.

4. Interview with Hermilo Salinas Jr. of Austin, Texas, by author, June 17, 2014, tape in Arnoldo De León's files; Arreola, *Tejano South Texas*, 53, 55; Montejano, *Anglos and Mexicans in the Making of Texas*, 247; Tyler, et al. (eds.), "Duval County," in *The New Handbook of Texas*, II, 742–744; Anders, *Boss Rule in South Texas*, 171.

5. Anders, *Boss Rule in South Texas*, 172; Arreola, *Tejano South Texas*, 112; *The Texas Almanac and State Industrial Guide, 1936* (Dallas: H. Belo Corporation, 1936), 458, 463; *The Texas Almanac and State Industrial Guide, 1943–1944* (Dallas: H. Belo Corporation, 1943), 226, 235.

6. Tyler, et al. (eds.), "Benavides," in *The New Handbook of Texas*, I, 486; Anders, *Boss Rule in South Texas*, 174.

7. Aida Garza, "The History of Benavides and Its Surrounding Area," 14, and author unknown, "History of Benavides," 1, both in *Feria en Benavides*, Sept. 14, 15, 16, 2001 (privately printed, 2001), pamphlet in Arnoldo De León's files; *The Texas Almanac and State Industrial Guide, 1945–1946*, 358; Arreola, *Tejano South Texas*, 81, 185.

8. Garza, "The History of Benavides and Its Surrounding Area," 13; Forrest H. Clark Sr., *The Crosswinds of Duval County* (Houston, TX: 3C Publishers, 1991), 98.

9. Julie Leininger Pycior, *LBJ & Mexican Americans: The Paradox of Power* (Austin: University of Texas Press, 1997), 79.

10. Interview with Wally Rodríguez by Jorge Iber, September 2, 2005, transcript in Arnoldo De León's files; e-mail correspondence with Amando González of Corpus Christi, Texas, October 12, 2014, in Arnoldo De León's files.

11. Copy of Emiliano Rodríguez's death certificate, courtesy of Amando González of Corpus Christi, Texas, in Arnoldo De León's files; interview with Wally Rodríguez by Jorge Iber; e-mail correspondence with Amando González; letter from Wally Rodríguez Jr. of Corpus Christi, Texas, Summer 2014, in Arnoldo De León's files; interview with Hermilo Salinas Jr. by author.

12. E-mail correspondence with Amando González.

13. *El Cenizo,* Benavides High School annual, 1941–1942, courtesy of Amando González of Corpus Christi, Texas, in Arnoldo De León's files. Photo images may be found in *El Cenizo,* 1941–1942 to 1944–1945 annuals, courtesy of Amando González of Corpus Christi, Texas, in Arnoldo De León's files. Tribute of Hermilo Salinas Jr. in obituary to Wally Rodríguez, January 19, 2014.

14. Information derived from reading of *El Cenizo,* 1941–1942 to 1944–1945; interview with Wally Rodríguez by Jorge Iber; interview with Hermilo Salinas Jr. by author.

15. *El Cenizo,* Benavides High School annual, 1943–1944.

16. Ibid.

17. Letter from Wally Rodríguez Jr.; interview with Hermilo Salinas Jr.

18. E-mail correspondence with Amando González.

19. Interview with Hermilo Salinas Jr.; *El Cenizo,* 1944–1945.

20. Letter from Wally Rodríguez Jr.; Edinburg *Daily Review,* Edinburg, Texas, January 7, 1979, 7.

21. Interview with Hermilo Salinas Jr; letter from Wally Rodríguez Jr.; interview with Wally Rodríguez by Jorge Iber.

22. Interview with Wally Rodríguez by Jorge Iber; Corpus Christi *Caller-Times,* Corpus Christi, Texas, September 26, 2006, n.p.

23. *La Prensa,* San Antonio, TX, August 11, 1946.

24. Interview with Wally Rodríguez by Jorge Iber; interview with Hermilo Salinas Jr. by author; letter from Wally Rodríguez Jr.

25. Interview with Wally Rodríguez by Jorge Iber; Corpus Christi *Caller-Times,* June 3, 1976, 19.

26. Undated newspaper clippings, courtesy of Linda Saldaña of Corpus Christi, Texas, in Arnoldo De León's files.

27. Interview with Wally Rodríguez by Jorge Iber; Corpus Christi *Caller-Times,* June 3, 1976, 19; Abilene *Reporter-News,* Abilene, Texas, August 5, 1949, 8.

28. Corpus Christi *Caller-Times,* June 3, 1976, 19; Brownsville *Herald,* Brownsville, Texas, May 27, 1949, 10; letter from Wally Rodríguez Jr.

29. http://www.baseball-reference.com/minors/team.cgi?id=-c8a00c41; Corpus Christi *Caller-Times*, June 3, 1976, 19; undated newspaper clippings, courtesy of Linda Saldaña; Abilene *Reporter-News*, August 5, 1949, 8; Lubbock *Morning-Avalanche*, Lubbock, Texas, August 5, 1949, 9; Lubbock *Evening-Journal*, Lubbock, Texas, August 5, 1949, 9.

30. Corpus Christi *Caller-Times*, June 3, 1976, 19; Valley *Morning-Star*, Harlingen, Texas, September 7, 1949, 9.

31. Undated newspaper clippings, courtesy of Linda Saldaña; http://www.baseball-reference.com/minors/team.cgi?id=660f829f.

32. Corpus Christi *Caller-Times*, June 3, 1976, 19; Galveston *Daily-News*, Galveston, Texas, May 23, 1950, 9; *The Southwest Citizen*, Lake Charles, Louisiana, May 20, 1950, n.p., May 23, 1950, n.p., May 30, 1950, n.p.; Corsicana *Daily-Sun*, Corsicana, Texas, May 26, 1950, 9; Sweetwater *Reporter*, Sweetwater, Texas, May 30, 1950; Mexia *Daily-News,* Mexia, Texas, May 30, 1950, 6.

33. *The Southwest Citizen*, May 26, 1950, n.p.; undated newspaper clippings, courtesy of Linda Saldaña; Galveston *Daily-News*, June 4, 1950, 17, June 22, 1950, 10.

34. Undated newspaper clippings, courtesy of Linda Saldaña (although this particular story appeared circa June 3, 1950).

35. *The Southwest Citizen*, July 9, 1950, n.p.; Galveston *Daily-News*, July 16, 1950, 15, July 19, 1950, 11; Lubbock *Avalanche-Journal*, July 16, 1950, 16; Abilene *Reporter-News*, July 16, 1950, 15; *Valley Morning-Star*, Harlingen, Texas, July 16, 1950, 9; http://www.baseball-reference.com/minors/team.cgi?id=5243d49e.

36. Interview with Wally Rodríguez by Jorge Iber; Corpus Christi *Caller-Times*, January 21, 1951, 35; Odessa *American*, Odessa, Texas, March 14, 1951, 16, March 23, 1951, 9; Abilene *Reporter-News*, March 25, 1951, 50; Sweetwater *Reporter*, April 19, 1951.

37. Pampa *Daily-News*, Pampa, Texas, May 25, 1951, 8; Clovis *News-Journal*, Clovis, New Mexico, April 22, 1951, 14, May 20, 1951, 14, May 31, 1951, 8, and June 1, 1951, 2; http://www.baseball-reference.com/minors/team.cgi?id=658fe93a.

38. Corpus Christi *Caller-Times*, June 3, 1976, 19.

39. Interview with Wally Rodríguez by Jorge Iber.

40. Corpus Christi *Caller Times*, March 9, 1952, 43.

41. Ibid., June 2, 1976, 17, June 3, 1976, 19, September 26, 2006.

¡PONTE EL GUANTE! BASEBALL ON THE US-MEXICAN BORDER:

The Game and Community Building, 1920s–1970s

Alberto Rodriguez
Texas A&M University–Kingsville

AS A YOUNG MAN, I remember my father asking me to put on my glove, so he could hit fly balls to me in our front yard in the Lower Rio Grande Valley. I still recall that voice calling: "¡*Ponte el guante, Beto!* He had never played the game at school or professionally, but we spent every summer following the Los Angeles Dodgers and the St. Louis Cardinals. Fernando Valenzuela and Ozzie Smith were his favorite players, but Vince Coleman and Willie McGee did not stray far behind. Much like most Texas boys, I preferred playing football to baseball, but the times we spent talking about and viewing games are some of my fondest family memories. My father was part of the golden age of baseball in the Lower Rio Grande Valley, the period from the 1920s to the 1970s. Although the game has roots going back to the 1800s, it was not until the early 1900s that the area was engulfed by what many have called America's game. For many Mexicans and Mexican Americans, baseball would allow advances in education, economics, and spaces for community building.

The Lower Rio Grande Valley has a long history of Mexican and Mexican American baseball teams. Teams such as the Brownsville Brownies, Brownsville Tigers, Brownsville Charros, San Benito Nine, Mission 30-30s, and many more have been part of the Lower Rio Grande Valley history since the 1800s.[1] All-Mexican, African American, and Anglo teams challenged Mexican American teams from the Lower Rio Grande Valley and, as a result, Mexican American baseball players often had social encounters that would challenge race and ethnicity on the borderlands. The following are a few of the pro and semi-pro teams that many Mexican Americans played against or for and the year they were established (Est.):

> Brownsville Brownies (Est. 1910)
> Brownsville Tigers (Est. 1928)
> Donna Cardinals (Est. 1949)
> Donna-Weslaco Twins (Est. 1950)
> Edinburg Bobcats (Est.1926)
> Harlingen Capitols (Est. 1950)
> Harlingen Hubs (Est. 1938)
> Harlingen Lads (Est. 1931)
> La Feria Nighthawks (Est. 1931)
> McAllen Dusters (Est. 1927)
> McAllen Giants (Est. 1949)
> McAllen Packers (Est. 1928)
> McAllen Palms (Est. 1931)
> Mission Grape Fruiters (Est. 1928)
> Mission 30-30s (Est. 1920s)
> San Benito Saints (Est. 1931)[2]

The many semi-pro teams allowed for Mexican Americans to play baseball at a young age and against the best in Texas and even the best in the United States.

According to Rene Torres, a local baseball historian who played for many of the teams in the Lower Rio Grande Valley and who is part of the Rio Grande Valley Sports Hall of Fame, "The games were popular and usually drew healthy well-dressed crowds that often engaged in wagering for the home team."[3] Teams such as the Brownsville Tigers and the Mission 30-30s produced local heroes who are still remembered today and helped foster the growth of the game. Two former players who made a mark on the Mexican American community were Adolfo Arguijo and Leonardo "Leo Najo" Alaniz.

Adolfo Arguijo "was an icon on the diamond but, unfortunately, was just as well-known around the beer taverns."[4] Locals remember that Arguijo wore a Yankees cap and carried a photo of himself in a Yankees uniform. It is believed that Adolfo tried out for the Yankees and the St. Louis Cardinals in the 1920s. The baseball career of the 6-feet 6-inch player from San Diego, Texas was cut short by service in WWI, but he returned to professional baseball as a thirty-year-old.[5] According to Rene Torres, "Arguijo's most famous pitch came against the game's most famous player: Babe Ruth. The year is not known, but Arguijo was pitching for the Mexico City Aztecs in an exhibition game when he sent a pitch down the middle of home plate. Ruth nailed it. The crowd went wild, and as Ruth rounded third, [he] tipped his hat to Adolfo, thanking him for the gift."[6] Much like Ruth, Arguijo was a showman; locals remember him asking all his outfielders to sit down as he struck out the side.[7] Later in life he turned to managing and played for the Brownsville Tigers at Charro Park in Brownsville.

Other players also became the pride of the Mexican American community in the Lower Rio Grande Valley. Leonardo "Leo Najo" Alaniz — "*El Conejo*" (the Rabbit) — came to Mission, Texas, as a young boy in the early 1900s. Leo played for the Mission 30-30s from 1918 to 1923 before moving north to play for the San Antonio Bears in 1924. In his seven years in the Texas League, he played in 463 games. As a player he was fast, "twice stealing second base, third base, and home in succession and recording 12 outfield putouts in one game."[8] In 1926, *El Conejo* played for the Chicago White Sox, batting .310 for the season.

After his baseball career, Alaniz returned to Mission to manage the Mission 30-30s and coached Tom Landry and other local baseball players. Alaniz earned many honors, including his induction into the Mexican Baseball Hall of Fame and the Rio Grande Valley Hall of Fame; also, he had a street and a high school baseball field named after him. The city of Mission declared that October 12, 1971, would be designated Leo Najo Day.[9]

Other local baseball players have made history both on and off the diamond. Many Mexican American players made their marks at the University of Texas–Pan American before moving into the American, Mexican, and semi-pro leagues. These players became trailblazers for the Mexican American community and opened the doors of higher education and college sports for years to come.

THE PAN AMERICAN BOYS

The University of Texas–Pan American has a history of Mexican/Mexican American baseball players that dates back to the institution's founding in 1927.[10] Max Cavazos captained the first baseball team at Edinburg College, until recently known as University of Texas–Pan American. The team included five players with Spanish surnames: Guerra, Chavez, Garza, Perez, and J. Perez. Cavazos played catcher and first base and was part of the football team before becoming a well-known umpire in the South Texas region.[11] The university baseball team would continue to be home for many Mexican American players who would excel on the baseball diamond.

In the 1960s and 1970s, Pan American produced an array of great Mexican/Mexican American pitchers, many of whom would go on to play in the majors and who still hold collegiate records today. Two classmates from Brownsville's Saint Joseph Academy dominated on both the hardwood and the diamond. Guadalupe "Lupe" Canul and Felipe Leal were standout basketball players before they played baseball. At Saint Joseph Academy, they won two state titles in basketball, with Leal scoring 1,000 points in his high school career. Canul would score 1,221 points and became JUCO All-American at Texas Southmost College, averaging twenty points and twenty rebounds, before moving to the baseball diamond.[12]

Both Brownsville natives took their talents to the baseball team of what was then Pan American College (later the University of Texas Pan-American and now the University of Texas–Rio Grande Valley) in 1963. Canul pitched for the college from 1963 to 1966, leading his team to their first postseason appearance. In 1964, Canul led the team with an 8–2 record. After his collegiate career on the hardwood and the pitching mound ended, Canul played ten seasons in the Mexican Baseball League and became a semi-pro and high school coach.

Leal also made the transition from basketball to baseball, becoming one of Pan American's best players. Felipe Leal pitched for Pan American College from 1963 to 1965 and was named NAIA All-American in 1963 and 1964. Leal pitched a no-hitter in 1963 versus Trinity University and ranks as one of the top pitchers in program history. In his career, Leal pitched 248.1 innings, had a 1.92

career ERA, and struck out 107 batters in one season and twenty batters in one game in 1963. Felipe played for both the Baltimore Orioles and the California Angels. The line of great Mexican American pitchers at Pan American College would continue with other Mexican –American players.[13]

Only one other pitcher surpassed Tony Barbosa's career at Pan American College. Barbosa pitched for the college from 1967 to 1970, becoming the first pitcher in program history to beat the University of Texas at Austin. Barbosa's career at Pan American was a remarkable one, finishing with many records: 290 innings pitched, 351 strikeouts, career 1.24 ERA, and .89 ERA single season in 1968. In 1969, he was an NCAA All-American, pitching a no-hitter versus the University of Houston. A year later he pitched a one-hitter against Houston Baptist and was drafted by the California Angels.

Barbosa's freshman teammate would become the best pitcher Pan American College had ever seen.[14] Lupe Salinas was a fearless fireball thrower who dominated batters during his collegiate career. Salinas played for Pan American College from 1970 to 1973 and is known for beating the University of Texas 1–0 in 1971, sending his team to the College World Series, their first and only trip to the series. Salinas was an NCAA All-American, finishing his career with many records that still stand today: one hitter (1972) versus St. Mary; one hitter (1971) versus Missouri; 41 complete games; 356.2 innings pitched; 1.16 career ERA, .39 ERA single season in 1972; 309 strikeouts. Salinas is one of the best pitchers to ever come out of South Texas. However, other NCAA All-American players at Pan American College also made great contributions to the area and the establishment of baseball in the Rio Grande Valley.[15]

Mexican/Mexican American pitchers at Pan American were the foundation of the success of its baseball program. Of the twelve no-hitters delivered by Pan American College pitchers, five (42 percent) were pitched by Mexican/Mexican American players. Following are the names of these players, year of the season, and the teams against which they achieved no-hitters: Tony Rico, 1955, versus St. Edward's; Felipe Leal, 1963, versus Trinity University; Tony Barbosa, 1969, versus University of Houston; Mando Reyes, 1976, versus University of Dallas; and Carlos Hidalgo, 1982, versus Baylor.

Mexican/Mexican American players also account for 44 percent of all one-hitters thrown in the history of Pan American College. The following is a list of those pitchers who threw one hitters, their opponents for those games, and the year in which the accomplishment was attained.

> Aaron Guerra, University of the Incarnate Word, 2003
> Alan Maria, Oklahoma State University, 1981
> Alan Maria, Northwestern College, 1980
> Alan Maria, Morningside College, 1980
> Hector Rios, East Tennessee State University, 1979
> Mando Reyes, University of Texas–Arlington, 1976
> Mando Reyes, Dallas Baptist University, 1976
> Jesse Trinidad, Dallas Baptist University, 1976
> Jesse Trinidad, Morningside College, 1976
> Jesse Trinidad, Dallas Baptist University, 1974
> Lupe Salinas, St. Mary's University (TX), 1972
> Lupe Salinas, University of Missouri, 1971
> Tony Barbosa, Houston Baptist University, 1970
> Richie Flores, Texas A&M Corpus Christi, 1962[16]

For many, the success they had on the diamond continued in their personal lives and the communities they shaped. Baseball for them became the foundation of their lives and their legacies.

Hector Salinas was born in Elsa, Texas, and became a great player at Pan American College, but he also made huge contributions on the baseball diamond as a coach at the college level. Along with his teammate, Tony Barbosa, Salinas became an NCAA All-American in 1967 for Pan American College. As an outfielder, Hector hit for power and was always dangerous on the base path, having twenty-seven doubles from 1965 to 1968. Salinas's greatest contributions to South Texas baseball, however, occurred after his collegiate player days were over.[17]

At the high school level, Salinas has been called "the father of Moody Trojan Baseball [Corpus Christi, Texas], having served the nationally renowned high school program as head coach from 1974 to '78 and again for two seasons in 1989–90."[18] In 1978, Salinas took Moody High School to its first state tournament appearance. A year later, he was called up to the college level, becoming the coach of Southmost College in Brownsville, Texas, where his teams went 145–98–2, with four trips to the playoffs between 1979 and 1985. Hector had a long relationship with the Lower Rio Grande Valley as both a player and a coach.

Two of the biggest contributions by Mexican American ex-baseball players to college baseball both happened in the Costal Bend Area. In 1993, Salinas was asked to resurrect the Texas A&M University–Kingsville baseball team. The baseball program had opened in 1926 and closed by 1930. Texas A&M University–Kingsville had been a trailblazer for Mexican American athletes and students since it opened its doors in 1925. For example, Simon Gomez played third base for South Texas Teachers State College (now Texas A&M University–Kingsville) from 1926 to 1930. As a freshman, he was one of the team's best hitters. Both South Texas Teachers State College and Edinburg College were open to Mexican Americans and continue today to be categorized as Hispanic Serving Institutions. As a result, Salinas, who had ties to the Costal Bend Area, understood what Texas A&M University–Kingsville meant for Mexican/Mexican American athletes and students.

As a coach at Texas A&M University–Kingsville, Salinas won 192 games in six seasons, winning the Lone Star Conference in 1995 and 1998 and leading his team to the university's first NCAA tournament. His achievements as a coach are extremely impressive: "1995 LSC Coach of the Year, trained 25 first-team all-conference players and two All-Americans (Juan Sanchez 1995; Steve Foley 1998). He had no athletic scholarships to offer the first four years."[19] Salinas's ability to bring back to life a baseball program that was ended in 1930 and have great success would make him a highly desirable college and university coach in Texas.

In 1998, Texas A&M University–Corpus Christi would call on Salinas to develop a new baseball program. The Texas A&M University–Corpus Christi Islanders, with Salinas as coach, defeated the 2003 NCAA champion University of Texas–Austin 5–0 and in 2005 defeated nationally ranked Oklahoma State University. In 2005, Salinas was named NCAA Independent Coach of the Year and finished his baseball-coaching career with a 172–191 record at Texas A&M University–Corpus Christi. Salinas was not only a great player but also a great coach; as a result he is a member of four halls of fame: "Moody High School Hall of Fame (2000), Rio Grande Valley Sports Hall of Fame (2009), Texas A&M University–Kingsville Javelina Hall of Fame (2013), and Leo Najo Sports Hall of Fame (1980)."[20]

Other Mexican American ex-baseball players would use Pan American College as a stage to have great success in their communities. Arnie Alvarez also played baseball for Pan American College: from 1967 to 1970 the Brownsville, Texas, native played the infield for the Broncs. Alvarez is the only man to be part of the University

Interscholastic League (UIL) State Tournament both as a player and a coach. In 1965 he played third base for Brownsville's Hanna High School and served as coach at Mercedes High School in 1974. Much like his Pan American College teammate, Hector Salinas, Alvarez helped developed collegiate baseball at Southmost College and the University of Texas–Brownsville as a coach and athletic director. Others would follow their Pan American College baseball careers with great success.[21]

Rene Torres, also a teammate of Hector Salinas and Arnie Alvarez, took what he had learned on the diamond and implemented it into a successful life. Torres has a long history in Brownsville, Texas, in baseball, as a politician, and as a scholar. Torres, who played for many of the Brownsville Mexican American baseball teams, was also instrumental in the preservation of its history. Torres was shortstop for the Brownsville High School team that advanced to the final game in the Class 4A tournament in 1965. Rene "later started in center field for Pan American College and committed only one error in three seasons. He was a member of the first Bronc ball club to defeat the Texas Longhorns in 1968."[22]

If anyone is to be called "Mr. Baseball" it is Rene Torres, who played centerfield for Pan American College from 1965 to 1969. Torres is a scholar of all South Texas sports and has single-handedly recovered the history of baseball on the Texas borderlands. Torres has served his community as a member of the Texas Southmost College board of trustees, leading the Hispanic Serving Institution to a new road. People can only dream they affect the world they live in the way Rene Torres has.

Part of the successes that many Mexican/Mexican American baseball players enjoyed was due to the integration of their baseball teams. Pan American not only became home to many Mexican American players in the 1950s and 1960s but included African American players as part of the team. Murray Grant was a pitcher in 1957 and was a member of the Joe Davis Ginners semi-pro team that won the Texas World Series and advanced to the National Baseball Congress World Series in Wichita, Kansas in 1963. The second African American to play baseball at Pan American College was Gary West, centerfielder, in 1964.

Pan American College/University of Texas–Pan American has been home to many Mexican/Mexican American baseball players since it opened its doors as Edinburg College in 1927. Players have had great success in baseball after leaving their institute of higher learning.

The following is a list of Pan American Mexican/Mexican American players who went on to play in the Major Leagues, Mexican Leagues, and Independent Baseball Leagues.

MAJOR LEAGUE BASEBALL ORGANIZATIONS

Jesse Banda, Atlanta Braves
Rafael Barbosa, Atlanta Braves
Tony Barbosa, California Angels
Camilo Estevis, Los Angeles Dodgers
Danny Firova, Seattle Mariners
Kiki García, Pittsburgh Pirates
Lonnie Garza, California Angels
Marco Garza, Cincinnati Reds
Jesse Gutierrez, Cincinnati Reds
Joe Hernandez, Chicago Cubs
Albert Molina, Pittsburgh Pirates
Jody Moore, Florida Marlins
Jorge Ortiz, San Francisco Giants
Omar Ortiz, San Diego Padres
Hector Rios, San Diego Padres
Mark Rodriguez, Cincinnati Reds

MEXICAN PROFESSIONAL TEAMS

Kiki Beltran, Mexico
Lupe Canul, Mexico City
Luie Chavez, Mexico
Richie Cortez, Reynosa
Joe Lara, Reynosa
Felipe Leal, Mexico City
Eric Martinez, Mexico
Arturo Puig, Reynosa
Arthur Rodriguez, Reynosa
Hector Salinas, Vera Cruz
Lupe Salinas, Reynosa
Jorge Sanchez, Reynosa

Tommy Sandoval, Reynosa
Ricky Soliz, Monterrey

INDEPENDENT BASEBALL ORGANIZATIONS

Aldo Alonzo, Edinburg
Kelly Casares, Edinburg
Gabe de la Garza, Independent
Ray DeLeon, Independent
Marco Garza, Edinburg
Aaron Guerra, Edinburg
Rick Pena, Harlingen
Bert Reyes, Independent
Danny Roma, Utica
Roy Sosa, Harlingen
Kiki Trevino, Independent
Jesse Trinidad, Laredo[23]

The list of the many University of Texas–Pan American Mexican American players who joined professional leagues after their collegiate days ended demonstrates the level of athleticism showcased in the Rio Grande Valley. Many Mexican American baseball players who called the University of Texas–Pan American home played in the highest levels of the minors and in the Major Leagues. For other Mexican American baseball players, the Mexican Leagues served as an avenue to continuing their careers in hopes of making a living and leaving a mark on the game they loved. The Mexican Leagues also served as a summer training camp for many local baseball players, allowing them to perfect their craft against much older and more established players. Other University of Texas–Pan American alumni played in the many independent Texas organizations that served as a de facto minor league for the Mexican Leagues and the A, AA, and AAA teams of the United States. The fact that so many Mexican American players from the University of Texas–Pan American continued their baseball careers after attending college must not be overlooked. Such players had talent and commitment to their craft and as a result were rewarded with opportunities to keep playing.

According to historian Adrian Burgos, "Latinos adopted America's game and gave the sport meaning that went beyond athletic competition. For them, baseball also became a site for building community, class behavior, and displaying masculinity. And as the game became professionalized and opportunities to play in the United States increased, baseball also developed into a possible avenue of escape for impoverished Latinos."[24] Baseball games became instrumental to the identity of Mexicans on the borderlands of the Lower Rio Grande Valley.

Others understood that the love of the game felt by Mexicans and Mexican Americans would produce profits. Much like the Negro Leagues that had a large African American following, the same can be said for the Lower Rio Grande Valley teams that were made up of a majority of Mexican American players who had links and roots to the area. In turn, when a game was played, the whole city would partake in the event. Locals used such events to promote their businesses and even their political candidacies. If such people could influence the crowd or players to partake in their interest, they could benefit and profit from the games in their community.

THE 1963 JOE DAVIS GINNERS AND THE 1967 SALAZAR GROCERY ALL-STARS

Ramon Cantu — whom locals called "Mr. Baseball" — was considered the Lower Rio Grande Valley's most useful baseball promoter. As a semi-pro promoter, he sponsored and organized teams throughout the Rio Grande Valley, with two teams that came to fame in the 1950s: the Harlingen Capitols and the Edinburg Merchants. Cantu's greatest success, however, would come with the Salazar Grocery All-Stars, who were dominant in the late 1960s in the South Texas League of the National Baseball Association. In 1963, his sponsored team won the National Baseball Congress state title in Lubbock. The championship was an integrated one and included top players such as Felipe Leal (Mexican American) and Johnny Flowers (African American).[25]

In 1967, Ramon Cantu once more led an integrated team to the National Baseball Congress World Series with the Salazar Grocery All-Stars. Major League players such as Tom Seaver, Dave Winfield, Don Sutton, Ozzie Smith, Roger Clemens, and Tony Gwynn all played in the National Baseball Congress World Series. The following is a list of Mexican/Mexican American players who were part of the 1967 team, many of whom were Pan American College greats:

Luis Alamia
Arnie Alvarez
Tony Barbosa
Lupe Canul
Richard Cortez
Queenie Cortez
A.C. Deanda
Ray García
Juan Guzman
Roger Luna[26]

Luis Alamia — of what locals call the first family of the University of Texas–Pan American baseball — and brother Richy played in 1963; son Louie Alamia was a standout in 2003–2006 and still holds records for most base hits at 762, longest hitting streak (24 games in 2006, with 22 and 21 hitting streaks in 2003 and 2004 respectively). In 2003, Louie was named First Team All American Freshman. In four years, he averaged .352 for his career, had 267 hits, and scored 149 runs.[27]

Other Salazar Grocery All-Stars had great careers at Pan American College and in their semi-pro careers. Nieves "Queenie" Cortez and his brother Richard Cortez played for Pan American College in the 1960s. The Cortez brothers led the Salazar Grocery All-Stars of Edinburg Texas to the National Baseball Congress World Series in Wichita, Kansas in 1968. During the first at bat, Queenie led off his team with a home run in the Salazar Grocery All-Stars' opening game. Queenie remembers how community played an important role in baseball: "When we played in Lubbock for the state title, old friends from the Valley that were working in the cotton fields came out to see us play. We even put on a baseball camp for the local Mexican American community."[28] Queenie and his brother had lengthy careers in the Lower Rio Grande Valley and Mexican League and became instrumental in passing the game on to youngsters in and out of the Rio Grande Valley.

As the 1980s began, the golden age of baseball ended in the Lower Rio Grande Valley. As new coaches led the University of Texas–Pan American, Texas A&M University, and Texas A&M–Corpus Christi University baseball teams, few Mexican American athletes became part of the teams from 1980 to 2000. In turn, with the growing popularity of other high school sports, especially football, few athletes found baseball as desirable an option. With the invention of the internet and growing telecommunications alternatives, local businesses and political candidates had limited use for local teams. Others would find playing in the Mexican Leagues a dangerous endeavor, because of the increase in cartel violence on the border and in Mexican cities.

The many Mexicans/Mexican Americans who played the game in their communities, college, and pro leagues changed South Texas and the lives of many people. Baseball became an avenue for social, cultural, and economic mobility. Collegiate programs such as those in Edinburg, Kingsville, and Corpus Christi allowed for these men to showcase their talents as players, coaches, and teachers and, as a result, influenced and trained a whole new generation of Mexican American ballplayers. For many, baseball was the beginning of a long life of service to and activism on behalf of their communities, people, and race. For people such as my father, baseball was more than a game: it was a blueprint for life and all its challenges.

QUESTIONS:

1. What role did baseball play in the Mexican American community?

2. How did Mexican American college players change higher education and improve their personal situations?

3. Are there any links between the experiences of African American and Mexican American baseball players?

NOTES

1. The historiography of Latino and Mexican/Mexican American baseball athletes has been at the center of many recent works, e.g.: Jorge Iber and Samuel O. Regalado, eds., *Mexican Americans and Sports: A Reader on Athletics and Barrio Life* (College Station: Texas A&M University Press, 2007); Jorge Iber, Samuel Regalado, José M. Alamillo, and Arnoldo De León, *Latinos in U.S. Sport: A History of Isolation, Cultural Identity, and Acceptance* (Human Kinetics, 2011); Jorge Iber, ed., *More Than Just Peloteros: Sport and US Latino Communities* (Lubbock: Texas Tech University Press, 2015); Francisco E. Balderrama and Richard A. Santillan, *Mexican American Baseball in Los Angeles* (Charleston. SC: Arcadia Publishing, 2011); Richard A. Santillan, Mark A. Ocegueda, Terry A. Cannon, *Mexican American Baseball*

in the Inland Empire (Charleston, SC: Arcadia Publishing, 2012); Richard A. Santillan, Christopher Docter, Anna Bermúdez, Eddie Navarro, Alan O'Connor, *Mexican American Baseball in the Central Coast* (Charleston, SC: Arcadia Publishing, 2013); Richard A. Santillan, Susan C. Luévano, Luis F. Fernández, Angelina F. Veyna, *Mexican American Baseball in Orange County* (Charleston, SC: Arcadia Publishing, 2013); Richard A. Santillan, Mark A. Ocegueda, Alfonso Ledesma, Sandra L. Uribe, Alejo L. Vásquez, *Mexican American Baseball in the Pomona Valley* (Charleston, SC: Arcadia Publishing, 2013); Adrian Burgos Jr., *Playing America's Game: Baseball, Latinos, and the Color Line* (Berkeley: University of California Press, 2007); Noe Torres, *Baseball's First Mexican American Star: The Amazing Story of Leo Najo* (Llumina Press, 2006).

2. Noe Torres, *Ghost Leagues: A History of Minor League Baseball in South Texas* (Llumina Press, 2005). See also http://www.baseball-reference.com.

3. Rene Torres, "Neighborhood Leagues Kept Kids off the Streets and on the Diamond: The 'Solar Vacante' Served as the Perfect Diamond," (provided to author by Rene Torres, who states that the story was featured in the *Brownsville Herald*, date unknown).

4. Jeff Raymond, "Serving It Up: Pitcher Found Niche as Local Waiter after Pro Baseball Career," *Brownsville Herald*, April 24, 2005. Rene Torres, Personal Collection, Brownsville, Texas, 2014.

5. Ibid.

6. Ibid.

7. Ibid.

8. Leonardo "Leo Najo" Alaniz, https://missiontexas.us/about-mission/famous-people/leonardo-alaniz.

9. Torres, *Baseball's First Mexican American Star.*

10. University of Texas Pan American, *El Bronco Yearbook Collection: 1928*, Lower Rio Grande Valley Collection, The University of Texas Pan American: Edinburg, Texas, 2014.

11. Rio Grande Valley Sport Hall of Fame, http://rgvsportshalloffame.org/?inductee=max-cavazos, 2014.

12. Rio Grande Valley Sport Hall of Fame, http://rgvsportshalloffame.org/?inductee=guadalupe-lupe-canul, 2014, and http://rgvsportshalloffame.org/?inductee=felipe-leal-garcia.

13. Ibid,, and *Baseball Media Guide University of Texas Pan American*, 45–52.

14. *Baseball Media Guide University of Texas Pan American*, 45–52, and http://rgvsportshalloffame.org/?inductee=tony-barbosa-jr, 2014.

15. *Baseball Media Guide University of Texas Pan American*, 45–52, http://

rgvsportshalloffame.org/?inductee=lupe-salinas

16. *Baseball Media Guide University of Texas Pan American*, 45–52.

17. Ibid.

18. Corpus Christi Hooks News, "Lifetime Achievement Award: Hector Salinas," http://www.milb.com/news/article.jsp?ymd=20140114&content_id=66611138&fext=.jsp&vkey=news_t48 2&sid=t482, 2014.

19. Ibid.

20. Ibid.

21. Rio Grande Valley Sport Hall of Fame, http://rgvsportshalloffame.org/?inductee=arnoldo-arnie-alvarez, 2014.

22. Roy Hess, "Brownsville Well-Represented in '07 RGV Sports HOF," *Brownsville Herald*, June 8, 2007; On Deck - Program History: 2007 *Baseball Media Guide University of Texas Pan American*, 50.

23. *Baseball Media Guide University of Texas–Pan American*, 44.

24. Adrian Burgos Jr., *Playing America's Game*. Also see Jorge Iber, et al., *Latinos in U.S. Sport*, and José M. Alamillo, *Making Lemonade out of Lemons: Mexican American Labor and Leisure in a California Town, 1880–1960* (Champaign, IL: University of Illinois Press, 2006).

25. Rio Grande Valley Sports Hall of Fame, http://rgvsportshalloffame.org/?inductee=ramon-o-cantu, 2014.

26. Rene Torres, "Edinburg Win State National Baseball Congress Crown in 1967: The Valley 'Dirty Dozen' Captures Second Title," *The Monitor*, March 20, 2011, Personal Collection, Brownsville, Texas, 2014.

27. *Baseball Media Guide University of Texas Pan American*, 47–52, http://rgvsportshalloffame.org/?inductee=luis-prince-of-thieves-alamia-jr, 2014.

28. Nieves "Queenie" Cortez interview with author, summer 2014.

"A DIVIDED COMMUNITY UNITED ON THE DIAMOND":

The 1962 Hidalgo County Colt League Baseball World Series Champions

Juan David Coronado
Central Connecticut State University

"OUR CONNECTION TO THE WORLD was through sport."[1] In 1962, Hidalgo County, Texas, formed an all-star team comprised of fifteen- and sixteen-year-old boys (the age requirement of the Colt League) that qualified for and competed in the 1962 Colt League World Series in Shawnee, Oklahoma. The team transcended ethnic and social barriers, as boys from across the Rio Grande Valley in deep-most South Texas came together to represent their community. The gravest challenges to several of the boys were extreme poverty, prejudice, and racial restrictions.

In a pre-Civil Rights society in the early 1960s, towns in South Texas with sizable Mexican American populations remained segregated as an Anglo American minority still in power applied a unique form of Jim Crow laws and practices (enforcing racial segregation) that had become so prevalent.[2] Baseball was one of the few activities that became integrated by both Mexican Americans and Anglos. The makeup of the Hidalgo County team was split down the middle: eight Mexican Americans and eight Anglo Americans, one Mexican American head coach and one Anglo American assistant manager. Contrary to a South Texas society that remained divided, the team demonstrated unity in its efforts to fulfill a true Cinderella story.

During the era of the 1940s–1960s, baseball was the community's favorite pastime in the Rio Grande Valley as families flooded local ballparks in support of their teams and family members who played at various levels ranging from Little League all the way to semi-professional. The impact of the great Leonardo "Leo Najo" Alaniz, who had been drafted by the Chicago White Sox in 1925, could be felt not only in his hometown of Mission, Texas, but also in the surrounding communities of McAllen, Pharr, Edinburg, Peñitas, and the rest of the Rio Grande Valley. Semi-pro baseball had a cult following, as Sunday matinees were regularly enjoyed and youngsters dreamed of one day representing their local teams.[3]

In a post-World War II society, a large number veterans returned to their homes in the Rio Grande Valley, and baseball served as a therapeutic distraction from their memories of war. In Mission, Leo Najo — along with Bernardo Peña, Jose Carreon Garza, and other ballplayers — founded the Mission 30-30s. Edinburg had the Joe Davis Ginners, McAllen had the Palms, the Merchants represented Pharr; the small communities outside of Mission also had teams, as the Madero Valley Brickers and the Granjeno Lions played ball. Even the King Ranch Cowboys, a semi-pro team from Kingsville, made the rounds to challenge Valley squads.[4]

Empowered by their war experiences, Mexican Americans sought to become more integrated into their everyday society, and baseball became a vessel for integration. Mexican Americans became integral participants in the American pastime for several reasons, including the popularity of baseball soaring in the postwar years. The sport served as entertainment for the players and community, and the changing demographics allowed the sport to become more integrated as the Anglo population dwindled in South Texas. In the border region, baseball was inclusive, as it connected a society that otherwise was disjointed by a political border and by de facto segregation. The popularity of baseball was a transnational phenomenon. Teams from Monterrey, Nuevo León, and from the border town of Reynosa, Tamaulipas, along with other teams, travelled north across the Rio

Grande to challenge their South Texas neighbors and often hosted games as American teams travelled to Mexico for an attractive outing as well.[5]

Semi-pro teams such as the Mission 30-30s set a precedent for integration and a limited interaction among Mexican Americans and Anglo Americans. The legendary Tom Landry, also a Mission native, suited up for the 30-30s. Through the early 1960s, Mission, like most Valley towns, remained segregated, as the Anglo community lived north of the railroad tracks and the Mexican American community lived south of the tracks. As a result, Mexican American barrios such as *Monterreyito* arose in South Mission.

Sports served as an avenue for interaction between both groups, easing racial tensions. During the 1946 season, the 30-30s played primarily on the road as they lacked a home field.[6] The team eventually nestled itself at the 30-30 ballpark located in Southwest Mission in what traditionally was the Mexican American part of town. Similar to the phenomenon José M. Alamillo noted with the Corona Athletics Baseball Club in California, the Anglo American community soon found itself cheering for the 30-30s in South Mission, an area almost never frequented by Anglos.[7]

Racial animosity was not the only obstacle plaguing the community in South Texas. Historically, unity has not come easy for the Mexican American community in the Rio Grande Valley. Stemming from a legacy of colonial conquest in which their native and Mexican ancestors were divided, conquered, and killed, while those that survived were forced to assimilate, Mexican Americans in South Texas have carried a legacy of division.[8] Even though geographically and politically isolated from the rest of the United States, South Texans have often remained divided among themselves instead of forging everlasting bonds.

With an institutionalized and regionalized mentality, South Texans viewed themselves not as a united region but rather as Bobcats, Cardinals, Bulldogs, Eagles, and Bears — the local high school sports teams. By 1962, running on the recent high that took Donna High School to a Class AA State Football Championship in 1961, the Valley was shaping for more sports success and ready for cross-county unity. Jorge Iber, in his piece "On Field Foes and Racial Misconceptions," has shed light on the efforts by the Donna boys in fulfilling what many thought was impossible for a Valley team: suiting up Mexican Americans.[9]

In summer 1962, the Mission Colt Team won the Hidalgo County League championship, earning Mission's coach Reynaldo Valadez the opportunity to coach an all-star team that would emerge with the top players from the entire county. Valadez, a Mission native, grew up in Leo Najo's neighborhood in the Mexican American barrio. There the former Major League Baseball prospect spent endless nights mentoring the younger Valadez.[10] Eventually, Valadez developed into a star pitcher for the Mission High School Eagles and led them to a district title in 1952. "La Zorra was a heck of a pitcher," recalls Francisco Estevis, who pitched against Valadez in the post-season that year and would later become a college teammate.[11] The nickname "La Zorra" (The Fox) was given to Valadez by Najo himself as a testament to his crafty and cunning ability on the mound.[12] Many of the ball players from the area were affectionately bestowed nicknames.

After playing semi-pro baseball for various teams including the Mission 30-30s, Valadez's passion for baseball continued and he began coaching. Selecting the 1962 all-star team would not come easy, as Hidalgo County fielded plenty of talent. Coach Valadez knew he could rely on the Mission youngsters, fresh from winning the league, to carry the load. Still, to give all young boys an opportunity, tryouts were held at McAllen's Cascade Park.[13] Not surprisingly, seven of the sixteen boys selected had played for the Mission team. Of the seven boys, Francisco Santiago and Roberto Zamora were from the neighboring farming community of Peñitas and the remaining five — Miguel "Mike" Santana, José Torres, Ted Gerlach, Gary Robinson, and Norris Lewis — lived in Mission. Representing McAllen were Michael Cline, Leslie Saunders, and Conrado "Conrad" Villarreal Jr. Edinburg sent three ballplayers: Ted Larson, Jack Williams Jr., and Roy Lee Hinojosa Jr. Pharr contributed two players, Gabriel Serda Jr. and Lizandro "Lee" Gonzalez, and representing the Mid-Valley town of Mercedes was Sherwood Lucas Jr.[14]

While cohesiveness and racial harmony existed on the field, tensions mounted among the coaching staff off the field. Pharr manager Glen Robie, who had been a rival, approached Valadez seeking an assistant coaching position on the team and Valadez kindly agreed. However, on the Tournament Team Eligibility Affidavit, Robie listed himself as "Manager" and Valadez as "Coach."[15] Despite the paperwork, Valadez remained in control of the team as Robie positioned himself for a key role that summer.

The racial tensions that plagued the community and restrained the older generation contrasted with the racial attitudes of the boys on the field. "We were happy we were gonna play ball," recalls pitcher Miguel Santana. "We didn't care who was from where or whether you were Hispanic or Anglo. We loved to play and that was the main thing. We didn't treat anybody different. No racial issues. We were of a different generation. We interacted better. We didn't see no difference."[16] The Colt League youngsters did not allow skin color or surnames to dictate the fate of their squad, as their love for baseball trumped the racial tensions and barriers that existed in their communities and were not always addressed by the Mexican American community nor fully acknowledged by the Anglo American community.

In many ways, the Colt League boys reflected the changing times, as by the 1960s the Mexican American community challenged the status quo that had relegated them to a second-class status. In one instance, shortstop, pitcher, and left-fielder Francisco Santiago quit the team in response to the imposition by an Anglo parent. "I stopped going to practice because they didn't want me to play shortstop. After Robinson's father put pressure on Coach Rey Valadez to play his son, he came to my home asking me why I stopped going to practice and I explained to him in my broken English and he asked me to return to the team even though it would affect his son's playing time. I didn't question it. I wanted to play," remembers Francisco Santiago.[17] The passion for the sport overcame the divisions and tensions and baseball became the priority, as if something special was brewing among the boys that summer.

More important, baseball allowed an interaction between Anglos and Mexican Americans that was otherwise limited in Rio Grande Valley society. Right fielder José Torres, who lived in the Mexican American barrio, remembers the segregation in Mission: "Monterreyito, it's across the tracks. There's two tracks, one that runs north and south and one that runs east and west. The east and west separated the well-to-do from the poor neighborhoods. We lived in the poor neighborhood. Whites lived to the east [and north] of the tracks, where all the businesses were located. There was no such thing as interaction." Segregation for Mexican Americans extended to the public school system, as Torres recollects: "I started going to Roosevelt [elementary], *era puro Mexicanos* (it was all Mexicans). They had their own schools for sure."[18]

Team co-captain and catcher Roberto Zamora attests to the tense racial atmosphere in Mission. "We were isolated from the rest. We knew that if we would go to Mission there were places like the swimming pool that we couldn't get into. We had heard stories. In our schools, we were told not to speak Spanish."[19]

"In Mission there was discrimination," confirms pitcher Miguel Santana. "Crystal Waters was a swimming pool in Mission. They wouldn't allow Hispanics in there, only Anglos. In downtown, there was Mission Theater and Border Theater. Mission Theater was for Hispanics and Border Theater was for Anglos. In Mission, there was a restaurant, Manhattan Café, they also didn't serve Mexicans. There was a sign: 'No Mexicans or Dogs Allowed.'"[20] Middle-class and upper-middle-class Mexican Americans, however, often intermingled with Anglos and found themselves in North and East Mission.

Racial segregation may have been the rule in South Texas, but socioeconomic mobility became the exception to the rule. Outfielder Lizandro "Lee" Gonzalez's family, who owned a successful service station in Pharr, moved into the Anglo part of town. "Pharr was a place in my day divided by the railroad," summarizes Lee. "North of the railroad was the Hispanic community and south of the railroad was the Anglo community. Our family moved to the south side in 1956. I went to school with Anglos. I grew up in the Anglo community. In my school, I was one of the few Mexican Americans. My friend at the time was Chinese, Pete Lee. It's not like I grew up in the *barrio* 'cause I didn't."[21] Upward social mobility challenged segregationist patterns, and several Mexican American families left the barrio for the more affluent middle-class neighborhoods.

While social prosperity tore down those walls, baseball momentarily blurred the divisions. "The only reason I would interact with them: I had to walk from my home all the way to Lions Park," confirms Torres, as he recounts crossing into northeast Mission. "Walking all the way. I would play Little League and I would walk back. And Lions Park was in the White part of town."[22] Baseball exposed some of the Mexican American players to an Anglo world that had not been previously open to them.

Segregation and racism were so rampant in the town of Weslaco that Mexicans and Mexican Americans were restricted from living south of the railroad tracks that ran across Highway 83. Supporting segregation in Weslaco was despicably racist ideology. "The wind blows from the southeast in the Valley," explained historian Juanita Elizondo Garza. "Anglos did not want Mexicans living in South Weslaco because they would have to smell them as the wind blew from the southeast into the north. My God, can you believe that?"[23]

In summer 1962, however, a group of fifteen- and sixteen-year-old boys put behind South Texas racism and segregation and came together to play in the Colt League World Series. For several of the Mexican American boys, the biggest challenge came in convincing their parents to allow them to play. Typically, many Chicano families left the Rio Grande Valley during summertime, following the migrant trail north. "[During] our summertime as a migrant family we migrated. It just happened that particular summer we were not migrating. One of the expectations from my parents was that we had to work," declares Robert Zamora. "So, my initial interaction with my parents was 'you are not playing because you are gonna have to work.' I still remember having a big argument. 'If you want to play you are gonna have to work. You are going to have to find a way to the games. Wherever we are you are gonna have to get home and go to the ballpark'"[24] During the morning, Zamora would work doggedly in the fields with his family and would have to run home in order to make it to baseball practice.

Francisco Santiago found himself in a similar situation to Robert's and was overjoyed with not having to migrate and work that summer. "Some people call them the good ol' days. For me, they were not. *A veces ni me quiero acordar.* (I do not even want to remember.) We were poor, but we didn't know we were poor. Life was hard growing up," admits Santiago. "It was my best summer. *No fui a piscar. No fui a trabajar en el labor.* (I did not go pick cotton. I did not go work in the fields.) I was just playing ball. *No sé cómo le hizo apa* (I do not know how dad could afford) to let me go and play ball. We would go to Sinton [Texas] to pick cotton. I don't know how dad made it, but he let me play ball. It was a sacrifice they made. It was the best summer I had. It was good."[25] For Santiago, playing ball in the South Texas summer heat that regularly rises to the triple digits was preferable to working in the fields in one-hundred-degree weather.

Summers in the Rio Grande Valley were challenging, as agricultural work was virtually nonexistent due to the intense heat. Following the cotton trail and other crops, many families migrated north in search of seasonal work. José Torres's family also headed north following the migrant trail. "I was a cotton-picker, migrant farmworker," affirms Torres. "We would start in San Antonio, picking cotton, then go to El Campo, migrate to Houston or Dallas. Then Altus, Oklahoma: around October, of course, school had already started. We did that up to my age of sixteen. Then back home to school."[26] The typical life of migrant farmworker children involved the curtailing of the academic school year due to travel.

It was not only the struggling Mexican American boys who worked during summertime, as some of the other boys worked as well. Ted Gerlach worked construction with his father during the summer, while Ted Larson worked on the family farm in Edinburg. Lee Hinojosa worked at his father's service station and pulled a newspaper route in Pharr. The youth of that time were expected to contribute to the household and still made time to play ball.

On July 12, 1962, the Hidalgo County Colt team initiated the Colt League Tournament, seeking qualification to the Colt League World Series at the area level by playing and defeating Brownsville. They moved on to the district level, challenging Corpus Christi Seaside who forced a third game in a two-loss elimination match-up. "We played Corpus and we got beat the first game," recalls first-baseman Ted Gerlach. "Game was over at ten o'clock at night and we practiced 'til one in the morning. Coach made us stay there and practice. Then we won two in a row."[27] A soft-spoken Coach Valadez kept the team focused on the task ahead and ironed out sloppy creases with practice.

Hidalgo County moved on to sectionals, defeating a Monterrey, Mexico team and qualifying to regionals where they faced a team from the neighboring town of Harlingen and then a team from Houston. Without major difficulties, Hidalgo County moved on to the divisional round in Abilene against El Paso. For many of the boys this would be their first time out of South Texas. Edinburg resident and volunteer firefighter Johnny Economedes joined the team as bus driver, trainer, and personal assistant to the boys. After seeing the deplorable bus assigned to the team, Economedes momentarily disappeared and returned with a borrowed bus from the Edinburg School District to transport the team; he took on several roles for the team, becoming an asset on the road.[28] He assumed personal responsibilities such as washing clothes for the boys who were unaccompanied, especially since many of the parents could not afford to travel to see the Colts play.

While the social and racial atmosphere in Abilene may have not been much different from that of South Texas, the unfamiliarity in the West Texas town lent itself to open discrimination. At least in the Rio Grande Valley, the boys knew where they were not welcome, but in Abilene they would have to identify locales of racism themselves. Mike Santana remembers:

José Torres and I, when we got to Abilene, we went for a walk around town. We saw one of those five-and-dime stores. We walked in and they had a fountain where they sell hamburgers and malts. We sat and there were only Anglos. We wondered when they would come take our order. Norris Lewis came over and sat with us. One of the girls came over and asked Norris what he wanted. He asked for a hamburger and malt. He asked us if we had ordered and we told him no. He called the girl back and the girl said they didn't serve Hispanics there. So, we got up and Norris got up with us and he didn't even pay or wait for his meal. He walked out with us. That was one experience that I will not forget.[29]

This incident of discrimination would not sidetrack Santana and Torres; if anything it brought them closer to their teammate, Norris Lewis, who demonstrated solidarity with his friends.

In a three-game series, Hidalgo County would top El Paso for a chance to enter the Colt World Series in Shawnee, Oklahoma. After forcing a third game, El Paso fell 2–1 in a tight game where Frank Santiago pitched a fine outing and Conrad Villarreal closed the game and sealed a trip to Shawnee.[30] Although Hidalgo County secured a trip to Shawnee, entry to the Colt League World Series was not guaranteed. They still needed to face a team from Pensacola, Florida, in a three-game series to see who would represent the Southern Division in the 1962 Colt League World Series.[31]

After the victory against El Paso, the boys began to believe that their Cinderella story was possible and would not come to an end at the strike of midnight. Arriving in Shawnee felt like a homecoming to the Hidalgo County Colt team. "The town of Shawnee was behind us. It was like playing [at] home. We had all the support from them. They invited us and welcomed us everywhere in town. We were always the underdog. They called us the Border Bandits," remembers Ted Gerlach.[32]

In Game 1 against Pensacola, Ted Larson pitched a three-hit shutout, striking out thirteen as Hidalgo topped Pensacola 2–0 and inched closer to a World Series berth. The following night Hidalgo clinched the final World Series spot in a 4–1 victory over Pensacola, becoming the Southern Divisional Champion. They now joined the Northern Divisional Champion—Hamtramck, Michigan, a Detroit suburb team that had won the Pony League World Series the previous year and now was in line to repeat at the Colt level.[33] Norfolk County, Virginia, the Eastern Divisional Champion and Riverside, California, the Western Divisional Champion rounded up the final four in the 1962 Colt League World Series.

On August 20, 1962, the night before the World Series was set to start, all four teams were invited to a banquet at Oklahoma Baptist University. Comedian Joe E. Brown and former Major League ballplayers Allie Reynolds, Dale Mitchell, Lloyd Waner, Lou Kretlow, and Pepper Martin served as guest speakers at the banquet and reinforced positive values to the Colt leaguers.[34] For the first time, Hidalgo County felt undersized and overmatched as their opponents seemed bigger and stronger. "We were little guys compared to giants," admits Conrad Villareal.[35] But, here they were and there was no backing down for the Texans.

The phenom at the 1962 Colt League World Series was Bobby Bonds, who starred for Riverside, California. Pro scouts would be in attendance throughout the series watching Bonds' every at-bat. Unsurprisingly, he would make his Major League Baseball debut only six years later. Perhaps watching Bonds even closer were coach and strategist Rey "La Zorra" Valadez, whose nickname was very fitting in these occasions, and catcher Robert Zamora. Conrad Villarreal recalls Coach Valadez's scouting ability. "He knew his baseball. He would tell you: pitch here, throw him a fastball, or a curve. He would study the opposing batters and their stance and then he would say this guy did this in the first inning. He was a strategist."[36] If Hidalgo County was going to prevail, they were going to have to outsmart and outhustle their stronger opponents. Strong pitching, good defense, good coaching, and small ball would be key for the Texans.

The first game in a double-elimination tournament matched Hidalgo County against favorites Hamtramck, Michigan. Frank Santiago and Conrad Villarreal combined for a 6–3 victory and moved on to the winners' bracket in a showdown with Riverside, California. The heat may have been a factor, as the Michigan players seemed to be bothered by the "100-degree temperatures Monday and Tuesday while Hidalgo County, Texas from the Mexican border seemed to think it was kind of cool."[37] Being comfortable in the heat, the Hidalgo County boys preferred day games to night games, which they were not accustomed to play as most ballparks in the Valley were not equipped with lights.

On the second day of the tournament in the losers' bracket, Norfolk eliminated Hamtramck and would move on to face the loser of Hidalgo County and Riverside. With a late start of 10 p.m. local time, Hidalgo County went up 4–0 in the top of the third inning. Riverside pulled three runs back in the fourth and Bobby Bonds blasted a four-hundred-foot, two-run home run to dead centerfield, which would eventually give Riverside a 5–4 victory.[38]

Hidalgo County was now on the brink of elimination and faced a Norfolk County team riding the momentum after eliminating Michigan. Robie, Valadez, and co-captain Zamora came together to game plan and decide on a starting pitcher. "We would scout the players, I remember us doing it, and we noticed that Norfolk was a very impatient team," comments Zamora. "They would get up to the plate and start swinging. We went down our list of pitchers and came up with one player that hadn't been pitching: Gabriel Serda! Why Gabriel? He is very patient. He gets off the mound and takes his time. And sure enough, he did all that. Gabriel pitched the only shutout in the World Series and that allowed the rotation to keep going like it had done before."[39] Gabriel Serda pitched a five-hitter, and Hidalgo's bats showed up for an 8–0 shutout and went on to eliminate Norfolk.

Revenge was on the minds of the Rio Grande Valley boys as they now faced Riverside again and would have to beat them twice for the Colt League Championship. Ted Larson got the start for Texas, and unfortunately Bobby Bonds' bat showed up again as he went 3 for 3, driving in three runs including a home run which would be his third for the series.[40] Fortunately for Texas, a series of costly Riverside errors in the sixth inning would give Hidalgo a 9–4 lead and force one final championship game.

The stage was set at Shawnee's Memorial Park as a 4,000-plus crowd shuffled in to witness the deciding game of the 1962 Colt League World Series. Daryl Farnsworth got the start for Riverside and Coach Valadez trusted Francisco Santiago to pitch in the deciding game. In the top of the first inning, California jumped to an early lead, driving in two runs including an RBI single for Bonds. In the bottom frame of the first, Hidalgo County answered with three runs of their own including an RBI double for Santiago; Roy Hinojosa batted in two more himself. Both pitchers settled down and after three shutout innings Coach Valadez turned to Conrado Villarreal in the fifth inning to close out Riverside. "I was thinking I could have gone more innings," remembers Santiago. Instead, "I went to left field. We were used to playing in the day. We were not used to playing under the lights. That summer was the first time we played at night. So, I wasn't comfortable with the dim lights."[41] Hidalgo County would have to secure the victory in the dimming light of Memorial Park, and an error would be costly to the narrow margin.

Security runs showed up in the bottom of the fourth and bottom of the sixth innings for Texas; still, a swing from Bonds and Riverside could easily make a comeback. Catcher Robert Zamora, counseled by Coach Valadez, noticed a flaw in the future big leaguer's at bat. "To Bobby Bonds it was a curve outside and low. I would see him on TV and he would still miss those," asserts Zamora.[42] After Coach Valadez shared his advice with Villarreal, Bobby Bonds struck out on his final plate appearance. The 6–2 lead was insurmountable, and Hidalgo County claimed the 1962 Colt League World Series. Santiago and Villarreal held Riverside to three hits, a feat that the two remain very proud of today. "We were never favorite," recalls co-captain and now Colt League World Series Most Valuable Player Robert Zamora. The Hidalgo County Colts defied all odds and won the prestigious title. "We felt like we could do it and we did it," interjected Ted Larson.[43]

Co-captains Sherwood Lucas and Robert Zamora received the championship trophy for Hidalgo County. The boys prepared for a team photo and all seem overjoyed, including Valadez and Robie. The entire team, with the exception of Valadez, wore "Pharr 101" uniforms from sponsor American Legion, Post No. 101 from Pharr, Texas. Evidently, these had been the best uniforms that the team with limited resources could acquire.[44] Robie, who had managed the Pharr 101 team, donned an identical uniform. Valadez, who for whatever reason was not given a Pharr 101 uniform, proudly wore his Mission Spikes 30-30 uniform from his semi-pro days.

A more direct division would ensue between Valadez and Robie as the pair would feud over the championship trophy. Robie, who had listed himself as manager in the tournament paperwork, kept the trophy. Upon Robie's death in 2005, his widow Maysie Marie Robie returned the trophy to Coach Valadez; it currently sits in a corner of the Valadez family home in Mission.[45]

The championship had a resounding impact on the team. "For me, from there on out it made a big difference," points out Robert Zamora. "I felt like if I could play like that, I could do anything. [My] confidence was boosted. I think athletics played a big part. I got a lot of confidence. I got the opportunity to meet other people. I was captain of the team. I was given responsibilities. My first experience with the media was at that age. I learned very early — be careful who you talk to."[46] Sports served as a springboard for a successful life as young boys gained respect beyond their neighborhoods.[47]

For the South Texas boys, this victory meant more than just a championship. They saw their community unite like never before as they were paraded across the Rio Grande Valley as local heroes. They rubbed elbows with Anglo elites in Oklahoma and in South Texas. The tight social order that had been strictly followed crumbled as community leaders from numerous Valley towns planned celebrations in honor of the Colt leaguers. One of the biggest honors came the following May at the Mission Chamber of Commerce Banquet where the team was introduced to Texas Governor John Connally. State Representative and former Mission 30-30s ballplayer Kika de la Garza delivered on his promise made the previous summer and cemented a political career that would shortly take him to the U.S. House of Representatives.[48]

The times were changing, the Rio Grande Valley was changing, and the boys were also changing. To some of the ballplayers the experience in partaking in the 1962 Colt League World Series brought them into an integrated world that previously had not been fully accessible to them. "It changed me a lot," comments José Torres. He continued, "I don't think I would have finished high school if it had not been for baseball. I probably would have dropped out. I even skipped eighth grade to play with Mission High School. That pushed me and that encouraged me. Socially, I got to hang out with Anglos. We rubbed elbows with the English-speaking people. It opened the doors. It opened my mind that there was a better world crossing the tracks."[49]

The boys returned home from Shawnee not only with a championship trophy but with the self-confidence to succeed in life. Most of the boys went on to have notable baseball careers in high school. Torres, who had struggled with school, went on to graduate from college and obtained a graduate degree. He had a successful career as an administrator in the Dallas Independent School District. Robert Zamora went on to complete a doctoral degree at The University of Texas–Austin and served his home district of La Joya as Superintendent of Schools. Ted Gerlach continued in his father's footsteps and operates a successful construction company in South Texas. Conrado Villarreal received a scholarship to play college baseball at Sul Ross State University and then moved on to Saint Mary's University in San Antonio where he continued on a baseball scholarship.

Francisco Santiago, Mike Santana, and Lee Gonzalez were drafted into the military during the Vietnam War era. Santiago opted to serve in the Air Force, and as soon as his time was fulfilled returned to the Rio Grande Valley and went to work for the U.S. Post Office. Santana returned home after not qualifying for the service due to health-related issues. Gonzalez remained in the Air Force and reached the rank of captain and then became a schoolteacher afterwards. Ted Larson went to work for Southwestern Bell, while Roy Lee Hinojosa went on to have a successful career in the oil business. Norris Lewis worked for Central Power & Light Company for thirty-five years and lost a lengthy battle with an undisclosed illness in 2014.

In 2012, at the 41st Annual Leo Najo Day Celebration, the entire team was inducted into the Leo Najo Hall of Fame. The men continued to be bound by the memorable summer of 1962 when they rose from one of the most impoverished regions of the country as true underdogs to triumph in a national competition. More important, the team defied social and ethnic barriers as unity prevailed throughout South Texas in support of the Hidalgo County Colt League Champions.

Today, it is questionable whether baseball continues to serve as an avenue for interaction as it did fifty years ago. Although the number of Puerto Ricans, Dominicans, Venezuelans, Cubans, and other Latin American ball players has grown exponentially in Major League Baseball in the last twenty years, the number of domestic Latino and African American ball players has not seen the same rate of growth. The same is true for semi-professional baseball leagues that have ceased to exist at the level they once did when baseball was at its apex in the US. In revisiting the 1962 Hidalgo County Colt League World Series Championship team, the ball players and populace were moved by the nostalgia of yesteryear, where baseball played an important role in their social interactions, created a sense of community in South Texas, and further connected them to the larger society.

QUESTIONS:

1. Given the segregation that existed in South Texas in the 1960s, why do you think the baseball team was integrated?

2. Did the boys on the team share the same racial attitudes as those of many of the parents in Hidalgo County at this time? Is this significant? Why or why not?

3. Does sport serve as an "avenue for interaction" between groups today? Why or why not?

NOTES

1. Roberto Zamora, interviewed by author, Edinburg, TX, September 25, 2014.

2. David Montejano, *Anglos and Mexicans: In the Making of Texas, 1836–1986* (Austin: University of Texas Press, 1987), 162. Arnoldo De León, *Mexican Americans in Texas: A Brief History* (Wheeling, IL: Harlan Davidson, Inc. 1993), 110–112. The terms Mexican American, Chicano, Latino, Hispanic, and Mexican will be used interchangeably. When noting political or national differences, the terms will be explained as pertaining to such differences.

3. Pikey Rodriguez, "Roadrunners Latest Team to Call Edinburg Home," *The Monitor*, May 13, 2001, 6C.

4. "Cowboys to Invade 30-30 Park," *The Mission Times*, July 18, 1952, 4.

5. "Monterrey Invades Jax Field Sunday," *The Mission Times*, August 1, 1952, 2. "Independent Nine Meets Reynosa at 30-30 Park Sunday," *The Mission Times*, September 12, 1952, p. 4.

6. "Mission Baseball Team Seeks Park for Home Games," *The Mission Times*, April 26, 1946.

7. José M. Alamillo, "Peloteros in Paradise: Mexican Americans in Baseball and Oppositional Politics in Southern California, 1930–1950," in Jorge Iber and Samuel O. Regalado, eds., *Mexican Americans and Sports: A Reader on Athletics and Barrio Life* (College Station: Texas A&M University Press, 2007), 55.

8. Daniel D. Arreola, *Tejano South Texas: A Mexican American Cultural Province* (Austin: University of Texas Press, 2002), 22.

9. Jorge Iber, "On Field Foes and Racial Misconceptions: The 1961 Donna Redskins and Their Drive to the Texas State Football Championship," in Jorge Iber and Samuel O. Regalado, eds., *Mexican Americans and Sports: A Reader on Athletics and Barrio Life* (College Station: Texas A&M University Press, 2007), 123–24.

10. Irene Villarreal Valadez, Esther Ramirez, Jose Alfredo Valadez, and Ray Valadez Jr., interviewed by author, Mission, TX, November 5, 2014.

11. Francisco Estevis and Vicente Estevis, interviewed by author, Edinburg, TX, October 24, 2015.

12. Irene Villarreal Valadez, Esther Ramirez, Jose Alfredo Valadez, and Ray Valadez Jr., interviewed by author, Mission, TX, November 5, 2014.

13. Roberto Zamora, interviewed by author, Edinburg, TX, September 25, 2014.

14. "Colt League Tournament Team Eligibility Affidavit," McAllen, TX,

July, 11, 1962.

15. Ibid.

16. Miguel Santana, interviewed by author via telephone, McAllen, TX–Edinburg, TX, October 31, 2014.

17. Francisco Santiago, interviewed by author via telephone, Brownsville, TX–Edinburg, TX, October 17, 2014.

18. José Torres, interviewed by author, McAllen, TX, May 28, 2014.

19. Roberto Zamora, interviewed by author, Edinburg, TX, September 25, 2014.

20. Miguel Santana, interviewed by author via telephone, McAllen, TX–Edinburg, TX, October 31, 2014.

21. Lizandro Gonzalez, interviewed by author via telephone, Pharr, TX–Edinburg, TX, October 17, 2014.

22. José Torres, interviewed by author, McAllen TX, May 28, 2014.

23. Juanita E. Garza, conversation with author, Weslaco, TX, December 4, 2010.

24. Roberto Zamora, interviewed by author, Edinburg, TX, September 25, 2014.

25. Francisco Santiago, interviewed by author via telephone, Brownsville, TX–Edinburg, TX, October 17, 2014.

26. Jose Torres, interviewed by author, McAllen TX, May 28, 2014.

27. Ted Gerlach, interviewed by author via telephone, Pharr, TX–Edinburg, TX, October 17, 2014.

28. Roberto Zamora, interviewed by author, Edinburg, TX, September 25, 2014.

29. Miguel Santana, interviewed by author via telephone, McAllen, TX–Edinburg, TX, October 31, 2014.

30. "Hidalgo County Beats El Paso Colts, 2–1," *Valley Morning Star,* August 14, 1962, 8.

31. "Hidalgo Edges EP Colts Out, 2–1," *El Paso Times*, August 14, 1962, 8.

32. Ted Gerlach, interviewed by author via telephone, Pharr, TX-Edinburg, TX, October 17, 2014.

33. "Colt World Series Notes and Quotes," *Shawnee News-Star*, August 21, 1962.

34. Ibid.

35. Conrado Villarreal, interviewed by author via telephone, Laredo, TX–Edinburg, TX, October 17, 2014.

36. Ibid.

37. "Colt World Series Notes and Quotes."

38. "Bonds' Home Run Leads Colts to Finals, 5–4," *The Press*, August

23, 1962.

39. Roberto Zamora, interviewed by author, Edinburg, TX, September 25, 2014.

40. Garland Rose, "Colts Face Showdown," *The Press*, August 25, 1962, A8.

41. Francisco Santiago, interviewed by author via telephone, Brownsville, TX–Edinburg, TX, October 17, 2014.

42. Roberto Zamora, interviewed by author, Edinburg, TX, September 25, 2014.

43. Roberto Zamora, interviewed by author, Edinburg, TX, September 25, 2014. Ted Larson interviewed by author via telephone, Kennewick, WA– Edinburg, TX, November 19, 2014.

44. Roberto Zamora, interviewed by author, Edinburg, TX, September 25, 2014.

45. Irene Villarreal Valadez, Esther Ramirez, José Alfredo Valadez, and Ray Valadez Jr., interviewed by author, Mission, TX, November 5, 2014.

46. Roberto Zamora, interviewed by author, Edinburg, TX, September 25, 2014.

47. E. Anthony Rotundo, *American Manhood: Transformations in Masculinity from the Revolution to the Modern Era* (New York: Basic Books, 1993), 42.

48. "Colt Team Meets Governor," *Valley Evening Monitor*, May 5, 1963, 10.

49. José Torres, interviewed by author, McAllen TX, May 28, 2014.

SHAPER OF SPORTS HISTORY:
An Interview with Latino Football Pioneer Hank Olguin

Frederick Luis Aldama
The Ohio State University

HANK OLGUIN WAS BORN in Albuquerque, New Mexico; his family moved to California when he was young. There he grew up in a bilingual/bicultural family and became involved in creative endeavors as early as elementary school: singing in the boys' church choir, playing the cello in a string quartet, and getting leading parts in school-play skits. By the time he reached junior high, he had taken up the piano and was performing regularly at weddings and dances with a combo he helped form.

In high school, Hank switched his focus to the athletic arena and became a football and track star but still managed to play in bands, act in school plays, and write and produce radio shows. His college career at the University of California at Berkley involved more of the same. While there, he earned letters in football and track and was the leading rusher in Cal's Rose Bowl appearance. Later, he was awarded the Sara Huntsman Sturgess Memorial Prize (for outstanding artistic achievement in dramatic art) and earned a degree in rhetoric with an undeclared minor in theater arts.

Hank spent the majority of his career working in communications and advertising. He is a former vice president and associate creative director for GSD&M Advertising where, for eleven years, he was responsible for developing dual-language advertising for major national and regional clients in the early days of Latino market development. He was a leader on the team that put the Coors Brewing Co. on the Latino market map — called "One of the most dramatic marketing turnarounds in modern corporate history" by *Advertising Age*.

In addition, he has won numerous advertising awards, including two Clios and a National Addy; has written a book on creativity; written songs for *Sesame Street*; and performed as voice talent for several major companies, including Ralston Purina, Busch Entertainment, Holt Rinehart & Winston, and Microsoft Games; and currently facilitates seminars and conducts lectures on creativity. (www. CreativeIdeasForSuccess.com)

Throughout his career, Hank has been on a mission to creatively counteract stereotypes and improve the image of Latinos in the mass media. Toward that end, he and a partner have formed a company, Creative Media Development Group (CMDG), to identify and develop entertainment content with Latino themes, characters, and stories that are positive, inspiring, and historically accurate — focusing on the English-dominant and bilingual Latino market segments. They are available to producers, writers, and investors to evaluate and consult on content appealing to the various tastes and interests of Latino audiences.

Always looking for ways to give back, Hank is also developing a program to help college-bound Latino students to more effectively use their creative potential toward academic success. In addition, he published an article in *The Salinas Californian* — "Who Let the Mexicans Play in the Rose Bowl" — about his relationship with Joe Kapp, legendary All-American and NFL quarterback and former Cal teammate.

FREDERICK LUIS ALDAMA (FLA): You were born in Albuquerque and moved to LA when you were five years old, then a year later to San Jose. Were sports a big part of your life growing up? How did you get into football as a Latino?

HANK OLGUIN (HO): I sort of stumbled into it. This is a real shaggy-dog story. When I was in junior high school, I was more into music. I played piano in the eighth and ninth grades, with Johnny Orosco and a band called The Melodiers. We played small gigs. I wasn't too terribly interested in sports. At the time a lot of my buddies in the neighborhood were in sports, participating in all the city recreation leagues for kids. I wasn't.

While in junior high school, it was discovered that I was the fastest guy in the world. I was running around the track, beating everybody. In ninth grade my PE teacher told me that I was going to compete in this junior high school track meet — that I was going to learn how to do the broad jump. I didn't even know what that was. The ninth grade record was seventeen feet, eleven and one-half inches. I shattered the record by jumping twenty-one feet, two and three-eighths inches. The next day my name appeared in big headlines and I liked that.

Because I hadn't been involved that much in sports growing up, when I got to Lincoln High I didn't have the skill set other kids had. I was third-string junior varsity my sophomore year in high school, but the first time I touched a football, believe it or not, I ran 99 yards for a touchdown. At that point, I think the coaches decided I was worth developing. As I participated more and more in sports all through high school I just got better and more skilled. I lettered in track and football. We won championships, and my senior year I ended up as the leading scorer in our league.

FLA: As a Latino, did you feel different from the other guys on various sports teams you played on?

HO: I have always been firmly anchored in my Latino heritage, growing up in a bilingual home. We would travel to meet my mom's family in Mexico, even spending a couple of months there when I was ten. And my dad is a US Latino, Mexican American, so there was a constant reinforcement of my ethnic roots. Still, growing up I considered myself a regular American kid, so didn't see myself as terribly different. And San Jose was pretty much a multicultural city. There were Italians, Japanese, Portuguese, Chinese, Filipinos, Latinos, and of course white folks in my neighborhood and schools.

FLA: Clearly, you showed talent at sports. Did you know already in high school that you'd be playing football in college?

HO: I was kind of a naive kid. I simply engaged in activities I enjoyed. This included sports, but also music and theater. I produced music concerts at the school, acted in plays, and created a high-school sports-news show. I took them all seriously and was self-disciplined. I got good grades, and I took some college prep courses. That said, when Cal recruited me, I did have to take some math and language classes at San Jose City College that brought me up to speed. Once those were behind me, I got into Cal easily.

FLA: Who were some of your role models — athletes or otherwise — growing up?

HO: There weren't any Latino role models visible back then. I looked up to good football players like Ollie Matson, Hugh McElhenny, and Joe Perry as well as my coaches at high school. But I picked my role models from all over the map, including actors in films. Thursday nights I would go to see Mexican films with my parents. I think of Mexican role models such as Pedro Infante and Jorge Negrete but I also had American role models like Bogart, Brando, Tracy, and others.

FLA: You and Joe made Latino history in 1959. Two Latinos taking Cal to the Rose Bowl. What was it like to be one of a few Latinos (you and Joe Kapp) playing sports at Cal — and only a few others nationally?

HO: You could count those Latinos playing football on one hand: myself, Joe, Tom Flores, and Rene Ramirez at the University of Texas. We were few, but I never felt any scrutiny because of my ethnic background, I guess because I was light skinned, didn't have an accent, and could pass. My name wasn't Martinez, it was Olguin — a name that could also sort of pass. I don't think anybody questioned whether I was good enough. In addition to Joe Kapp, there was a Latino guy on the Cal basketball team, Mike Diaz. We also had a Mexican American assistant basketball coach, Rene Herrerias, who later became the head coach at Cal. There were also some black guys on the team at the time. It seemed pretty egalitarian. Nevertheless, back in the '50s it was not exactly cool or fashionable to be Mexican, so we weren't down at Sather Gate waving Mexican flags and yelling "Viva Zapata." This racial consciousness came a few years later, in the '60s when we would more publicly embrace and celebrate our ethnic background.

FLA: You were always strongly encouraged to be proud of your Latino roots. And while you are light skinned and although you are bilingual you spoke English without an accent. Yet, you chose not to pass as Anglo.

HO: Shadow boxing with my background became a bit of a burden. I wanted to declare to the world who I was as a Latino. It was during this time, too, that I started really taking notice of what was going on in the mass media. I became more aware of all the negative stereotypes of Latinos and wanted to do something about this. After college I worked as a talent agent for Pacific Artists in Hollywood. During the time that I was voiceover director there, I became interested in combatting the terrible stereotypes that existed in the media about Latinos in general and Mexicans in particular. Helping to foster this activist spirit was my growing friendship with Emilio Delgado, who has played the Fix-it Shop Owner, Luis, on *Sesame Street* for many years. He was registered as an actor with the agency. We both looked for opportunities to more forcefully change the ridiculous stereotypes that were so prominent then and, I hate to say it, to some degree still are.

FLA: Scholarships (athletic or otherwise) and the GI Bill have proved so important for those coming from the socioeconomic margins, Hank.

HO: I fell in between the crack of two wars, so I didn't receive a GI Bill, but I know it has certainly been a great help to Latinos. The tuition at Cal back then was something like $300 per semester, so it wasn't much. I received a grant-in-aid that I had to work for but was grateful for it getting me through school. Scholarships are terribly important, especially today, with the exorbitant costs of education.

FLA: You chose not to pursue a career in the pro leagues, Hank.

HO: I actually signed with the Dallas Texans in 1960, the first year of the AFL. As I recall, to sign, I got a huge bonus of around $1,000 and my annual salary would have been around $6,800. [Later, the Dallas Texans became the Kansas City Chiefs, owned by Lamar Hunt.] It wasn't exactly the most lucrative thing in the world to do. I gave it a shot and went to camp, but at the beginning of the first week I tore up my knee pretty badly. I think subconsciously I wanted something like this to happen because my heart wasn't in it. I had other interests and other passions I wanted to pursue, including theater. When I was in college I changed my major in rhetoric and took many courses in theater for an undeclared minor.

FLA: You went on to work in programs like Pacific Artists and others where you began to focus your sights on making a difference for Latinos.

HO: After leaving Pacific Artists, I began to do freelance work for the national program, SER, Jobs for Progress, allowing me to be involved in the community. I became the director of communications for this federal employment and training program primarily serving Latinos at the time. I worked for eight years helping with their outreach, public affairs, and PR efforts. I created public-service announcements, films, brochures, and newsletters, among other media to help grow projects all over the country. The job sent me to cities like Miami, Detroit, and Dallas — and so many more. It was a tremendously valuable experience, allowing me to learn firsthand the breadth, complexity, and pluralism of our community. During that whole time, I was actively working to improve the image and change the perception of Latinos in the minds of other Americans. At the time, I also put together a presentation that I delivered to nonprofit organizations and business groups on stereotypes in the mass media. To draw awareness to the Latino stereotypes, I juxtaposed slides of the stereotypes with those showing slides of the accurate, diverse, complex range of Hispanics in the real world.

FLA: You also worked for the group Nosotros.

HO: I shared the same point of view as actor Ricardo Montalbán. We both knew that we had to change perceptions in Hollywood and in the media generally about Latinos. This was the push behind Nosotros so I jumped on it. Joe Kapp was also a part of the organization, but somehow we missed each other during those years.

FLA: Moving our conversation back to Latino athletes, why don't we have more Kapps, Plunketts, and Floreses, among others, in the Football Hall of Fame?

HO: Speaking cynically, I'd say we're being shortchanged. The committee making these decisions is made up of media professionals, and I assume many, perhaps not all, of them carry some of those misperceptions of Hispanics that I've been working hard to change. So I can see how some may be as ignorant as anyone else about what we are and what we have to contribute.

FLA: I know our numbers are nowhere near the other racial demographic numbers that make up the NFL, but today we certainly have more Latinos playing football than when you played for Cal.

HO: Yes, no doubt about it. Today, we have a growing young Latino demographic playing sports. They are doing well and being recognized for this, winning awards and such. I think our main effort right now should be to see that more of this young generation of Latinos gets to college. When Latinos do graduate from high school, many tend to feed into community colleges, and I understand that many of that number fail to go on to four-year universities. We need to work hard to improve the numbers of Latinos going to and graduating from four-year, degree-granting colleges.

FLA: Looking back over your lifetime, is there something you might have wanted to do differently? Any regrets?

HO: Not really. I played sports that led to great friendships, taught me the value of hard work, self-discipline, and teamwork. I'm grateful that I was able to apply what I learned playing sports in the pursuit of other interests and in my professional career. No regrets.

QUESTIONS:

I.   How did Hank Olguin get involved with sports? What impact did they have on his life? What were some of his other interests?

2.   Of what significance were Latino role models to Mr. Olguin (both in and beyond sports)?

3.   Why did he decide to focus on Latino issues (how they are presented/perceived) in the world of media?

ADIOS, AMIGOS:
Bean Bandits and other Mexican Americans in the Golden Age of Drag Racing

Andrew T. Harris
Independent Scholar, Pueblo, Colorado

EL GUAPO IS THE MEXICAN VILLAIN in the 1980s comedy movie ¡Three Amigos! El Guapo, which is Spanish for "The Handsome One," is anything but that in the movie. He is most likely younger than he looks, with a leathered faced and salt-and-pepper hair and beard. In El Guapo's birthday celebration scene, El Guapo's best henchman, Jefe, raises his bottle of tequila to toast his boss and says in a thick Mexican accent, "Today, he is..." Before Jefe can finish, El Guapo snaps his head and gives Jefe a look that says, "Do not even think of telling them my real age or I will kill you." Jefe finishes by saying, "Thirty-three years old!"[1] Two-time National Hot Rod Association (NHRA) Funny Car Champion Cruz Pedregon posted the YouTube video of the scene on Facebook with the comment, "I guess I'm 33 today."[2] He was actually celebrating his fifty-second birthday. The connection between the YouTube video and Cruz Pedregon is that he named his funny car "El Guapo." He also has another funny car that has the logo from the movie *Scarface* inside the body of the car.[3] As a Mexican American drag racer, Pedregon stays connected with his Latino roots by giving his funny cars familiar Latino names, just like his drag-racing father, "Flaming" Frank Pedregon, did in the 1960s. Frank Pedregon would paint *Adios Amigos* on the back of his dragster or name it "Taco Taster."[4] Like father, like son.

In recent years, several scholars have been studying Mexican Americans and their contribution to sports in America. Richard A. Santillan's books focus on Mexican Americans and baseball in different regions across America. Jorge Iber's book, *Latinos in U.S. Sport: A History of Isolation, Cultural Identity, and Acceptance*, is an effort that explores the different sports Latinos have touched in America. It focuses on sports with which any in academia would be familiar: football, baseball, basketball, and boxing. This offering even discusses some not as widely followed endeavors, like tennis and horse racing. However, there is a gap in these scholarly works: no mention of auto racing. Iber's *Latinos in U.S. Sport* has only a half-page dedicated to NASCAR's recruitment of Latinos into the sport.

Historians have explored other ethnic groups in auto racing, such as African Americans, in the past. Wendell Scott, the first African American to race in NASCAR in the 1950s and 1960s, and Charlie Wiggins, who wanted to be the first African American to race the prestigious Indy 500 during the 1920s and 1930s, are just two examples. Both examples have also been brought to the attention of the public through film. The movie *Greased Lightning* is based on the true-life story of Wendell Scott, as portrayed by Richard Pryor. Charlie Wiggins's story is outlined in the PBS documentary *For Gold & Glory*, narrated by African American film actor and National Medal of Arts winner Ossie Davis.

Mexican Americans' involvement in the early days of drag racing has not received the attention it deserves. This study is intended to begin this process of filling a void in scholarly works on Mexican Americans and their contribution to auto racing. In particular, this study will focus on the early days of drag racing — the so-called golden age — from the 1950s through the 1970s.

Some will argue that auto racing is not a sport. However, if we use sports historian Allen Guttmann's definition of sport, we can see that auto racing *is* a sport. Guttmann states, with drag-racing examples in brackets:

A distinctive set of systematically interrelated formal-structural characteristics; these qualities, taken together, differentiate "sport" as such from other forms and traditions of physical culture. Five of these characteristics help us identify sport as the representative physical culture of modernity: specialization [having a gamut of specialized roles: e.g., driver and mechanic], rationalization [rules: e.g., maxium engine size, minimum weight of racecar], quantification [stats: e.g., low elapsed time (ET) set the racing bracket], obsession with records [e.g., number of wins, top speed], and bureaucratization [modern sports are typically governed: e.g., NHRA, IHRA].[5]

Drag racing and auto racing demonstrably meet the five characteristics that Guttmann lays out.

This chapter on the history of a few Mexican Americans' involvement during the early days of drag racing will build on the current theories of Latinos in United States sports. This includes a theory that Iber has stated elsewhere: "Spanish-surnamed people in the United States had used sport to break down social barriers, discredit stereotypes, and facilitate assimilation."[6] Additionally, unlike in other sports, some Mexican American drag racers also gained a trade by becoming machinists and mechanics. Building on these theories, this chapter will explore the lives of four Mexican American drivers, mechanics, and/or owners of their own drag-racing cars: Joaquin Arnett, Fran Hernandez, Bobby Tapia, and Frank Pedregon. Some of these men were at the forefront of drag-racing technology while others explored speed and entertainment. Their stories are important because they demonstrate the treatment of Mexican Americans in Southern California during the 1950s and 1960s and how the latter were able to overcome typical stereotypes — such as being illiterate, uneducated, or ignorant — attributed to their having darker skin. However, they held onto their Mexican heritage throughout these troubled times.

A BRIEF HISTORY OF DRAG RACING AND THE NHRA

One could argue that drag racing started after the second automobile came off the production line when two horseless carriages, daring to go as fast as they could, raced from one end of town to the other. However, historians agree that drag racing started in the late 1930s when Americans were building hot rods by stripping down jalopies, mainly Ford Model Ts, to achieve higher speeds and better handling for racing on dirt tracks and city streets. The men who built these hot rods were known as "hot rodders." Drag racing became more organized at remote dry lakebeds such as El Mirage and Muroc, California. The Southern California Timing Association (SCTA) and the Russetta Timing Association supervised the races and installed timing lights at half-mile, one-mile, or two-mile markers. Even in the 1920s and 1930s, racers were able to achieve speeds of above 100 miles per hour. Of course, street drag racing or outlaw drag racing was also going on in cities and towns across America. As access to suitable dry lakebeds declined, and more racers were showing up to race, a search began for a workable substitute to dry lakebed racing. The idea of a shorter race also was appealing to some of the lakebed racers.[7]

Organized drag racing, as we know it today, was started by the NHRA in 1953 at Pomona, California, where timing lights were put a quarter mile (1,320 feet) away from a starting point on a paved section of the LA County Fairgrounds parking lot. The creation of the NHRA in 1951 by Wally Parks, who was also an elected official of SCTA, preceded the installation at the Fairgrounds. The NHRA created rules, standards, and operating procedures to try to move outlaw drag racing from cities and towns to purpose-built drag-racing facilities. The first NHRA national event, which pitted East Coast drag racers against West Coast drag racers, was held in 1955 at a World War II airstrip in Great Bend, Kansas.[8]

The NHRA formed a group of people called "Drag Safari" to go on a coast-to-coast crusade to get cities to build proper drag-racing facilities, mainly from old landing strips abandoned after World War II. "The Drag Safari were a team of experienced hot rodders led by an energetic California police officer."[9] For three years they led a campaign to explain the meaning behind NHRA and educate car clubs, civic leaders, law enforcement officials, media, and the general public on the benefits of running an organized drag-racing event and providing information about building a permanent drag-racing facility, public safety, and drivers' safety.[10] Today the Drag Safari is known as the Safety Safari, going to each national NHRA-sanctioned event, making sure the track is safe to run and at the ready for any mishap, such as a crash or a fire, that might happen on the track.

With the NHRA's creation of standards, the cars drag racing in the early days were mostly roadsters, Ford Model Ts and As with the roof cut off and racecars left over from dry-lake racing. Gassers were full-body cars, but with larger modified engines under the hood. Some gassers were street legal and were often used in outlaw drag racing. Mechanics built altered drag cars by taking the car frame, shortening it, putting on a roadster or coupe body, and leaving the engine exposed. However, the top-of-the-line, fastest things on wheels were the Top Fuel front-engine dragsters.[11] A long wheelbase with lightweight, large supercharged engines was the winning formula in dragsters, which people knew as "slingshots." The nickname derives from a dragster designed by Marion Lee "Mickey" Thompson, who put the driver behind the rear wheels, making the driver look "like a rock in a slingshot."[12] By the end of the 1960s, these big-block, blown, nitro-fueled dragsters were running the quarter mile in 6.43 seconds and reaching speeds of over 231 miles an hour. This was a gain of almost fifty mph and two seconds per quarter mile from the beginning of the decade.[13]

Among some of the other standards the NHRA imposed was the creation of different classes of drag cars. This structure was created to keep each racing classification competitive, so that one racer would not have an advantage over another. Cars are classified into a number of groups and then divided into classes according to the power-to-weight ratio. Because the different car classifications can be complicated and lengthy to explain, this chapter will examine only a few of these classifications relevant to this research. Stock Eliminator comprises new-factory-production automobiles running original equipment. Middle Eliminator rules allow some of the car to be modified, while Top Eliminator consists of custom-built drag cars.[14] Most of the men mentioned in this article raced dragsters, which run in Top Eliminator — also paying out the most money for wins.

The first three decades of drag racing — the 1950s, 1960s, and 1970s — are considered the "golden age" of drag racing. These were the formative years of the sport. However, during the 1970s, racers and fans agreed to what constituted top-level drag racing. Gone were the roadsters, gassers, and "altereds," replaced by Top Fuel Funny Cars, Top Fuel Dragsters, and Pro Stock.[15] Additionally, major sponsorship had come into the sport, pushing out smaller teams.[16] This chapter will validate that the golden age of drag racing was a time when these four Mexican Americans came out of the barrios and demonstrated how fast they could go.

THE BEAN BANDITS

Joaquin Arnett II was born in Old Town, San Diego, California on November 27, 1927. His mother, Esperanza, was born in Bisbee, Arizona and his father, Joaquin, was born in La Paz, Guanajuato, Mexico. She was a seamstress, and he was a successful, self-employed landscape gardener who built the house Arnett grew up in on Market Street. Joaquin, or Joaq (pronounced wäk), as his friends called him, got interested in automobiles at a very early age. By the age of thirteen, he was driving his mother and her friends around town to do their shopping and errands in his first automobile, a junked car bought by his grandfather. While Spanish was the language spoken in the household, Arnett learned English while attending school. He did not enjoy high school and joined the Merchant Marines during World War II. He received an honorable discharge in 1945 after serving on the ss *Ina Coolbrith*. He ultimately did not finish high school but instead learned how to weld and fix cars from a shop near his house.

By the early 1950s, he was successful at building, chopping, and modifying automobiles. According to his daughter, Jacqueline Arnett Sonka, he took a 1934 Ford Model A Coupe, modified it, and sold it for $3,000 ($26,000 at today's rates). His welding skills were well known, as he built racing frames for other drag racers. His welds were strong and were so unique that other racers could tell if they were done by Arnett.[17] Arnett's claim to fame came from understanding the proper 50/50 blend of nitro and methanol for racing. "It's easier to mix that way. A gallon of this and gallon of that."[18] It is also possible that he was one of the first to run a dragster with twin engines.[19] The early days of drag racing were well known for experimentation with different body configurations and engine combinations to produce the fastest speeds and quickest times.

Old Town, San Diego, where Arnett grew up, was part of a multi-cultured neighborhood. The ethnic groups included Mexicans, African Americans, Hawaiians, Japanese, and some whites. When Arnett started drag racing he created a club of enthusiasts called the "Bean Bandits." Members of the Bean Bandits consisted of Arnett's school friends and their associates. According to Jacqueline, her father did not drag race stock cars, or Stock Eliminator; he built custom drag cars, running in what would later be known as Top Eliminator.[20] Arnett was their leader, building cars, building engines, and, most of the time, being the main racecar driver.

The club's name came about because the white drag racers were calling the Mexican American racers the derogatory term *beaners*.[21] Instead of taking it as an insult, Arnett embraced it and created the Bean Bandits. Also included in their club was a Native American, Billy Galvin, who designed the club's logo.[22] Not only did they have a club logo that was part of their Mexican heritage, but they also dressed the part in basic white cotton shirts, matching pants, and straw hats.[23] The racing team did get two sponsors, Schaeffer's Automotive and Schneider Racing Cams, and placed their emblems on the sides of the cars. However, they never got money from these sponsors, although they may have provided oil and parts. Most of the team's financial assets came from member dues and race winnings. But when they were called *beaners*, it was not about the cash from race winnings; all they wanted to do was see who was the fastest on the drag strip.[24] Most of the time, Arnett, and the Bean Bandits, were the fastest.

While the Bean Bandits were very successful on the racetrack, both winning at local drag strips around Southern California and also setting land-speed records on the dry lakebeds, there was more than racing to being part of the club. From the beginning, even as they were bandying the provoking name *beaners*, the other racers started to put their prejudice aside with every race the Bean Bandits won and slowly started to discredit the Mexican stereotypes. This was especially the case after the Bean Bandits started to break speed records and post the quickest times at the drag races. However, when traveling in other parts of the Southwest, they often would have to sleep outside because Jim Crow laws applied not just to African Americans but also to Mexican Americans. Jacqueline Arnett Sonka recalls a story her father told her: "While traveling cross county, possibly in Texas, they went into the hotel and the hotel told them they were too dark to stay here. Arnett says, 'I'm not black.' The hotel replied, 'We don't care, you are too dark to stay here.' So they had to camp outside."[25]

The Mexican Americans who were members of the Bean Bandits were proud to be part of the club because it got them out of their neighborhood and helped many of them learn a trade, such as being a machinist, welder, or auto-body mechanic.[26] Arnett created a successful body repair shop due to his accolades as one of the top drag racers and his success on the dry lakebeds during the late 1950s and early 1960s. People of all colors would bring their cars to him. He was a true master of reshaping metal back to looking like new after an accident.[27] Arnett and his Bean Bandits broke down social barriers by winning on the racetrack, discrediting stereotypes by putting their Mexican heritage up front and center and proving their worth on the race track, and facilitated assimilation by promoting employment throughout the Southern California community.

FRAN HERNANDEZ

The story of Fran Hernandez is very different from that of Arnett and the Bean Bandits. He was born Francisco Arturo Hernandez on February 8, 1922 in Chihuahua City, Chihuahua, to a Mexican father and a French mother. Because the French were not welcome in Mexico, life became difficult for the Hernandez family. The Mexican government had been in turmoil from 1914 to 1934, with eight different leaders over those twenty years. Each regime brought its own ideas on how to control Mexico, frequently mandating the exile of the opposion and their followers. The Hernandez family often found itself being exiled, depending on the ruling government. The family decided to move to Southern California when Fran was an infant.[28] He grew up in a Spanish-speaking household, but the family thought it best for their children to learn proper English. He attended St. Catherine's School, a Catholic military academy, for a year or a year and a half, until illness forced him back home. Hernandez later attended Polytechnic High School where he was a gymnast and trained as a machinist. While in high school, he got the car bug and conned his mother into taking him to the DMV to get his driver's license early (age fifteen) so he could drive and help his mother to do her errands.[29]

After high school Hernandez worked at Dooling Bros., a manufacturer of special tools, dies, wrenches, jigs, and high-grade precision products, where he learned about nitromethane by racing tethered cars, similar to today's gas-powered remote-control cars, on a wooden racetrack in the back of the shop. He started to run fast cars at the dry lakebeds until he enlisted in the Navy during World War II. After the war, he continued to pursue fast speeds at the dry lakebeds as well as applying his knowledge of nitromethane from the small tethered cars to full-size V8 engines. To test their newfound speeds, most of the hot rodders started to drag race in towns, often resulting in arrests. Hernandez met his future wife the day after he got out of jail. Her friends told her there was this cool guy she needed to meet, but he was in jail. He got thrown in jail because he was doing outlaw drag racing and the cops had had enough. They charged him with "unsafe equipment" because he took the running boards and fenders off his 1932 Ford coupe, which was a popular thing to do among the hot rodding crowd. The cops planned to make an example out of him to try to stop street drag racing. He got thirty days in jail but obtained his release after two weeks for good behavior. This was in 1941 or 1942. However, in 1949 outlaw drag racing was about to undergo a revolution.[30]

According to *Hot Rod Magazine*, the first organized drag race was on a service road at the Goleta Airport near Santa Barbara, California, in April 1949. Hundreds of spectators showed up to see who was faster, Tom Cobbs racing out of Los Angeles or Fran Hernandez out of Santa Monica. Both drivers were dry-lakebed veterans, but this race was much shorter. Cobbs drove a 1929 Ford Model A roadster that had been channeled to fit over a 1934 frame. It had a '34 Ford V8 with a Roots blower from a GMC diesel truck or bus fitted on top as a supercharger. Hernandez raced his fender-less, 1932 Ford Model A three-window coupe with a Mercury V8 that had been over-bored and stoked. The '32 did not have a supercharger but instead had three Stromberg carburetors on a special manifold Hernandez build that ran nitromethane.

So, who won the first organized drag race? Hernandez won by a car length. This was due to Cobbs's losing traction at the line with the wrong gears in the rear-end. Even after the '34 Ford gained traction, it could not close the gap.[31] After the race, Hernandez connected the tow-bar back on his '32 and towed it back home after the race. He had nothing else to prove. He won, and if he kept going, he might lose. He just wanted to go as fast as he could and win the race.[32] This race would later be known as "the day drag racing began."[33]

Through his mastery of machining and his popularity from winning the first organized drag race, Hernandez was able to get jobs with Peter DePaolo Engineering, which won the Indy 500 in 1925, and later with Vic Edelbrock, who still today builds performance parts for both street cars and racecars. Hernandez then worked at the Ford Motor Company in the Lincoln-Mercury division. While Hernandez started out as a driver for drag racing, he was better known for being behind the design and engines used in drag racing. Factory Experimental (FX) cars, according to NHRA rules, allowed for a change in certain elements of the car but required that the car continue to look as if you could buy it off the showroom floor. Some credit Hernandez with coining the term "Funny Car," used to describe FX cars with their shorter wheelbase and forward front wheel. In 1966, he created the first generation of funny cars based on a 1966 Comet Cyclone GT. He built it with a fiberglass body that was able to "flip," with attachments in the back of the frame to allow access to the engine.[34]

Hernandez was able to enjoy success throughout his career and life, and he never was treated like a "typical" Mexican American from Southern California. This might be attributed to his European bloodline, which rendered him light skinned. According to his son, Randy, "Dad seem to have a permanent farmer's tan. When he wore shorts or a sleeveless shirt, he was very white."[35] Even though he had a recognizable Spanish surname, he did not have to break down social barriers and discredit stereotypes as much as did Arnett and the Bean Bandits. However, with his involvement as a winning drag racer, his machinist knowledge and hard work, he was able to be heavily involved in the sport of drag racing and facilitate assimilation by working for a major corporation such as Ford Motor Company.

BOBBY TAPIA

The Robert "Bobby" Tapia story is both similar to and different from those of the other Mexican Americans in this chapter. His parents moved to the United States from Mexico when they were teenagers. Tapia was born in Santa Monica, California, on March 25, 1938. He did not grow up in the barrios of Southern California but in a tract home in Torrance. He grew up in a Spanish-speaking household and was taught English at school. He played football in high school for two years, but his need for speed was too irresistible; he dropped football to work on cars. He graduated from high school in 1956 but had been working on cars since age twelve. Tapia remembers his first time, at the age of fourteen or fifteen, going to Santa Ana Drag Strip in Southern California where he got the drag-racing bug.[36]

Tapia did not have the money or experience to start his drag-racing career at the top; instead he started at the bottom. In 1957, he won thirteen weeks in a row at Lions Drag Strip in a 1957 Chevrolet two-door that he had modified for drag racing. In 1958, he started racing dragsters in Middle Eliminator, winning 50 out of 52 races.[37] He served in the Army from 1961 to 1963 and afterward attended UCLA, where he got his bachelor of science in math.[38]

While working at a muffler shop during college, Tapia spent his weekends drag racing. Before he left for the Army, he raced for Ed Donovan. Donovan built drag cars and engines and helped many drivers as they came through town. His shop was a hangout place for famous drag racers, such as "Big Daddy" Don Garlits, Wayne King, and Tom "Mongoose" McEwen. While working with Donovan, Tapia learned how to tune engines and weld. He noted, "[Donovan] could not find anyone to drive while I was away in the Army; that is how I got into fuel cars."[39]

"Fuel cars," running nitro and supercharged, was the term used for Top Eliminator Funny Cars or dragsters. And Tapia was fast. In October 1964, Tapia was able to set a low E.T. (estimated time) at two different drag strips on the same day.[40] Tapia was driving Donovan's "Pegasus" dragster at Lions Drag Strip to an 8.10 seconds pass but decided the track was too slick to go any faster and was getting too dangerous to run fast speeds, so they loaded up the car and drove forty miles to Fontana. There they set a low E.T. of 7.54 seconds. Because Tapia had set a time at Lions early in the day, his E.T. stood for the lowest of the day, and he pulled a rare double low E.T. from two different racetracks.[41] There is also evidence of Tapia running close to 200 miles per hour in June 1964 and over that speed in 1966 in front of 2,000 drag-racing fans in San Fernando Raceway. He was often a featured driver at Lions and San Fernando Raceways for his outright top speed in the quarter mile, as noted in the *Los Angeles Times*.[42]

According to Tapia, "I never saw myself as a Mexican American drag racer. I just wanted to go fast."[43] Once he got the taste of achieving 200 miles per hour with 3,000 to 4,000 horsepower, he just wanted to race. He enjoyed the feel of g-forces; the tires would often smoke from start to finish. "You lived and breathed drag racing," Tapia commented. While driving for Donovan, he took in 30 percent of the winnings; Top Eliminator would pay out $2,000 to $3,000 over the course of a weekend. If there was not much money to go around, he drove for free. Running these engines to max cost money, and Tapia knew that.

Tapia's story is somewhat different from but still similar to those of the Mexican Americans discussed above. He grew up in a Spanish-speaking household, and while he finished high school and served in the military, he still had to fight stereotypes. Some of his fellow racers would tease him about his Mexican heritage. Tapia handled the situation with a cool head and always wanted to settle it on the track, proving time after time he was faster than they were.[44] Through his winning, he started to discredit Mexican stereotypes held by fellow racers. Tapia demonstrated assimilation by attending college and playing football, but his love for drag racing is what broke down social barriers.

"FLAMING" FRANK PEDREGON

Frank Pedregon was born Francisco Lopez on July 9, 1940, in Freestone County, Texas. The reason why Frank changed his name from Lopez to Pedregon is lost to family history, but according to Cruz Pedregon, the middle son, "there must have been some bad blood between my father and his parents."[45] Frank took his mother's maiden name of Pedregon. Unlike the other Mexican Americans listed above, Pedregon's parents were born in the United States. One would have to go back a few generations in Pedregon's family tree to find a direct relative who was born in Mexico. However, Pedregon, like the others discussed here, grew up in a Spanish-speaking household and learned English while attending school. During high school he was working at a garage, learning about fixing cars, when he got the drag-racing bug. He did not start at the bottom but instead built a dragster by himself.[46] He grew up in El Paso and San Antonio, Texas, before moving to Southern California to be closer to the "scene" and opening a trucking business.[47]

Pedregon got his nickname "Flaming" because his tires would often catch fire. He claims he did not use any chemicals or tricks. He just ran the tires so hard they would sometimes ignite. It became part of his trademark, along with the style of dragster he ran.[48] Pedregon did not run an open-top dragster like the others; he fabricated a 1938 Fiat coupe body that was chopped and cut down to fit on a dragster body.[49] While Pedregon was able to race with just the frame in Top Eliminator, with the body on he was able to race in Competition Coupe, where he won more often. Track promoters, in newspapers ads, often featured his supercharged Chrysler coupe to try to get more fans into the grandstands. The *Los Angeles Times* noted, "Frank Pedregon will attempt to break his world's coupe record of 7.98 seconds and 201.60 m.p.h. at San Fernando Raceway Sunday afternoon."[50]

Like the Bean Bandits, Pedregon accentuated his Mexican heritage when he raced. Several pictures of his coupe dragster show it with "Chicken Coupe" painted on the side. According to Tony, the youngest son, "It sat in the back of our house in Chino (California) and chickens lived in it. That's why we called it the 'Chicken Coupe.'"[51] One time, Dave Wallace Sr., track reporter and photographer, named Pedregon's dragster "Taco Taster"; the next day Pedregon painted the moniker on the dragster.[52] Pedregon would wear t-shirts advertising "Genuine

Mexican Parts" with the traditional tricolors of Mexico in the background. He would tell people that his dragster was "powered by genuine Mexican horsepower."[53] While he did receive some help from Clay Smith Cams, Horsepower Engineering, Coburn Glaze (Bill Coburn), and a few others, he never collected any real money to use for racing. Pedregon would pull used pistons, bearings, and other used parts out of trashcans or request worn-out parts from other racers and rebuild them to almost new condition. According to Tony, "He once got some used pistons from Dale Armstrong and rebuilt them, then went out and ran faster than Dale."[54]

Pedregon would also bill himself as the "World's Fastest Mexican," which track promoters used in their promotions. Fellow Mexican American drag racer Tapia responded, "What am I, Irish?"[55] Thinking back to that time, Tapia said, "That was a thing for Frank, he would bring his kids and they were kind of grubby and stuff. I didn't think that was right (being called fastest Mexican). I was running faster than he was."[56] When asked if Pedregon was too proud of his Mexican heritage, always putting it out front, Tapia responded, "Probably true. Frank had to find something he could excel at. I didn't have to do that."[57] Pedregon not only wanted to run fast, trying to prove it every weekend at the drag strip, but he was also known for entertaining the crowd by lighting the tires of his coupe-bodied dragsters on fire.

Unlike other drag racers who had friends, family, or a shop to support the racing bug, Pedregon did most of the work himself. He welded his chassis, rebuilt engines, and even assembled the trailers they were hauled on.[58] He assimilated into American society through his successful trucking company, hard work, and ability to race on a shoestring budget, but moreover he undermined Mexican stereotypes with every race he won. He did race for other people, including Joe Winter and Don Madden, later in his career.[59] However, like the other drag racers, Pedregon just wanted to go faster than his opponents. With his tire burning and unique coupe-bodied dragster, he won over the racing fans, helping to break down social barriers and erode stereotypes.

OTHER MINORITIES

The four Mexican American men of the golden age of drag racing mentioned above share similar stories to those of other minorities getting into auto racing. As mentioned previously, Wendell Scott was the first African American to race in NASCAR in the Deep South during the 1950s and 1960s. During this time of segregation in the South, he fought social barriers, prejudice, and bigotry. Similar to the Mexican Americans mentioned above, Scott was a master mechanic who worked on his own racecars and also owned an auto repair shop that locals, both white and black, used. He competed against white racers, often winning, and chipped away at racial stereotypes held by his fellow racers. However, all too often, it was the track owners and the prejudice of the fans that fought against Scott. Like the Mexican Americans mentioned above, Scott just wanted to go out and run as hard and as fast as his car would allow. The race of the people against whom he was competing did not matter to him.[60] By racing hard and winning races, Scott was able to break social barriers and discredit stereotypes.

Another African American racecar driver, also mentioned earlier, was Charlie Wiggins. Wiggins wanted to be the first African American to race the prestigious Indy 500 during the 1920s and 1930s. Wiggins was an excellent mechanic, getting an auto mechanic job based on touch and hearing. He was able to fix automobiles that nobody else could fix. As a test to get a job at a garage, Wiggins diagnosed by hearing only that an automobile needed a new timing belt. This aptitude is similar to the way in which Arnett was such a good mechanic; the latter would visualize the engine as if he were crawling around inside until he could see the problem in his head.[61]

Wiggins fought social barriers and prejudice regarding letting black racecar drivers race at Indy. To address this problem, the Colored Speedway Association, which was only for black racecar drivers, was established. The association had its own version of the Indy 500, the Gold and Glory Sweepstakes. While black racecar drivers never got the chance to race the Indy 500 in the '20s and '30s, they were able to break down social barriers by creating a racing venue where thousands of white and black fans came to watch.[62]

Women have been racing almost as long as men, and they also have had to challenge social barriers. There was a time when women could not race because of the Victorian code. People thought that racing had become too dangerous for women, although the women themselves did not subscribe to this point of view. Camille du Gast is considered to be one of the earliest women competitive automobile racers. She first raced in 1901 in the 678-mile Paris to Berlin race, starting last and finishing 33 out of 121. Dorothy Levitt, Joan Newton

Cuneo, and Margaret Mabel Gladys feature among those women racers during the early 1900s who raced against men.

While there were a few women racecar drivers during the 1920s and 1930s, it was not until after World War II that society allowed women to race again. Drivers such as Denise McCluggage and Ruth Levy were well known in sports car racing circles. Shirley "Cha Cha" Muldowney became one of the first women drag racers in the NHRA. She fought against social barriers to receive her license to race a Top Fuel Dragster during the late 1960s and 1970s. She went on to win three NHRA Top Fuel Dragster Championships during her career.[63] All these women had to fight prejudices against letting these "frail creatures" race huge, fast racecars.[64] While some minorities in automobile racing have been covered, this author believes that further study needs to be conducted in this area.

CONCLUSION

This chapter explores the lives of four Mexican American drag racers from the golden age of drag racing: Joaquin Arnett, Fran Hernandez, Bobby Tapia, and Frank Pedregon. Each of these Mexican Americans has his own story. Arnett created a racing club, the Bean Bandits, to help his friends get out of the neighborhoods and learn a trade. They were not afraid to put their Mexican heritage up front and center, wearing the derogatory term *beaners* with honor. Pedregon also called attention to his Mexican heritage by wearing t-shirts showing his Mexican pride, painting Mexican labels on his dragster, and promoting himself as the world's fastest Mexican.

Hernandez and Tapia have similar stories. They did not have to fight against social barriers to the same extent as did the other two, possibly due to the fact that they did not emphasize Mexican heritage. However, when they were disparaged for their Mexican heritage, they preferred to settle it out on the track. Hernandez used his machinist and engineering knowledge to break down social barriers while Tapia used his right foot. Arnett, Hernandez, and Tapia served in the military. When they returned from service, they got back into drag racing; for Arnett and Hernandez it was when organized drag racing was just getting started. The Spanish-surnamed men discussed in this chapter used drag racing to break down social barriers, discredit stereotypes, and facilitate assimilation, each in his own way. These Mexican Americans, these El Guapos behind the wheel, deserve more attention by sports historians.

Other Mexican American drag racers deserve historical recognition, including Dave Marquez, Don Enrique, and Poncho Gonzales. Fran Hernandez, with his interesting resume at Ford Motor Company and Autolite Company, his involvement in the 100,000-mile durability run at Daytona in 1964, and other interesting endeavors, merits a separate historical monograph. The Bean Bandits, along with their leader Joaquin Arnett, also warrant a separate historical monograph. One can be sure that each of the Bean Bandits, and their families, have stories to tell. Sports historians should also take the time to study other minorities involved in drag racing, such as Hawaiian Roland Leong, and explore the formation of the Black American Racers Association, created by Leonard W. Miller, Ron Hines, Eugene Gadson, and Charles Singleton, to promote black racing development.

EPILOGUE

This chapter focused on four Mexican American men in their early years; but what happened to them later in life? Arnett stopped drag racing for a short time to raise his family. He had a successful career in the body shop industry around San Diego, with clients insisting that only he pound out the dents of the old metal cars. He was a true craftsman when it came to repairing dented cars, using very little Bondo (an automotive repair putty). Later in his life he focused on setting land-speed records, racing on dry lakebed with his sons. Unfortunately, he lost one of his sons in a racing accident in the mid-1990s and Arnett stopped racing altogether. He passed away September 24, 2010, in El Cajon, California. Some of the original members of the Bean Bandits have also passed away, but there are some still living.[65]

Fran Hernandez raised a family and worked for Ford Motor Company for over thirty-five years, retiring at age seventy. He then started his own business and, within a month, was back working with Ford as a consultant. While working at Ford, he helped with racing programs and car research and engineering. He worked on building Lincoln Presidential limousines for the Reagan/Bush administration in 1988. Unfortunately, two years after Hernandez opened his consulting business, he became ill; he passed away January 5, 2011. His son Randy has created a Facebook page to honor his father.[66]

Bobby Tapia is still alive and living in Tennessee. He too stopped drag racing to help raise a family. Tapia mentioned that, after moving to Houston to work at IBM, he found it difficult to take the time to load up the dragster and go across the country to the next NHRA racing event. Asked about racing at the local dragstrip, which would mean racing modified or lower-class drag racing, Tapia said, "Doing 220 miles per hour at night and feeling the G's, which is pretty healthy in those dragsters, it's hard to go back down."[67]

Pedregon stopped drag racing after his friend, Joe Winter, lost his battle with cancer. He had a successful trucking business that ran routes between California, Mexico, and Texas. He lost his life due to injuries from a private plane crash in Mexico in the early 1980s. Pedregon initially survived the crash but had significant blood loss from a severed arm. He managed to walk to a highway, but because of the dizziness resulting from his injuries, he made a wrong decision and walked away from a nearby town. All three of Pedregon's sons — Frank Jr., Tony, and Cruz — were involved in NHRA drag racing. Tony and Cruz have each won two NHRA Funny Car Championships, in 2003 and 2007 and 1992 and 2008 respectively.[68] Cruz was also the first motorsports athlete to receive the Premio De Oro award, a national award for Hispanic athletes, by the Argentine Círculo de Periodistas Deportivos (Association of Sports Journalists) in 1997.[69]

The four Mexican American racing pioneers featured in this chapter — Joaquin Arnett, Fran Hernandez, Bobby Tapia, and Frank Pedregon — lived full lives, having families and successful careers and enjoying their involvement in the golden age of drag racing.

QUESTIONS:

1. What is the author's main argument? Is there more than one argument?

2. How does the author use the four main characters in this chapter to demonstrate how they break down social barriers, discredit stereotypes, and facilitate assimilation through drag racing?

3. Is drag racing a sport? Why or why not?

NOTES

1. "Three Amigos El Guapo is 33," YouTube video, 0:10, posted by "HSeddiegilbert," April 26, 2012, https://youtu.be/2PGF42ONNmQ.

2. Cruz Pedregon, Cruz Pedregon Facebook Page, September 19, 2015, https://www.facebook.com/CruzPedregon/timeline.

3. See El Guapo photo on twitter page: https://twitter.com/cruzpedregon/status/ 467501643693428736 and *Scarface* photo https://twitter.com/cruzpedregon/status/ 655016516887252992.

4. Tom Madigan, *Fuel and Guts: The Birth of Top Fuel Drag Racing* (St. Paul: Motorbooks, 2007), 81.

5. Varda Burstyn, *The Rites of Men: Manhood, Politics, and the Culture of Sport* (Toronto: University of Toronto Press Incorporated, 2000), 15–16.

6. Jorge Iber, Samuel O. Regalado, José M. Alamillo, and Arnoldo De León, *Latinos in U.S. Sport: A History of Isolation, Cultural Identity, and Acceptance* (Champaign, IL: Human Kinetics, 2011), 290.

7. National Hot Rod Association, *The Fast Lane: The History of* NHRA *Drag Racing* (New York, NY: HarperCollins Publishers Inc., 2001), 14.

8. Bob McClurg, *Diggers, Funnies, Gassers & Altereds: Drag Racing's Golden Age* (North Branch, MN: CarTech, 2013), 5; *The Fast Lane*, 15–17; "NHRA history: Drag racing's fast start," NHRA, http://www.nhra.com/nhra101/history.aspx.

9. NHRA, *The Fast Lane*, 17.

10. Ibid.

11. Ibid., 10, 22, 44, 70. Much more could be said about the different specs of drag-racing cars, but many details were omitted due to space limitations.

12. Robert C. Post, *High Performance: The Culture and Technology of Drag Racing, 1950–2000* (Baltimore: The John Hopkins University Press, 2001), 34, 36.

13. Ibid., 333.

14. Mike Carr, "Understanding Class Racing: NHRA Competition Eliminator," *Dragzine*, http://www.dragzine.com/features/car-features/understanding-class-racing-nhra-competition-eliminator/; Mike Carr, "Understanding Class Racing – Stock Eliminator," *Dragzine*, http://www.dragzine.com/features/ understanding-class-racing-stock-eliminator/.

15. Pro Stock motorcycle racing was added in the 1980s.

16. McClurg, *Diggers, Funnies, Gassers & Altereds*, 5.

17. "US Inflation Calculator," *Coinnews Media Group* LLC, http://www.usinflationcalculator.com. Inputting 1953 as the "if in" year and 2015 as the "then in" year used to produce the calculation; Jacqueline Arnett Sonka, "Joaquin Arnett's Biography," *Joaquinarnettbio.blogspot*, March 23, 2009, http://joaquinarnettbio.blogspot.com; Jacqueline Arnett Sonka, interview with author, September 25, 2015. For more information

about the custom-built 1934 Ford see: http://www.macsmotorcitygarage. com/2013/07/23/the-arnettgranatellicouch-1934-ford-coupe/.

18. Post, *High Performance*, 22.

19. Ibid., 35.

20. Jacqueline Arnett Sonka, interview with author, September 25, 2015.

21. According to Jacqueline Arnett Sonka, they were often called "the damn beaners" after they won the race.

22. Jacqueline Arnett Sonka, interview with author, September 25, 2015.

23. Post, *High Performance*, 22–3.

24. Jacqueline Arnett Sonka, interview with author, September 25, 2015.

25. Ibid.

26. Ibid.

27. Ibid.

28. The history of the Hernandez family was written by Luis Felipe Hernandez, Dean of the School of Education at California State University, Northridge. The paper was given to the author by Randy Hernandez through email.

29. Randy Hernandez, interview with author, November 12, 2015.

30. Ibid.

31. Post, *High Performance*, 1–3; "Hot Rod of the Month," *Hot Rod Magazine*, April 1949, 15–7. *Hot Rod Magazine* scanned and emailed to author by Randy Hernandez.

32. Randy Hernandez, interview with author, November 12, 2015.

33. Post, *High Performance*, 140.

34. Ibid., 141; Randy Hernandez, interview with author, November 12, 2015.

35. Randy Hernandez, interview with author, November 12, 2015.

36. Bobby Tapia, interview with author, August 10, 2015.

37. Mark Hendon, "Bobby Tapia's Low ET Double of '64," *Drag Racing List*, November 18, 2006, http://www.draglist.com/artman/publish/daily_stories/article_001928.shtml.

38. Ibid.; Bobby Tapia, interview with author, August 10, 2015.

39. Bobby Tapia, interview with author, August 10, 2015.

40. According to NHRA, "Upon leaving the starting line, each contestant activates a timer that is, in turn, stopped when the same vehicle reaches the finish line. The start-to-finish clocking is the vehicle's E.T. (elapsed time), which serves to measure performance." http://www.nhra.com/

nhra101/etracing.aspx.

41. Hendon, "Bobby Tapia's Low ET Double of '64."

42. "Mulligan Takes Fuel Honors at Lions Strip," *Los Angeles Times*, June 21, 1964; "Auto Racing," *Los Angeles Times*, June 6, 1966; "Hot-Rod Finals Scheduled Today at Lions Strip," *Los Angeles Times*, September 11, 1965.

43. Bobby Tapia, interview with author, August 10, 2015.

44. Ibid.

45. Cruz Pedregon, interview with author, September 20, 2015.

46. Madigan, *Fuel and Guts*, 80.

47. Cruz Pedregon, interview with author, September 20, 2015; Greg Sharp, "El Paso Athletic Hall Of Fame," *El Paso Athletic Hall Of Fame*, March 7, 2011, http://elpasoathletichalloffame. com/docs/nomres2011/Posthumous-Pedregon.pdf.

48. Andy Kirk, "Behind the Rebirth of the Ultimate 'Tyre Fryer,'" *Drag Rod & Classic Review*, April 14, 2005, http://www.drcreview.com/news. asp?art=73.

49. Madigan, *Fuel and Guts*, 80.

50. "McEwen Top Eliminator at Fontana," *Los Angeles Times*, March 15, 1965; "'Funny Cars,'" *Los Angeles Times*, February 17, 1966.

51. "Pedregon Brothers Recreate Father's 'Coupe' Memories," NHRA, November 10, 2004, http://www.nhra.com/story/2004/11/10/1944/.

52. "$10,000 Purse Attracts Leading Drag Racers to Irwindale Strip," *Los Angeles Times*, October 20, 1966.

53. Sharp, "El Paso Athletic Hall Of Fame"; photo in Kirk, "Behind the Rebirth of the Ultimate 'Tyre Fryer.'"

54. Madigan, *Fuel and Guts*, 80–1.

55. Ibid., 81; Sharp, "El Paso Athletic Hall Of Fame."

56. Bobby Tapia, interview with author, August 10, 2015.

57. Ibid.

58. Sharp, "El Paso Athletic Hall Of Fame."

59. Ibid.; "Pedregon Brothers Recreate Father's 'Coupe' Memories."

60. For more on Wendell Scott see Brian Donovan, *Hard Driving: The Wendell Scott Story* (Hanover: Steerforth Press, 2008).

61. Jacqueline Arnett Sonka, interview with author, September 25, 2015.

62. For more on Charlie Wiggins and Gold for Glory Sweepstakes see Todd Gould, *For Gold and Glory: Charlie Wiggins and the African American Racing Car Circuit* (Bloomington: Indiana University Press, 2002).

63. Post, *High Performance*, 345.

64. For more on women sports car racing drivers see Todd McCarthy, *Fast Women: The Legendary Ladies of Racing* (New York: Miramax Books, 2007). Shirley Muldowney was featured in a movie, "Heart Like a Wheel," displaying how she fought through stereotypes to get her racing license and touching on her role as a wife and mother. She has also written a book, *Shirley Muldowney's Tales from the Track*.

65. Jacqueline Arnett Sonka, interview with author, September 25, 2015. For more information see http://beanbanditssandiego.blogspot.com.

66. Randy Hernandez, interview with author, November 12, 2015; https://www.facebook.com/ Fran-Francisco-Hernandez-157884174258948/. Randy Hernandez has sent the author documentation via CD-ROM about his father's career achievements.

67. Bobby Tapia, interview with author, August 10, 2015.

68. Sharp, "El Paso Athletic Hall Of Fame." Greg Sharp provided to the author a Microsoft Word document, and he wrote the introduction of Frank Pedegron Sr. (posthumous) into the International Drag Racing Hall of Fame.

69. "NHRA Driver: Cruz Pedregon Career Highlights," NHRA, http://www.nhra.com/drivers/funny-car/Cruz-Pedregon/. "News," *Cruz Pedregon Racing*, http://cruzpedregonracing.com/category/news/.

MEXICAN AMERICAN FASTPITCH

Ben Chappell
University of Kansas

IN ATHLETIC PARK in Newton, Kansas, an exuberant Tejano polka is blaring over the PA system while crowds arrive at the softball field. Handshakes, *abrazos*, and kisses accompany the music and laughter as people haul coolers, chairs, and softball gear onto the grounds. Groups of twenty or thirty wearing matching t-shirts stake out spots in the shade. Eventually, the music pipes down and the tournament director, dressed to play, introduces the local priest, who gives an invocation at home plate and sprinkles holy water on the field. Beyond the first-base foul line in the distance stands the vacant Harvey Building, where the Atchison, Topeka, and Santa Fe trains out of Kansas City used to stop to take on fresh linen and china on their way southwest.

A color guard of ROTC students advances on the pitching rubber, bearing flags of the Republic of Mexico, the USA, and Newton's Mexican American Athletic Club. The flag bearers split up so that Mexico ends up at first, and the N.M.A.A.C. at third, with the American flag in the pitching circle, while a young woman takes the microphone to sing an *a cappella* rendition of the "Star Spangled Banner." Arranged across the infield, the flags seem to map out a continuum or trajectory, echoed in the code-switching slogans that appear on the back of the t-shirts that men in their 60s and older are wearing for the old-timers' game that will open the weekend's competition: "Hecho in America" (made in America) "con Mexican parts." The mechanical metaphor gets picked up again in the jocular shouts of the old timers as play begins. A foul ball crashes into the fence, just missing a man who has wandered out of the dugout to watch the play from beside first base. *"Watch it!"* yells a player from the other side. *"I don't think they make parts for that year-model anymore!"*[1]

Two weeks later, in Houston, tarps have been stretched over the bleachers to provide shade at the pristine Field Number 1 in Memorial Park. The shaded sections are packed, but beyond them there are a lot of empty seats. On the PA system from the press box, a local radio personality is building anticipation for the games to come and urging the crowd to partake of the wares of the beer distributor who is a major sponsor. The space behind the grandstand has been turned into an impromptu museum, with rows of posters and photographs from decades of prior tournaments on display, alongside trophies, plaques naming the inductees to the tournament's hall of fame, and old tournament bracket charts. The bracket for this year is different from those of prior decades — more teams have shown up for the over-40 division than the open. An elderly gentleman sitting beside me as we watch the game takes up a refrain I have heard all weekend long at the annual Rusk Athletic Club softball tournament: *"You should have seen it back in the days in Settegast Park. The outfield was lined. All the stands were full, and everybody put their pits out there past the fence — smoking brisket, drinking beer, music. That was something to see."*

Between games, Ray Guerra, an umpire and Rusk tournament committee member, takes me around the park just outside the Memorial 1 stands to visit some barbecue pits. A few of the giant, welded contraptions on trailer wheels are parked near picnic tables for owners to smoke meat and feed an endless stream of family and friends who will stop by to visit awhile in the course of the weekend. I meet a pitmaster and compliment him on providing what amounts to a tailgate for the spectators and players at this sporting event that would probably draw a couple of thousand people. Once I am properly weighed down with a sagging paper plate of brisket, ribs, and sausage, I have to get eating and the conversation goes on without me. One middle-aged Latino man who stops by to chat with Ray nods toward the entrance to the ballpark. *"What's with the false advertising?"*

The wry rhetorical question comments on a banner decorating the chain-link fence: "Rusk Athletic Club 64th annual tournament — 'The Latin.'" Everyone on the Mexican American fastpitch circuit in Texas, and quite a few others beyond those borders, know this event as "The Latin." Over the seventy consecutive years that it has now gone on, the Rusk club's tournament has gone through some name changes, being called in various periods the "Latin American tournament" and the "Mexican American state championship." But it was colloquially known as "The Latin," which was explained to me by one old-timer as reflecting the preferred nomenclature of the Mexican American generation who founded it in the 1940s: *Back then, we were Latin American, not Mexican.* More to the point, though, the Rusk tournament, like all others I am aware of other than Newton, has recently made the decision to "open up," changing from an invitational format mostly restricted to players of Mexican descent to a "men's fastpitch" tournament of undesignated ethnicity. Ray diplomatically refrains from taking a position on the "false advertising" charge. We return to the game at Memorial 1; not all the players on the field are Mexican American, but it is still The Latin.

These vignettes convey the kinds of experiences I have pursued in field research in six cities, spread out roughly between Kansas City and Houston, since 2011. A loose circuit of annual men's fastpitch softball tournaments hosted by Mexican American communities has existed in this strip of the central United States since at least the 1940s. The longest running of these, which serve not only as recreational sport and local spectacle but also as family reunions, fundraisers, and sites of collective memory and popular archiving, are in the railroad town of Newton, Kansas, and the Southwestern metropolis of Houston, Texas. The Mexican American tournaments in these cities have occurred for seventy-one and seventy consecutive years, respectively. The timeframe is significant: both tournaments began at a historical moment in which de facto segregation was the norm. In the years before and after World War II, the generation of Americans whose Mexican parents had sought work and fled revolutionary upheaval in the 1910s and 1920s were coming of age, and softball was a popular recreation nationwide.

There was no single event that sparked the modern tradition of Mexican American fastpitch; in fact, it seems that numerous local traditions began simultaneously, or nearly so. If the various Mexican American communities that took up softball and invested it with a locally specific identity in the 1940s didn't all know about each other, many eventually would as these traditions continued. Tournament brackets from the 1980s provide evidence of teams carpooling from places like Kansas City to Austin, and the formidable Houston Nine was featured in the Newton local paper once when the entire team flew to Kansas to compete in the tournament. Attending tournaments over the past few summers, I have learned to wear a Kansas t-shirt to a Texas tournament, and vice-versa, increasing the odds that a stranger will notice and address me with *"Newton, Kansas? You know Gil Solis?"* or offer up stories of their road exploits in days gone by.

This essay is part of a larger project of multi-sited ethnography, which I have undertaken to "follow the game" of Mexican American fastpitch and gain a sense of the value that this softball tradition poses for the communities that invest so much time, money, and especially effort into making sure that their fastpitch teams and tournaments continue.[2] This research in turn joins a larger agenda reflected in this book — that is, a commitment by scholars to take seriously the long-standing and substantial attachments to sport that are salient in various Latina/o communities. As an ethnography, engaging with people's ongoing reconstructions of memory and their sometimes diligent, sometimes haphazard collections, my project does not always deliver precise facts and data to "correct the record." This may be to the chagrin of at least one of my interviewees, who began our conversation by declaring *"Statistics! That's the key!"*

But as I have struck up conversations in the bleachers; listened to announcers, players, and fans in the heat of competition; browsed the archives both of newspapers and memorabilia hounds; and recorded interviews with over fifty people, I have gained a sense of the importance of fastpitch in the ordinary yearly life of certain Mexican American communities. In what follows I hope to render something of this sense of fastpitch in order to suggest how a sport associated mostly with playgrounds can end up meaning a great deal to people, becoming invested with identity as a focal point for collective memory. To do so I will discuss the segregated conditions under which Mexican American fastpitch emerged, the specific value that participants have ascribed to the sport over more than a half-century, and some of the signs of change that indicate that the Mexican American fastpitch tradition remains dynamic and evolving.

THE CONDITIONS OF SEGREGATION

The question that might present itself to a curious outsider approaching the Newton tournament and its banner proclaiming "the oldest

Mexican American fastpitch tournament in the country" is: What exactly makes a tournament Mexican American? The simplistic answer for the Newton tournament is: the rules. The Newton tournament is not only the oldest of what some ballplayers refer to as the "Mexican tournaments," it is also sometimes mentioned as "the last," because the tournament remains "invitational," and according to the rules, no team may include more than two "non-Hispanic" players. No one without Mexican ancestry is allowed to pitch. Officially, these restrictions are enforced by a requirement that players bring birth certificates to show a Spanish surname from at least one parent, but in practice such documentation is rarely necessary because of the tight-knit nature of the fastpitch community — everyone generally knows everyone.

Other tournaments hosted by Mexican American communities — I have attended them in Kansas City, Topeka, Austin, San Antonio, and Houston — have changed to an "open" format, welcoming all teams who can come up with an entry fee. As I will discuss in more detail, "opening up" is spurred partly by the decline of fastpitch softball as a recreational activity — there are simply fewer players, fewer teams, and most of all fewer pitchers, so maintaining a competitive tournament with only Mexican American teams has become less viable. But if a dwindling participant pool makes the prospect of opening up seem inevitable, it also comes with a sense of loss. The Newton organizers talk about the identity restriction as maintaining "our tradition" and continue to draw justification from the history of segregation and exclusion. As Manuel Jaso, who directs the Newton tournament as his father Nicholas Jaso once did, put it to me in an interview, "From what I've gathered, my dad told me...they were not allowed to play alongside the Anglos, so they started...basically a league of their own.... Just a sign of the times, you know?"

"The times" referenced here were just before the mid-twentieth century, and segregation was taken for granted as the order of everyday life in much of the United States. Exclusion of Mexican Americans from public life was not always official or absolute, and economics played a key role. Railroad companies had actively recruited Mexicans to work on their track throughout the 1920s and before, in some cases providing housing in modest "casitas" that would form enclave communities in small towns along the line. The organizers of the Mexican American tournament in Newton trace its origins to 1946, although there may have been less formal "meets" among Mexican teams before then, and later a rain-out would set the count of consecutive annual events back a little. Regardless, 1946 was the same year that a judicial ruling began to push back official segregation, in the case of *Mendez v. Westminster School District* of Orange County in California. The district court in Los Angeles found in favor of Gonzalo Mendez and his fellow litigants that the so-called "separate but equal" elementary schools his children had been assigned to attend were unconstitutional, in a decision that some legal scholars see as an important precedent for the landmark case *Brown v. Board of Education*.[3] The case would eventually be affirmed a year later, although the final decision somewhat watered down the constitutional implications by pulling back from an assessment of the separate-but-equal doctrine established a half-century before by *Plessy v. Ferguson*.

If the immediate post-war era was a time of political awakening for Mexican Americans, this could be attributed as much to enduring oppression as to progress. This was also the time that US serviceman Felix Longoria's family, in Three Rivers, Texas, were waiting for his remains to be repatriated after Private Longoria was killed in action in the Pacific Theater in 1945. By the time Private Longoria was returned to the US in 1949, the funeral director in his hometown of Three Rivers refused to allow him to lie in state in the chapel of the funeral home because "the whites would not like it." This incident of segregation even after death was one among many that sparked a new era of civil-rights activism among Mexican Americans.[4] Thus Mexican American fastpitch was established in a period when cracks were beginning to show in the edifice of segregation. But even as the Mendez decision heralded desegregation advances that were still to come, the appeals process of that case and events like the Longoria affair showed that the struggle by Mexican Americans to demand full status as Americans would proceed unevenly, with steps forward and backward. They were far from the only such situations.

This is why anthropologist Jennifer Nájera, while providing context for her historical ethnography of race in a small South Texas town, argues that the history of segregation experienced by Mexican Americans is not a story of steady progress from pre-modern ignorance to equality. On the contrary, Nájera shows how patterns of segregation were cross-hatched with contradiction and exception, and the greater part of the twentieth century can be characterized not in terms of a binary between segregation and freedom but what she calls "accommodated segregation." In this social formation, certain individuals of

Mexican descent may have experienced a measure of social mobility and opportunity, often due to being deemed exceptional in their racial, financial, educational, linguistic, or other characteristics. And yet the notion of Mexicans as "racial others" could come back into play at any time to throw up and enforce social barriers.[5]

Nájera joins other scholars who argue that the segregation of everyday life and public space that is the focus of her study emerged in the early twentieth century as a response to what Anglos viewed as the "Mexican problem." An ascendant Anglo order was displacing traditional Texas ranch society with the coming of the railroad and new forms of commercial agriculture. The Mexican problem, for Anglo rule, was that people from Mexico filled an urgent need for labor and yet challenged the hegemonic project of associating "America" with specifically Anglo ethnicity, including English language use, uncomplicated national allegiance to the United States, and physically observable racial distance from both African and indigenous American descent. In other words, the order being established in Texas under Anglo rule in the early twentieth century needed the presence of Mexican bodies at work but equally desired the absence of Mexican bodies from the imagined community.[6]

These dynamics also played out in Newton, a town of just over 19,000 people (about 14 percent of whom are Latino), that sits a half-hour north of Wichita, Kansas. Newton is a railroad town that at one point played a pivotal role in the middle section of the Santa Fe system and that still is home to a sizable BNSF railyard. The families that first made up Newton's Mexican-descended community were drawn to Newton in the 1920s by what historian Jeffrey Garcilazo describes as the "seemingly insatiable demand for labor" that accompanied the construction of the Western railroad.[7] Members of this community today share memories of being denied service in downtown restaurants and barbershops, and no Mexican American athlete played on a Newton High School sports team until the early 1950s — more than a full generation after the community was established.

Yet there is evidence that despite these exclusions Newton's Mexican Americans embraced the mainstream of sports in American society, and to some extent were allowed to do so. The *Newton Evening Kansan-Republican* daily newspaper gave extensive coverage to city softball leagues that organized games on weeknights and occasional tournaments in the 1940s. During that era, the generation that would later found the Mexican American tournament fielded a team to be reckoned with that often appears in box scores as "the Mexican Catholics," later taking on the name of the church's Holy Name Society. Teams with entirely Spanish-surnamed rosters (with a lot of overlap among them) were sponsored variously by the Optimist Club and an Anglo potato-chip merchant named Magee. Yet just across the fold from the sports section in one of these papers appeared a letter from Ignacio Martinez, with the heading "No Mexicans Allowed." The letter reads in part:

> While in one page of the *Evening Kansan* it tells of the friend-ly welcome accorded General Eisenhower in Mexico City, in another page of the same paper, it had a commercial advertise-ment sponsored by a local public place that utterly and with-out provocation insults and humiliates the Mexican people of Newton....Not very long ago, the Mexican boys from all over the United States were fighting and dying side by side with your own friends and perhaps your own relatives....They were fighting and dying for Democracy![8]

Here we see a version of the narrative of post-war political awak-ening that has become canonical in Mexican American historiog-raphy: after joining the total war effort against fascism, Americans of Mexican descent would not settle for second-class citizenship. The social formation of accommodated segregation was crumbling, although it would hold on for decades longer in some quarters. It would take sustained and vigorous resistance, first by integrationist organizations such as the G.I. Forum and the League of United Latin American Citizens (LULAC), and later through more radical actions that made up the Chicano/a movement, to begin to dismantle the segregat-ed racial boundaries. Sports organizations served as a focal point for this emergent politics in some locales, such as Austin, Texas, where State Senator Gonzalo Barrientos was an active honorary member of the Jokers athletic club (fastpitch and basketball), and drinking loung-es located a short walk from the Pan-American Recreation Center were venues for political strategizing as well as rehashing the most recent game.[9] Yet this kind of engagement was not universal—Mexican American sports traditions cannot be identified entirely with militant politics, but neither can they be dismissed as purely assimilationist, or as a substitute for politics. Rather, they reflect the "messiness" of accommodated segregation and struggles to move beyond it.

The founding of local sports institutions represents a community that is at once resisting exclusion, making claims to play in leagues dominated by Anglos, and also turning the condition of segregation into an opportunity to build and exert their own authority, by forming teams and tournaments of their own. As Nájera argues, "It would not be until Mexican-origin individuals and groups began to challenge prevailing racist ideologies and claim cultural citizenship rights that sustained and long-lasting racial integration would occur."[10] As one example, through the entirely mainstream idiom of softball, Mexican Americans challenged the racist ideology of their own physical and mental inferiority. They also made it clear that a bid for acceptance by Anglo society was not without conditions, which is the dynamic that Nájera references with the theoretical concept of cultural citizenship.[11] They would be accepted as Americans but would not deny, and indeed would emphasize, the particularity of their experience and position as *Mexican* Americans.

THE VALUE OF SPORT

Apart from the Our Lady of Guadalupe church, one of the Mexican American institutions in Newton that was most widely known across all ethnic groups before it closed in 1999 was Chuck's Familia Restaurant.[12] Newton residents of all backgrounds remember enjoying Chuck's distinctively Midwestern Mexican food (including flour tostadas and pork chile-smothered burritos) for years, some without ever having learned that the nickname "Chuck" referred to the owner's former prowess as a softball pitcher. As numerous veterans of the Newton tournament related to me, Joaquin "Chuck" Estrada learned to pitch underhand in the military during World War II from a fellow serviceman from Connecticut. He brought the game back home to Newton after the war and was part of the original Mexican American Athletic Club (M.A.A.C.) team. Chuck was deceased by the time I began this research, but his family members remain active, with his son serving on the Newton tournament committee and his daughter, married to another committee member, sometimes working the concession.

At the Newton tournament in 2011, several people regaled me with stories of Chuck, making sure I knew that he threw without a glove, a habit he had learned from his first pitching coach in the war and that he passed on to his own first protégé in Newton, as if that quirk of playing style were the embodiment of a legacy. Its strategic advantages are not clear in hindsight, but as a means of identifying a pitcher distinctively, it was hard to beat.[13] Chuck Estrada's generation began the Newton tournament as part of a fundraising effort to build an Our Lady of Guadalupe church to replace the mission chapel that stood on Santa Fe railroad land. The church was finally constructed more than ten years after the initial tournament and a ballpark built behind it in 1961.

The centrality of softball in the Newton Mexican community reflects a dynamic that is evident elsewhere, at times in relation to different sports. Juan Javier Pescador, in an article on Mexican/Chicano soccer associations in the United States, presents a claim that also largely applies to fastpitch, that "organized sports among Mexican communities are forming strong roots within a U.S. working class and leisure culture that emphasizes hard work, discipline, masculinity, individuality, and competitiveness, and reflects both shortcomings and aspirations of the Mexican experiences in the U.S."[14]

By asserting themselves into this complex of values, what in the mid-twentieth century certainly would have been considered part of the repertoire of normative US cultural citizenship, Mexican Americans were pushing against a powerful discourse of racial pseudoscience that justified their exclusion from athletics by underestimating both their potential and their drive to compete. As Jorge Iber, et al. recount in the textbook *Latinos in U.S. Sport*, racial theories that were widely held in the first half of the twentieth century led to assessments like that of scholar and coach Elmer D. Mitchell, who in 1922 posited a hierarchy of "the races" according to their physical attributes. Mitchell argued that:

> The South American has not the physique, environment, or disposition which makes for a champion athlete. In build he is of medium height and weight, and not rugged....[He] has inherited an undisciplined nature. The Indian in him chafes at discipline and sustained effort, while the Spanish half is proud to a fault....[His] disposition makes team play difficult...the steady grind and the competition involved in winning a place on the Varsity has no attraction for them.[15]

The idea that mestizo heritage somehow prevented Mexican Americans from wanting to play varsity sports or pursue athletic success was the kind of proposition accepted at face value by much of society without ever being exposed to the test of evidence. Thus it justified keeping Mexican Americans off of high school teams. Meanwhile, some sought other avenues to develop and display their athleticism. As for the vantage point of Mexican Americans themselves, for many the question of their own "Americanness" was settled, but what remained open was the degree to which their inclusion into US society would be recognized, through what means, and at what costs. The Newton softball team known as the "Mexican Catholics," among other monikers, was in fact allowed to play in city league and often dominated the standings there. When weekend tournaments came along, however, with the chance to win trophies and even money, they were often invitational. The politics of getting invited to such events, or not, belong to the contents of history and are not recorded in the *Evening Kansan Republican* sports pages.

The collective memory formed around Mexican American fastpitch serves as a reminder that being formally allowed in a city league did not always equate with being made to feel welcome. The memory of informal but palpable boundaries and barriers to full inclusion is reconstructed annually in shared reminiscing at the Newton tournament and is key to understanding the history of exclusion and integration of Mexican American communities in the United States, which requires close attention to the finer points of de facto segregation. One theme in this history reported to me by interviewees is a pattern across decades and generations of Mexican American athletes being blocked in their desire and efforts to compete by a systematic underestimation of their potential. This alone would be reason enough to motivate a community to run tournaments of its own.

Bearing in mind that it was track work that drew many members of Newton's Mexican community to Kansas, the idea of non-athletic "South Americans" can be quickly dispelled. Garcilazo gives a sense of the variety and complexity of the work required of track laborers, or *traqueros*:

> Among other things, they dug ditches, shoveled rock, graded road bed, lifted and laid ties and rails, and drove spikes. *Traqueros* replaced ties, rails, fastenings, frogs (switches), and ballast. Track workers cut the overgrowth of grass and weeds on banks, handled new and old materials, kept ditches open, adjusted fastenings, and maintained gauge (distance between rails) by re-spiking, adzing (trimming ties), raising joints, and

ballasting. Then, in addition to all this, *traqueros* removed snow and ice and repaired the damage constantly being done by water and weather.[16]

This responsibility for maintaining a piece of ground and the infrastructure of the railroad resonates with countless stories I have been told about the improvisation and bricolage that goes into carrying off a local softball tournament, where the expectation and commitment to maintain an annual tradition may be in greater supply than resources and facilities. Every locale has its repertoire of tales about when the rains came and the fields were too wet — in the old days it was not uncommon to dump gasoline on the ground and burn the fields dry, but this practice fell out of favor. At least once a resourceful host dumped kitty litter on the infield. Another, who discovered that they were short on lime for lining the fields after the supply stores had closed for the weekend, confessed to me that he ran to the all-night grocery for sacks of flour to ensure the fields would be ready for an early start.

Besides the ingenuity to make things work, the athleticism inherent to track work occasionally caught the eyes of Anglos, but this was the exception, not the norm. Garcilazo reports on an industry magazine's account of an Anglo college athlete who worked as a track hand in 1915 and spoke of the skill he had witnessed in his colleagues. The college athlete recounted, "The regular hands laughed at me because I could do only half as much work as they could and the result of my labor was remarkably rough." He had trouble even hitting the railroad spikes correctly and described by way of contrast, "Time and again I have seen regular laborers drive spikes with the 'pointed end' of the spike maul, which has a diameter of only five-eighths of an inch or thereabouts. And these laborers take a full, free swing with all the recklessness and abandon of a Ty Cobb at the bat."[17] Other industry publications conveyed the more common view of *traqueros* held by management: "Constant reiteration of rules and orders is absolutely necessary in handling Mexicans. Like children, they soon forget. When properly handled they are willing to do a great deal for a man, often working for ridiculously low wages or giving the very best of service for common wages."[18]

Against the backdrop of such degrading views, Mexicans encountered North American sport as part of the same ironic pattern of inclusion and exclusion they found in economic and social realms. Historian

José M. Alamillo describes how Mexican citrus workers recruited to Corona, California, in the post-revolution, interwar period met with a double standard about who should play ball. On one hand, baseball was thought to embody national characteristics and, by that logic, ought to be played only by those fully integrated into society. Among the lemon growers in Corona, California, this took the form in the 1920s of an annual tournament among teams of landowners.[19] Hence, in this context, working-class Mexicans found North American baseball to be an activity of the idle rich, and specifically their own bosses. At the same time, the normative activity of sport lent itself to the management strategies of welfare capitalism, designed to manage the everyday life of workers in order to produce a willing and able labor force. Alamillo recounts how employers were advised by experts to "provide garden plots, a local society, baseball teams, musical bands, a community center, and English instruction classes."[20] Measured doses of the good life, in other words, were doled out to keep workers working and to keep them relatively peaceful. Playing ball seemed to promise both Americanization and social order. But citing C.L.R. James on cricket, Alamillo points out that sport is an unreliable technology of control, as Mexican American ballplayers put baseball to their own uses — in his words, "to promote ethnic consciousness, build community solidarity, and sharpen their organizing and leadership skills....In doing so, they transformed the ball clubs into a political forum from which to launch wider forms of collective action."[21]

The softball teams and tournaments that developed later in Kansas and Texas also fit into this pattern, although the political effects of building community solidarity noted by Alamillo were not necessarily the primary goal. When I ask former players about their motivation for getting involved in fastpitch, a more common answer is that the game offered intense competition. As a scaled-down version of baseball that could be played in more constrained settings like urban parks, softball nevertheless offered fast-paced action and required skill and strategy, especially before the "slo-pitch" version of softball appeared, with its regulated delivery of the ball. The intensity of fastpitch presented a thrilling opportunity for Mexican Americans whose athletic potential was constantly underestimated in Anglo-dominated sports scenes. As one interviewee put it to me, "You see, we were the first cut, without a tryout." Yet, a recurring theme in my interviews was how competitiveness ultimately fed solidarity among players. John Limon, tournament director for the Austin Jokers, a team rooted in the east side of the Texas capital with over fifty years of history behind them, told me,

> "That was the beautiful thing about what we have in softball, is that when we're on that field, we'll play — you know, bite, scratch, tooth, nail, you name it, you know? But when we're done, let's drink a beer together. Let's have a good time, let's talk and let's eat."

Tony Castillo, a former coach of the Jokers, elaborated on how the team was formed of close neighborhood relationships that became lifetime bonds. When asked who came together to form the Jokers in the early 1960s, Coach Castillo said,

> They were mostly friends. And some of these guys...we play golf every Wednesday. We still, since growing up in elementary school, we still gather today. We still socialize. They baptize my children, I baptize their children. Their birthdays, we all go. Especially when we were very young, anytime there was any kind of occasion — boom! We were there. All of us. En masse.

Coach Castillo went on to describe the Jokers as holding a place of prestige within the East Austin community.

> "Because we, you know, we weren't hot dogs. We were pretty good guys. We really were. You can count it on one hand the number of guys that, you know, that didn't pan out well....We were the leaders of the community, to be honest with you."

Ali Solis, the daughter of former Newton tournament director and coach Gil Solis and who was an elite club softball player in her own right, reflected on her experience growing up as a "dugout rat" in the Mexican American fastpitch scene. In an oral history interview collected and archived by historian Gene Chavez, she said,

> "Growing up and being a part of that team, I thought they were all my brothers. When I found out that they were not my actual brothers, and they had different moms and dads, oh, my gosh, that threw me for a loop....I was like, '"Huh? But you treat me like I'm your sister.'"

For Ali, who is raising her son in a south suburb of Kansas City, maintaining a connection to the fastpitch tradition of her childhood is crucial, a model of sociality in danger of being lost as an effect of social mobility. She observes:

> When watching my son play in his tee-ball leagues here in Overland Park, watching how the adults interact, the children interact, it's just so different from the leagues that I grew up in. I think the first thing that comes to mind is the area. These kids did not grow up in the area that my family did, that my ancestors did. And growing up in an area where wealth is common, you treat people different, and I don't necessarily want my son to treat people that way. We're all equal. And it's so important for me to get Andre to the Newton Mexican American tournament...to see that camaraderie, to see how everybody else in the world relates to each other, because you have to have that kind of base foundation first.[22]

Ali's reverence for the "area" of Newton, her parents' home, is not innocent of the struggles that earlier generations faced. But having experienced a measure of social mobility, Ali now sees a special form of authenticity in the working-class social bonds and camaraderie that her community of origin expressed through softball.

CHANGE IN A LIVING TRADITION

Fastpitch softball in general, and the Mexican American tournaments in particular, went through a golden age of popularity after the mid-century. As the boundaries of segregation loosened, many of the Mexican tournaments retained their specific ethnic character. In practice, such restrictions place priority on local and family connections to the original network of ballplayers. The valorization of fastpitch not only as recreation but as a tradition that continues to tie communities to their past also reinforces the gendered form that the sport took in the 1940s. While women played softball and sought to be recognized as athletes throughout this history, athleticism in general was normatively gendered as masculine for much of the history of Mexican American fastpitch. The more recent development of opportunities for young girls and women to play competitive fastpitch has become the mainstream of the sport in the US, leading many participants to describe the men's game by contrast as a "dying sport," lacking the recreational leagues and public investment in "playground ball" that built a broad base for the game in the past.

The "opening up" of nearly all of the traditionally Mexican American tournaments is one effect of these shifting circumstances. In Texas, this trend has also made Mexican American fastpitch a showcase for international men's softball, with some teams recruiting players from Mexico, Canada, Argentina, Venezuela, New Zealand, and Australia, shelling out substantial investments in travel expenses and player fees in order to win trophies and bragging rights. This more cosmopolitan, less locally rooted version of Mexican American fastpitch, like many other outcomes of the negotiation of identity and recognition at the heart of cultural citizenship, represents something gained and something lost. Participants with whom I've discussed it often express a kind of melancholy or nostalgia that suggests that the older Mexican tournaments held a special kind of value that is now out of reach. If asked about the now atypical identity requirement, people involved in the Newton tournament often say they are trying to maintain a tradition — an argument that carries weight because there are some teams that seem to exist primarily to compete in the annual Newton tournament, in lieu of the once-ubiquitous city leagues. Newton has hosted a national wood-bat softball tournament for the North American Fastpitch Association, producing a bracket so stacked with Mexican American teams that it almost resembled a replay of the invitational tournament. Likewise, a veteran of San Antonio's Mexican American tournament, hosted by the Rios family's "Glowworm" team, told me at their forty-eighth annual event, "If it wasn't for us, there wouldn't be no fastpitch in San Antonio."

The move to open up invitational tournaments is one response to a decline in softball as a men's sport, and especially to the scarcity of men learning the crucial and intricate skills of underhand pitching. Another possible response to the scarcity of male pitchers, of course, would be to relax the gender boundaries that govern virtually all sport in the United States. Despite the designation of many Mexican American tournaments as "men's" events, many women identify Mexican American fastpitch as their heritage as well. A "girls'" tournament was planned to accompany the men's event in Newton in 1947, and a *mexicana* team from Newton won sponsorship from a local cab company. This was the generation of a woman I met at a softball event who identified herself as "a Rosie the Riveter," having worked in aircraft production in wartime Wichita. Some of these same women approached the City of Newton in the 1940s, when there was no soft-ball league for women, and asked for one. They were also subject to the retrenchment of gender roles after the war, when across American public culture, competitive, physical sports were reconstructed as an arena of masculinity and women were encouraged to engage them only in supportive, rather than active, roles.

In the long term, though, women would not give up on playing ball, and especially after Title IX led to athletic scholarships for wom-en's team sports, softball became an important channel for women's athleticism and achievement. In fact, scholarships have effectively re-gendered the way that the highly specialized skills of playing soft-ball, and especially pitching, afford players the opportunity for social mobility. Whereas at one time in the heyday of industrial-league and military softball, it was possible for some men to find job opportu-nities opened up by their ability to play, the most significant social mobility available through the sport today is in college scholarships for women ballplayers. There is also a pattern throughout Mexican American softball-playing communities of young women learning the game from elder men and channeling this knowledge and expe-rience from the Mexican annual tournaments into more mainstream venues of club, school, and collegiate softball. Periodically, women ballplayers — particularly pitchers — will play in the traditional tournaments as well. The Rusk tournament in Houston has added an under-18 girls' division to the competition, and in the first year a member of the committee personally sponsored four elite club teams to play. Although this certainly was not the main event of the weekend, I had more than one conversation with spectators who admired the young women's passion for the game and mused over whether the legacy of the tournaments ought to belong to them for that reason.

The winning team in the new girls' division at the Rusk tourna-ment was "Elite 9," a select club team based in Settegast Park in the Second Ward barrio where the tournament got its start. Their coach, Lauren Bautista, was the recipient of a tournament-sponsored schol-arship in 2008 that supported her studies at the University of Houston. In email correspondence following the tournament, Bautista told me,

"My father is Richard Bautista, who played for many years in the Latin Tournament and was [part] of the Latin Legends team along with my godfather Earnest Shepherd. I grew up watching these guys play softball since I was a little girl. My little brother now plays in the Latin tournament with the Misfits."

Bautista goes on to list players from her girls' club team who have been recruited to play college ball and reports on her budding career as a middle-school PE teacher and coach for not only softball but also baseball, volleyball, and soccer. She concludes,

> "I believe that I am where I am today because I grew up around watching all these guys play fastpitch with my dad. I owe everything I have to him and this organization and it was an amazing feeling to come back and win a tournament that I once played in...but now as a coach."[23]

EPILOGUE

I drove to the Kansas City, Kansas, neighborhood of Armourdale looking for Shawnee Park on the occasion of the Stateline Locos' fiftieth anniversary fastpitch tournament in 2011. Armourdale was incorporated in 1882 and named after Armour & Company, the Chicago meatpacking firm that opened shop there and became one of the employers that would draw workers from Mexico to the area. Today around 65 percent of its residents identify as Hispanic or Latino, and about 35 percent of the population is "foreign born." Situated within an oxbow curve in the Kansas River, with Interstate 70 and railroads wrapping its other side, Armourdale is effectively an island. In the middle of the island is Shawnee Park, and a softball field. The outfield is bounded on the left field side by Kansas Avenue, a major thoroughfare and the beginning of an industrial area that includes railroad maintenance facilities. Beyond right field is a commercial street lined with businesses. Behind home plate and across a narrow street is a row of houses, leading to the Catholic church that was desanctified by the parish and is now home to a social services organization.

But before I found all this I had to stop at a used tire shop to ask directions. The proprietor was decked out in Norteño gear, including a cowboy hat, belt buckle, and the curl-toed ostrich boots that were high fashion at the time. He spoke Spanish with a customer who came in just before me, translating to English for his Latino employee behind the counter. When I asked for Shawnee Park, he said "*Oh, that's far, a long way from here. Shawnee Mission?"* No, I said, I was not looking for Shawnee Mission Parkway, a major route from the affluent southwestern suburbs to the Plaza shopping district. Not that, but Shawnee Park. I thought it was around here. *"Oh, for the baseball? It's right over there."*

Right over there, right in the center of town where, if I had taken a wrong turn and was looking for my way to the Missouri side of the city or the interstate, I might drive right past without noticing the ballfield and the players spread out over the grass and brick dust. So easy to miss, and yet rumor has it that someone's ashes lie buried in that ballfield, a decidedly unofficial tribute to the last wishes of a ballplayer to be planted in ground he held dear. Certainly plenty of dramas have played out there. When I did make the effort to approach the field, after learning of the Locos' anniversary tournament, I was still unaware of the site's geography that I would learn about in a later interview, an unwritten map drawn over years and generations of habit, something like what I remember from church in my small Midwestern hometown, where everyone knows which family sits in which pew. *The Talaveras sit on the concrete platform next to the concession stand behind third, the Garcías sit in the bleachers, the Moraleses sit on their abuelos' porch just across the street behind home plate.* Standing behind the Talaveras during opening ceremonies, some aging veterans (of both war and softball) reminisced about how things used to be done. One of the "old-timers" who was watching the game nodded towards the diamond and said, *"I played my first game of fastpitch here in 1946."* Other elderly men standing nearby chimed in, telling fragments of stories about teams, tournaments, and road trips gone by. *"Oh, we used to do it good here,"* one of them said. *"We had a guy out to play the national anthem on the bugle. See, we're pretty patriotic, pretty patriotic. But we love our culture, too."*

The Locos were struggling through their own bracket, lacking a standout pitcher. Other local teams that they would face in the Tuesday evening city rec league later that summer also gradually fell before two teams that had driven in from Iowa for the weekend. Even the mighty Kansas City Indios, who were tough to beat in the city league and in any given game might fill seven out of the nine positions with someone named García, eventually lost to make it an all-Iowa final. The old-timers I stood next to remarked that this might not have happened in the days when the tournament was "invitational," before the tournaments on the Kansas summer circuit of Mexican tournaments had "opened up" to "white" teams.

By the time of the final game in the early evening on Sunday, most of the eliminated teams had already departed, thinking of work the next day. Members of the host team and their friends were congregated on the lawn of a house across the street from home plate, drinking beer and eating barbecue from paper plates. Tony, the young tournament director, walked to the pitcher's circle and presented awards for the top four team places and all-tournament honors. He stumbled occasionally over names of German or other northern-European provenance, at one point shaking his head and saying, *"Man, give me some Mexican names!"* After congratulating the victors, he announced that the barbecue, which had been sold as a concession all weekend, was now free for the taking, and that there was cold beer for the hangers-on as well. Another tournament, and a half-century of fastpitch, came to a close.

QUESTIONS:

1. Do particular sports "belong" to certain nations or cultures? What processes or forces determine whether a sport is "American"?

2. What identities are at stake when people choose recreational activities? How do specific sports affect the way we understand race, class, gender, nation, locale, family, and other kinds of identity?

3. When does a sport become a "tradition"? Does this change the value of an activity or affect whether we think of it as important?

NOTES

1. Quotations in italics are representations drawn from my own memory. I mark them as such as a reminder that they do not carry a claim of absolute fact. Quotations in "block" format are transcribed from recordings.

2. The formulation "follow the x" was introduced to ethnographic methodology by George Marcus in his landmark essay, "Ethnography In/Of the World System: The Emergence of Multisited Ethnography," *Annual Review of Anthropology* 24 (1995): 95–117. Although multi-sited fieldwork is

hardly unusual or innovative at the moment, the trope of defining whatever is constant in the study's purview as something "followed" remains useful.

3. Richard R. Valencia, "The Mexican American Struggle for Equal Educational Opportunity in *Mendez v. Westminster:* Helping to Pave the Way for *Brown v. Board of Education*," *Teachers College Record* 107, n. 3 (March 2005), 389–423. See also the special issue of *American Studies* on "Latinx Civil Rights and Beyond," 56, n. 2 (2017).

4. Lorena Oropeza, ¡*Raza Sí!* ¡*Guerra No! Chicano Protest and Patriotism during the Viet Nam War* (Berkeley: University of California Press, 2005), 37–40.

5. Jennifer Nájera, *The Borderlands of Race: Mexican Segregation in a South Texas Town* (Austin: University of Texas Press, 2015).

6. Ibid.

7. Jeffrey Marcos Garcilazo, *Traqueros: Mexican Railroad Workers in the United States, 1870–1930* (Denton: University of North Texas Press, 2012), 36.

8. *Evening Kansan Republican*, August 19, 1946.

9. Tony Castillo interview.

10. Nájera, *The Borderlands of Race*, 105.

11. Renato Rosaldo, "Cultural Citizenship in San Jose, California," *Political and Legal Anthropology Review* 17, n. 2 (November, 1994), 57–63; William V. Flores and Rena Benmayor, eds., *Latino Cultural Citizenship: Claiming Identity, Space, and Rights* (Boston: Beacon, 1998).

12. The grandson of the original owner reopened the restaurant in a new location in 2011.

13. "Throwing without a glove" also situated Chuck and others who shared his pitching style in another era. One interviewee informed me that the catcher would throw the ball to the first baseman after each pitch, with the infielder passing it on to the pitcher. This method of returning the ball was rendered illegal at some point, which made the gloveless style less comfortable. No one who told me these stories gave any indication of a connection to the "mushball" Chicago-based game, which players traditionally play without gloves in all positions.

14. Juan Javier Pescador, "¡Vamos Taximaroa! Mexican/Chicano Soccer Associations and Transnational/Translocal Communities, 1967–2002," *Latino Studies* 2, n. 3 (December 2004), 355.

15. Elmer D. Mitchell, "Racial Traits in Athletics," *American Physical Education Review* 27, n. 3 (March 1922), cited in Jorge Iber, Samuel Regalado, José M. Alamillo, and Arnoldo De León, *Latinos in U.S. Sport: A History of Isolation, Cultural Identity, and Acceptance* (Champaign, IL: Human Kinetics, 2011), 75.

16. Garcilazo, *Traqueros*, 59.

17. Ibid., 62.

18. Ibid., 66.

19. José M. Alamillo, *Making Lemonade out of Lemons: Mexican American Labor and Leisure in a California Town, 1880–1960* (Champaign, IL: University of Illinois Press, 2006), 18.

20. Ibid., 27.

21. Ibid., 100.

22. From the oral history collected by Gene Chavez in connection with the Kansas City Museum exhibition and documentary video "Mexican American Fastpitch: Connecting Communities across State Lines."

23. Personal communication with the author.

LATINOS IN PROFESSIONAL SPORTS AND THE QUESTION OF ARRIVAL

Frederick Luis Aldama and Christopher Gonzalez
The Ohio State University and Utah State University

IN THE TRADITION OF the *conversación de sobremesa* (table-talk), this chapter's authors have created an ensemble of contrapuntal voices that discuss and analyze the history of Latinos in sports — especially in the West. This book examining Latinos and Latinas in American sport offers an excellent opportunity for us to build on the significant work of scholars such as Jorge Iber, Adrian Burgos, Samuel O. Regalado, José M. Alamillo, Arnoldo De León, and Fernando Delgado, among others, who have begun to make visible the important presence of Latinos in shaping all variety of professional sports in this country. We seek to continue to deepen and widen this living, breathing socio-historical and cultural archive, as Latinos are by no means a new feature to most professional sports. The media present Latinos as contributing only to sports such as baseball, fútbol, and boxing. Indeed, the inclusion and participation of Latinos within professional sports is intimately connected with various social and political circumstances that have impacted our community including, perhaps most important, access to education. While the history of Latinos in professional sports is filled with heroic exceptions — we discuss several, including tennis player "Pancho" González — education and socioeconomic position allow a greater number of Latino families the time and money for growing new generations of athletes. We invite you, the reader, to join us in this small but important chapter in the larger narrative of Latinos in sports in the West.

FREDERICK LUIS ALDAMA (FLA): We end our book, *Latinos in the End Zone* (2013), with a discussion about whether or not we Latinos have finally *arrived* in the world of sports. By this we mean sports other than fútbol and baseball where we tend to be represented relatively well.

CHRISTOPHER GONZALEZ (CG): As with anything, it is a process. I hesitate at any discussion of "arrival" because it conveys the idea that it is more about a destination rather than a journey. In our book, we discuss Latinos in the NFL such as Jim Plunkett and Anthony Muñoz — players who broke new ground in the premier sports league in the United States. These players certainly signaled the arrival of Latinos in professional football, but we also recognize that if other Latino players did not follow, Plunkett and Muñoz would be interesting footnotes in NFL history. Latinos in the NFL have steadily increased in number, though they remain a small minority within the sport, relatively speaking. In other high-profile sports, we are seeing a surge in Latino players, especially in the NBA. There are other sport leagues such as winter extreme sports, the NHL, the X Games, and others that seem a type of final frontier for Latinos in sports, and we are beginning to see Latinos in these sports as well.

FLA: Destinations, in the plural perhaps, as our work along with scholars such as Jorge Iber seeks to make visible those spaces we've not only been visiting but actively shaping within this larger journey we're identifying as Latinos in professional sports. Of course, sports in this country have traditionally been held up as a symbol of our meritocracy and an emblem of the grand narrative of the United States as a melting pot. Yet sports themselves have been, and continue to be, heavily racially guarded.

CG: Doesn't it seem to fit into the American Dream narrative, though? The idea that if you simply work hard enough, that if you just put in long hours honing your skill, you'll be the next superlative athlete with a multi-million-dollar contract, is a narrative rooted in American exceptionalism. Combine that with America's appetite for underdog stories and you have the recipe for a traditional values-laden understanding of sports. Thus, like in other arenas where racial guarding, as you put it, has and continues to exist, the subtext is that Latinos and other members of minority communities must not be working hard enough or that their determination to succeed is lacking. But the truth, as you well know, reveals the many economic and material barriers that impede Latinos from breaking into the professional ranks of sports in greater numbers. Imagine how difficult it would be for any working-class family to place children in an extracurricular sport such as hockey. And I've not even touched on other resources such as hockey rinks, resources that are quite scarce in Southwestern states where Latinos comprise a larger portion of the population. The myth of meritocracy almost always blithely ignores things like available resources; so too in sports.

FLA: You mention hockey; imagine the expense and difficulty for Latinos to enter the world of professional skiing. As you and I know well, today and historically Latinos have been generationally closer to our working-class roots — factories and fields. Thus, the assumption is that we're less likely to be in what we might identify as more bourgeois sports like skiing — but also golf. Yet we have pro golfers like the Mex-Texan Lee Trevino, the Puerto Rican Juan "Chi Chi" Rodríguez, the Nuevo Mexican-raised Lizette Salas.

CG: I think your point resonates with what I brought up about resources. Golf clubs, even of average quality, would be considered an extravagance to a working-class family, to say nothing of lessons and country club fees. By its nature, golf is exclusionary and elitist. The game itself requires acres of land and paid caretakers. As a result, this fact makes the sustained success of players like Trevino, Rodríguez, Nancy Lopez, and Salas all the more extraordinary. Like so many Latino athletes who become successful in American sports, so many rare and happenstance occurrences had to align in order for them to have the opportunity to flourish. In our book we talked about the case of Jim Plunkett, who had so many challenges in his way but also had a perfect storm of circumstances that allowed his physical abilities and cannon-like arm to make a difference at Stanford and later the Oakland Raiders. The crucial point to be made here is not a deficiency in any given Latino's or Latina's athletic ability. Ability will only take any potential athlete so far before resources come into play. Why are the best college football players to be found at Power Five schools such as Ohio State or Alabama? This doesn't mean that excellent players cannot come from smaller programs. But it virtually guarantees that a greater number of NFL-caliber players will develop and emerge from those schools that have the best coaches and facilities. Indeed, access to resources matter. The same is true for Latino/a athletes from working-class backgrounds.

FLA: Let's take pro golfer, Nancy Lopez. As you mention, she's all the more extraordinary because she wasn't born on the green wearing golf apparel. Her father was an auto mechanic and the family sacrificed a lot so she could practice and eventually win the amateur golf championships that launched her career. And there was no silver-spoon privilege in Lee Trevino's life, either. He began supporting his family as a five-year-old picking cotton and only had access to golf practice working as a caddy. He had to drop out of school to pursue his passion and gift.

CG: These are amazing stories. But perhaps they are amazing in ways that most people don't at first realize. It is easy to learn of Lopez's and Trevino's stories and think in terms of the American Dream, of meritocracy. Instead, we should be even more impressed when we understand that not only did they have to hone their golf skills, they had to do it by working in jobs at the same time. Think of Tiger Woods, who is arguably the greatest golfer of his time. Would Tiger Woods have been such a terrific golfer if his father, Earl, had not provided his son with every opportunity to enhance his innate potential? What if Tiger had needed to take a job in order to pay for his equipment, and so forth? We can apply this sort of thinking in order to understand that working-class athletes with all the potential in the world would still need material resources to actualize that potential. The success of Lopez, Trevino, and others should make us wonder at those Latinos who did not have similar turns in serendipity in their lives.

FLA: Yes, for every Lopez and Trevino there are hundreds of other Latinos who might have been golfers had there been a level socioeconomic playing field. We identify this in our book as a brown color line in sports. It's a glass (cement?) ceiling constructed to keep Latinos out. So when a Plunkett (who defied the odds by working while in school to help support his legally blind parents) or a Joe Kapp (who worked from an early age to support his mother, abused by a macho father) make it, it's all the more extraordinary. Another Latino professional athlete who made it against the odds was tennis pro, Richard Alonso "Pancho" González. He and his mother abhorred the racist nickname "Pancho" christened by the Anglo media. He taught himself to play on a less-than-a-dollar racket (all his mother could afford) by watching others then practicing by himself at courts at the nearby Exposition Park in South Central LA. After dropping out of school, doing time in juvenile detention, then joining and being discharged by the Navy (WWII), he climbed his way to the world's No. 1 — a spot he held for eight years.

CG: I'm glad we're talking about González and tennis. First of all, though his surname ended in a "z," the sports media insisted on using the variant spelling that ends in an "s." Because I share his surname, I can attest to how frustrating this is. Do a quick search on Pancho and you'll often find both spellings in the same article. Second, like golf, tennis is another sport that requires costly equipment in order to be competitive. And something else that we haven't mentioned here is the all-too-common fact that many young Latinos and Latinas raised in working-class families find themselves unable to devote the requisite hours to sports that are required because it takes away from time in which they might be earning a wage. For many Latino families, taking a job in one's youth is not an opportunity for earning a little spending money. González's story leaves me feeling frustrated. Despite having an impressive career, he was constantly under duress because of the brown color line in sports. It's an all-too-familiar story.

FLA: And this brown color line rears its ugly head in the most bizarre, but legal, ways. The Tennis Association told Pancho that in order to play tennis he would have to go to school. Yet, unlike his Anglo counterparts, there was no support for both tennis and education at his school.

CG: Pancho González cared little for his education when he was in high school, and that became a stain on him for the rest of his career. It was easy then for the sports media to paint him as a rebel, and due to his Mexican ancestry, that *bandido* aura was there for the media's taking. While he may have been less than enthusiastic about school, it was undeniable that González was a supreme talent in the tennis world. The Mexican government wooed him to represent the country of his parents, but he remained in the United States. The emphasis of education is understandable, but we can also rationalize perhaps why González did not take to school. Just how supportive of an environment would a high school in California have been for a Latino in the early 1940s? González knew that he had an aptitude for tennis, and naturally he wanted to devote most of his time to develop as a player.

FLA: One of Pancho's most memorable matches (at Wimbledon in 1969) was against a fellow Latino, Charlie "Charlito" Pasarell. Can you imagine the media on this one: Two Latinos — *bandidos* — toughing it out 'til the last, making this the longest match in history at the time (5 hours, 12 minutes), a record that held for nearly a half century.

CG: It was an historic match between mentor, González, and mentee, Pasarell. And this match occurred in an era before the official implementation of the tiebreak in 1973. The match was notable for many reasons, but González was so outraged at what he perceived as a missed call by the umpire, and his emotions got the better of him during the second set. One might imagine how this was interpreted. González let his "fiery Latin temper" cost him the momentum and potentially the match. It is interesting that the professional tennis player most known for his temper on the court is John McEnroe. Yet McEnroe's tantrums were never part and parcel of his Irish ancestry. That is to say, he wasn't relegated to a stereotype, though McEnroe did become a caricature of himself that out-lived his on-the-court achievements.

FLA: Absolutely. According to the media, when Latinos express emotion or action of any sort, it's linked to who we are in the deepest way — to our genetic makeup. Like so many Latinos in sports — recall Joe Kapp's scowl and the "Toughest Chicano" caption splashed across the cover of *Sports Illustrated* — the media fixated on Pancho's Latinoness, as a kind of taco-eating fiery *bandido* (he smoked and stole) who didn't belong in the civilized (i.e., white) world of tennis.

CG: Anything that fits the expected stereotype of the Latino, right? In part, this is indicative of lazy sports reporting. Rather than take the time to research and understand a player like González, the media often found certain things to criticize that were ostensibly explainable because of his Latinoness. As González was a trailblazer in the tennis world, a sports arena that knew little of Latino players, the public swallowed such ridiculous assertions from the media wholesale. Incidentally, I think sports reporting and sports media have come quite a long way since then. And I don't mean to generalize all sports reporting on González; there were many fair-minded reporters covering González such as Dave Anderson and Bud Collins. But it is embarrassing to read some of the more unfair articles in today's light.

FLA: Pancho's story is tragic. It's certainly not the embodiment of the United States as meritocracy we're told to swallow as Latinos growing up. In 1995 he died impoverished and alone.

CG: Pancho had won the respect of so many of the memorable players of his era, players such as Arthur Ashe, Billie Jean King, Jimmy Connors, and others. One wonders how a man who achieved such high levels of success in a professional sport could die virtually penniless and with few friends and family members at his side. Andre Agassi ultimately paid for Pancho's funeral expenses. Agassi's sister was Pancho's fifth and last wife.

FLA: Agassi paid for Pancho's funeral — and with this was also buried any Latino tennis legacy since. Today, out of the 300 professional tennis players, less than a handful are US Latinos.

I think readily of Ernesto Escobedo, Christina McHale, and Sabrina Santamaria. A couple of years back, USTA [United States Tennis Association] Florida created a Latino outreach initiative called "Tenis para Todos."

CG: This is surprising, though I can see why USTA would want to do this. We know that the Latino demographic is growing exponentially, and US tennis hasn't exactly been dominant in world tournaments of late, with the exception of sisters Venus and Serena Williams. I also wonder if this lack of Latinos in tennis might be a function of the rise in numbers of Latinos in sports such as football, basketball, and soccer. Then again, tennis and golf have some similarities in that they require a high degree of specialized coaching and training, even more so than extracurricular leagues for team sports. Such one-on-one training, and I'm thinking here of gymnastics as well, requires a great deal of monetary resources and sacrifice. I also don't discount the lack of visibility of Latino tennis players for younger players to want to emulate. Remember when children from minority communities in urban areas wanted to be like Tiger Woods?

FLA: No Pancho, no role model. That said, it seems we're cropping up in very counterintuitive places — no representation in the past like hockey. I think of the Alaskan Scott Carlos Gomez who plays for the New Jersey Devils and the now-retired East Coast Irish-Nicaraguan Bill Guerin, currently assistant general manager to the Pittsburgh Penguins.

CG: Yes, hockey is a sort of final frontier for Latinos. I'm not certain Latinos will ever be a significant percentage of professional NHL players, but they are beginning to appear slowly and steadily. Undoubtedly this is geographic in nature. Certainly Gomez, whose accident of birth had him grow up in Alaska where a winter sport like hockey is commonplace rather than a place like Arizona, found himself in the right circumstance to allow his innate ability to play hockey to come to fruition. But such successes have the feeling of serendipity, and they cannot be relied on to have a regular expectation that Latinos in professional hockey are nothing more than anomalous. Along with that, perhaps Latinos should begin to see themselves in all sorts of sports where they haven't traditionally found themselves. Not only is it a change in expectation for fans but for Latino athletes as well.

FLA: That goddess Serendipity seems to have smiled on a few others. We're in the water and on the dirt, Christopher. There was Olympic medal winner Dara Torres from Califas (southern California) who set all sorts of US swim records. There's pro BMX-ers like Mike "Rooftop" Escamilla who was voted one of the most influential BMX riders of the 1990s (*Ride* magazine) and later broke and set two world records at X Games: for the longest backflip and the longest 360 on a BMX bike.

CG: Dara Torres was a high-impact athlete not only because of her successes and her "Latinaness" but also her age. Still competitive in the Olympics while in her 40s — a career that spanned 24 years — Torres was doing the talk-show circuit and gracing the covers of magazines in the twilight of her career. Escamilla made his impact on the X Games as the innovator of BMX moves now considered a standard in the sport. He's done stunt work in Hollywood films and has appeared with Latina Kat Von D on the tattoo-themed show LA *Ink*. Both Torres and Escamilla have made such an impact on changing how Latinos are perceived and helping break the public's expectations for what sorts of athletic endeavors Latinos can be successful at.

FLA: Let's not forget Latinos in other counterintuitive terrestrial sports like the two Latinos who radically reinvented skateboarding as a sport: aerial whiz Tony Alva and Stacy Peralta — original members of those skateboarders known as Z-Boys.

CG: These guys were among the most influential, groundbreaking skateboarders in history. Without them, skateboarding might have remained a fringe pastime and not become the mega industry it has become. Yet unlike those in other sports such as golf and hockey that have established equipment that requires large sports equipment companies for innovation, Alva and Peralta were creating, improving, and inventing their own equipment. The openness of the sport, at least at that time, allowed them to help shape skateboarding in significant ways.

FLA: Two Latino innovators on so many levels; but few skate-boarders who use the Powell-Peralta skateboards, wheels, and trucks know of their Latino history. The balance in participation and representation continues to remain heavily skewed toward the Anglo athletes. This is even more starkly visible when we consider audiences. For instance, nearly 50 percent of all attendees at the 2008 X Games in LA were Latinos. With the exception of Califas-born-and-raised Paul "P-Rod" Rodriguez Jr. (son of comic Paul Rodriguez), who picked up the silver, we continue to have few Latinos competing.

CG: But remember that as the X Games continues its rise in popularity and competition, it is now much more difficult to break into the professional ranks. This is good for the sport, but I can't account for why there aren't more Latinos competing at the highest levels of events like the X Games.

FLA: We mentioned how participation in sports is linked to class. Could this be the case with Dara Torres — a Latina who grew up in Beverly Hills but who chose to swim for the very underfunded, working-class-populated Mission Viejo Nadadores? I don't want to think the worst, but maybe she was slumming it as a Latina to get ahead.

CG: I don't want to speculate as to what Torres's motives for swimming at Mission Viejo might have been. On the other hand, there is no question that class is a major factor in sports. Call it opportunity. Call it access to resources. It is all tied together. An athlete, Latino or otherwise, can have the genetic potential to be a superior athlete. But if the circumstances are not conducive for allowing those innate athletic traits the opportunity to flourish, athletes may never achieve their potential. It's hard to argue against this.

FLA: At six feet, Torres was unusually tall for a Latina. We're traditionally not a tall demographic group. But it seems to be changing. Indeed, we're tall and big enough to play some of the most important defensive positions in the NFL. And, we're slamming hoops. I think of the extraordinary rebounder, the Tex-Mexican Eduardo Nájera, who began his career with the Dallas Mavericks and ended with the Charlotte Bobcats.

CG: And don't forget Puerto Rican José Juan "J. J." Barea Mora, who helped the Dallas Mavericks win the NBA championship in 2011. The NBA has had many Latino players from Spanish-speaking countries for years. Dominican-born Al Horford, Puerto Rican American Carmelo Anthony, and Cuban American Brook Lopez are all current players with Latino heritage. It is clear that the NBA had recognized the importance of Latino players as well as Latino fans long before the NFL began its recognition of Hispanic Heritage Month.

FLA: Latinos are talented, tall, and mixed race. Many miss the fact that NFL-er Victor Cruz and NBA-er Luis Flores (he played with Nájera when he was with the Denver Nuggets) aren't black, they're Afrolatinos.

CG: The same applies with the aforementioned Al Horford and Carmelo Anthony. The United States has always been a phenotype-first nation, meaning people are first defined by what they look like. Unless an Afrolatino player speaks with a heavy Spanish accent such as David "Big Papi" Ortiz or Sammy Sosa, such players are thought of as African American because they "look" black. Victor Cruz, who does a salsa dance when he scores a touchdown, embraces and honors his Latino heritage in a very public way. Someone like Victor Cruz explodes easy understandings of Latinos and African Americans in the United States. For many, this is apparently too much to handle.

FLA: Yes, historically, it's been so much all about black versus white that any complex shades of brown throw a wrench into the mainstream media's representations in this country. For browns, this radicalized representation snaps into places as stereotypes of the lazy, dim-witted, athletically incapable buffoon. And this happens even when we've hit it out of the field, as with Clemente — a figure you've written extensively about.

CG: Roberto Clemente is like Jackie Robinson with the added burden of not knowing American culture or even English. Not to take anything away from Robinson. He is an icon in American sports history, as he should be. But Clemente looked like a black man but was insecure about his poor English skills. He was able not only to join a small number of

Major League Baseball players to achieve 3,000 hits, one of the gold-standard statistical achievements, but he did it while feeling like an outsider to everyone but his family and close friends. The sports media interpreted his insecurity as arrogance. Clemente's lasting legacy is grounded in how he was able to have a superlative career despite the constant barrage of vitriol, prejudice, and racism he experienced along the way.

FLA: It's no wonder Clemente was terrified to speak English. Even today when we don't speak the Queen's English we're automatically identified as dim-witted. When we moved from Mexico to Califas when I was a young boy, the teacher took a ruler to the back of my hand when I spoke Spanish — or English with a Spanish accent. My mother fought back. She went to Sacramento State and, while working full time, managed to get her teaching credentials. She dedicated her life to educating Latinos, and bilingually. It's because of dedicated teachers and heads of schools — you yourself are a one-time public school teacher — that education continues to make a difference for Latinos. It opens doors, but unfortunately also closes doors because there's still a lot of prejudice within the hallowed halls of learning. Without access to education — and especially higher education — we'll never have the presence of Latinos in the professional sports that we should.

CG: No question. Higher education, from an athletics point of view, is an opportunity for athletes to develop and hone their skills. Earlier I mentioned how college football players who are in a Power Five conference have a greater chance of refining their abilities on the field in preparation for a potential professional career. The same applies for other professional sports. If an athlete cannot enter a university program, it certainly impacts his or her chances of making it in professional sports.

FLA: To this end, athletic scholarships have played a huge role for Latinos. Yet, some consider athletic scholarships akin to charity giving — to tokenism. For those kept out of education, it can be an important way in. This is the case historically with so many Latinos in sports, including those like Joe Kapp with his basketball scholarship to Cal (even though he, along with Hank Olguin, ended up taking Cal to their first Rose Bowl in 1959) and more recently the pro golfer Lizette Salas from Califas. The first of her family to go to college, she received a golf scholarship that got her through the otherwise prohibitively expensive USC.

CG: First of all, athletic scholarships are not charity. Let's set the record straight. Collegiate athletes who compete at a high enough level to be offered a scholarship bring added value to their university. College football is the largest cash cow for universities and the NCAA, raking in billions of dollars every year. The players are the ones who generate that revenue, and for all of that they receive an athletic scholarship. Players like Lizette Salas are afforded the opportunity to further their athletic development and get an education in a way that would not happen otherwise.

FLA: Hence, the momentum today behind college athletes struggling to unionize to seek protection as exploited bodies. Speaking of exploited bodies, perhaps this is most clearly seen with boxing. This is a sport in which the US media and imagery have more easily fixed brown bodies. Boxing and Latinos and mean urban streets — drugs, violence, and decay — seem to go hand in hand. The reality has been that boxing has offered not so much a way out as a way to survive for many Latinos. Historically, boxing youth clubs have served an important role here.

CG: I agree, Frederick. Unfortunately, professional boxing is dying a very slow death. Mixed Martial Arts (MMA) is dominating revenue and opportunity. But Latinos have had a rich tradition in boxing, and youth clubs have done and continue to do great work in providing a community-based outlet for Latino youth.

FLA: The boxer José "Rocky" Galarza from the Latino-dominant, poor El Segundo Barrio of El Paso, Texas, just two blocks from the Mexican border, ran one such club. He mentored young athletes from the area for over thirty years.

CG: Yet another example of how there is a void in resources for so many young Latino athletes. Galarza, as others have done, helped establish boxing schools and programs to give Latino kids an outlet for their energy and ability. For many, these are the kinds of programs that help level the playing field in terms of resources. Unfortunately, there are only so many Galarzas in the world.

FLA: Boxing clubs are going the way of the dinosaurs, and yet our demographic numbers have surged across the country. Still our numbers in professional sports continue to be shamefully low. In 2006, for instance, we only had nineteen Latinos out of 1,700 or so in the pro football leagues. Yet, we do have a track record of significant Latino athletes shaping the world of Latino sports.

CG: I think in years past, the scarcity of Latinos in professional sports was thought of as an indication that Latinos are by and large unathletic. As time goes on, however, we're seeing that Latinos can compete at the highest levels. If we look for a reason why Latinos are becoming more of the professional sports landscape, we might look to the rise in economic status among the expanding Latino demographic. With more disposable income to spend on private lessons, sports clubs, equipment, and so on, Latino athletes are becoming more and more competitive in athletic endeavors.

FLA: Of course, there have been important non-Latino figures like Al Davis with the Raiders — in sharp contrast, of course, with George Preston Marshall.

CG: It appears that the majority of sports team owners and general managers are more like Davis than Marshall. Davis was ahead of his time, drafting and bringing in players and coaches from minority communities long before it became acceptable. Many, like Marshall, seemed motivated by racial animus and prejudice. That's not to say things are a sports utopia. Far from it. In 2014 Donald Sterling, the owner of the NBA team the Los Angeles Clippers, essentially lost his team because of racist language he used in a recorded phone conversation. Yet I think it is becoming much more difficult for owners to uphold these color lines we've been discussing.

FLA: We've been focusing on Western and Southwestern athletes. But we've mentioned athletes, too, like Victor Cruz who hails from the East Coast. Cruz is from Paterson, New Jersey, and recently retired after playing seven seasons with the Giants. And, of course, there's Willie Colon from the Bronx who played offensive guard for the Jets.

CG: It's nice to see more Latino athletes that hail from places other than California and Texas. These states have been bastions for producing Latino athletes, and now we are seeing a surge in the East. I think it's a great reminder to fans and audiences that Latinos are not only Mexican American.

FLA: Speaking of Mexican Americans, what are they feeding us Latinos in places like Texas where you grew up, Christopher? We certainly have some big fellas coming out of the Southwest like Louis Vasquez from Corsicana, Texas, who played offensive guard for the Broncos. And, there's Roberto Garza from Rio Hondo who played center/guard for the Bears — a six-plus feet, 300-plus pound gargantuan who was told that Mexicans don't play football.

CG: As a native Texan, I can assure you there is a mindset about being bigger. It may not be the reality, but it is a way Texans tend to think about their state and, of course, themselves. Indeed, Texas has been producing some large NFL athletes that are Latino. Garza, along with other NFL offensive linemen such as Manny Ramirez and Louis Vasquez, who played for the Denver Broncos, help dispel the myth that Latinos are small-framed people adept at running long distance. (I'm sure the film *McFarland, USA* will reinforce the image of the small Latino distance runner.)

FLA: What do we make of the ups and downs of one of the most visible Latino players from the West — Mark Travis John Sanchez from Long Beach, Califas? After getting centerfolds in GQ and the like as well as showing some promise with the Jets, he's now a B-list quarterback....Nobody hears about the guy anymore.

CG: Sanchez found new life, however briefly, as a backup for Nick Foles for the Philadelphia Eagles. Twice in the 2014 season Sanchez and his Eagles met with Antonio Ramiro Romo, aka Tony Romo, and his Cowboys. After some success after taking Foles's place, Sanchez became a turnover machine. Despite his intermittent success, it seems that Sanchez may never be the franchise quarterback he once was with the New York Jets.

FLA: While on the topic of Romo, before he retired and when he was still quarterback for the Cowboys, his *abuelita* told a reporter that she thought her Chorizo Power would lead to Romo's victory over the Green Bay Packers. She wasn't right in her prediction, but what's interesting is how much he's tied to his roots and how the media choose to make visible some aspects of his cultural identity and not others.

CG: It's curious. The media didn't spend much time on Romo's Latinoness, except in rare cases. His grandmother was interviewed because Tony was returning to his native Wisconsin to play against the Packers, and he was going to spend some time with family. While his family was interviewed or invoked when the media mentioned Romo's Latino roots, he rarely raised or addressed the issue. But he was without question one of the most high-profile Latino athletes in the United States of his day. Now a much-lauded color commentator on CBS, Romo is known for his enthusiasm and uncanny ability to predict a play before it happens.

FLA: One way or another, the captains of the industry capitalized on Romo — with his Chorizo Power or not. Let's tilt more toward the capitalist aspect of our presence in sports, Chris. To increase Latino audiences, the NBA created Noche Latina where the teams from participating cities would wear t-shirts with team names in Spanish and there would be Banda (music) and tacos and such. How much cultural work and value of Latino community is going on versus consideration of profit margins?

CG: Let's not forget that professional sports organizations such as the NFL and the NBA are businesses (although they are strangely coded as nonprofit organizations). As such, they are always looking for new revenue streams. The NFL continues to toy with the idea of establishing a team in England because it might open a new market for them. Similarly, I think these forays into the Latino community by the NFL and the NBA are first and foremost an opportunity to increase revenue. Additionally, these high-profile sports organizations go to great lengths to engage substantively with the community. So, there is certainly cultural work going on, but let's also remember that there is potential revenue involved.

FLA: Cashing in on the Latinos, or more? I think of the NBA's Basketball without Borders Americas (a basketball development and community outreach program), and there's NASCAR's Drive for Diversity where clearly those seeking to profit see no borders, only pockets. In spite of profit margins, players do things for the communities while they are there, like build infrastructure in the poorer areas. With evil comes some good.

CG: I don't know if I would put it in such a dichotomy as good and evil. As I mentioned, these are businesses and they want to increase revenue. On the other hand, I think a lot of good does result in these sorts of community engagements. Cynics will always find an angle, and that's necessary as well. The NBA or NASCAR may want to foster a new generation of fans because it helps their bottom line. But it also reveals these organizations' understanding that Latino purchasing power is real and it is growing. That is another positive result we might look to.

FLA: Sports is an important revenue source for Spanish-language TV, radio, and the Latino websites.

CG: And American sports organizations recognize this. More and more you can find the NFL and NBA on Spanish-language TV. It's simply another opportunity to grow the game, which means it grows the fan base, which results in higher profits.

FLA: Fan base is so important to the vitality of professional teams, yet the captains of capitalism often overlook impact on communities when deciding where to build stadiums. The stadiums cost the tax payers, do little for the community, and yet generate massive profits for pro team owners and shareholders.

CG: It is a difficult issue. Communities are both positively and negatively impacted by local sports teams. An NFL team such as the Cleveland Browns means everything to its community. Remember how agonized Cleveland was when the Browns were relocated to Baltimore? Or remember the frenzy when LeBron James left (and later returned to) Cleveland? On the other hand, a city like Los Angeles doesn't seem to care much for an NFL team, and the league recognizes it. Even a stadium can mean a great deal to a community. Since Cowboys' owner Jerry Jones built AT&T Stadium in 2009, the venue has hosted a Super Bowl, an NCAA Final Four, and an NCAA College Football Playoff Championship Game. The stadium itself cost over a billion dollars to build, but it also generates amazing amounts of revenue for the Arlington, Texas, area.

FLA: Where are our icons? Given our demographic numbers, shouldn't we have our own LeBron James, Tiger Woods, David Beckham?

CG: The icons you mention are all very recent; they're each still playing or at the end of their careers. I think Latinos have had icons, but they are far enough in the past that they seem like ancient history in an age of instant social media. Roberto Clemente may be a Latino sport fan's patron saint. Pancho González was one of the true greats of tennis. Jim Plunkett, winner of two Super Bowls yet not in the Pro Football Hall of Fame, might have been another icon. Perhaps Tony Romo still has the best chance of becoming an icon because he was the feature player (quarterback) on one of the premier teams (Dallas Cowboys). He has recently begun to shuck the label of being a choker that dogged him for much of his career, thanks in large measure to his skill as a color commentator for CBS. But to your point, we should already have a Latino sports icon over the last decade.

FLA: There's been some appropriation of Latino culture along the way. Think of the rodeo. This was a sport, brought to the Americas by the Spaniards, known as *charreria* and that evolved into *vaqueros* or cowboys who would ride horses (*charros*) to round up cattle.

CG: And now the great bull riders of today are Anglo or Brazilian. This might have been a Latino tradition at one time, but we really can't say that at the moment.

FLA: While it gets a lot more play than other areas of Latinos and sports, we'd be remiss to not mention fútbol. Cuba, the Dominican Republic, and Puerto Rico — and Latin America generally — have become repositories of talent for fútbol.

CG: Yes, and more recently, baseball and basketball.

FLA: There's clearly exploitation of Latinos in the professional sports. However, there are some exceptions, like Cuauhtémoc Blanco. When he signed as striker for the Chicago Fire he came in as second-highest-paid soccer player in Major League Soccer — right behind Beckham.

CG: Blanco is a great example that earning potential in sports isn't necessarily predicated on race or ethnicity. Tony Romo is another. His contract worth over $100 million was not impacted by the fact that he's Latino. In other words, if the player can help a team win, the team will pay. Nothing motivates team owners and general managers like winning.

FLA: Profit margins are the great motivator in professional sports, and within this Latinos have proved to be a bountiful resource of exploitable arms and legs. We could say that without Latinos (those Cubans in the early days of the game) there would be no fútbol or baseball in the United States.

CG: Or at least it wouldn't be the baseball we know today. I'm interested to see how the recent lifting of sanctions on Cuba may impact American sports. Remember the saga of half-brothers Orlando and Liván Hernández, and how their baseball careers were affected by the US-Cuba relationship? In fact, Latinos have effectively displaced African American baseball players — an unfortunate development in recent years.

FLA: With US Latinos Aric Almirola, Bryan Ortiz, and Jack Madrid having broken into the traditionally all-white NASCAR sports space, perhaps we can say we've finally *arrived*, Chris.

CG: We're certainly players in the game. As the Latino demographic continues to swell, I expect our numbers will finally begin to grow in all manner of sports in America.

QUESTIONS:

1. Have Latinos/as, in your view, really "arrived" on the American sporting scene? Why or why not?

2. How does a lack of resources impact the opportunities for Latinos/as to participate in sport in the US?

3.   How does the presence of "brown" athletes throw a "monkey wrench" into the racial imagery/reality of American sport?

HILLS TO CLIMB:
A Historical Analysis of Latina Participation in Texas High School Basketball

Gregory Selber
University of Texas Rio Grande Valley

IN WHAT HAS BECOME an iconic article in sports and gender research, MaryJo Sylwester, writing for *USA Today* in 2005, attempted to explain the low level of participation in athletics by high school-age Latinas. Her impetus was the fact that in Colorado, as in the rest of the country, the number of girls of Mexican American descent playing sports at the time lagged far behind that of youths from other ethnic groups.

Sylwester noted that although this was the case, a recent series of events had jolted the numbers, including the performance of a handful of Latinas on the national collegiate stage. Her article suggested that having to overcome family tradition, among other obstacles, kept many Latinas from going out for sports in high school, but she added that the situation seemed to be on the verge of improving.[1]

The seminal article outlined the benefits of athletic competition, particularly regarding health and fitness, highlighting recent research indicating that such participation tended to lessen the chances of teen pregnancy, drug use, and other negative occurrences.

Sylwester focused on Latinos' family values and mores, writing that boys tended to have more freedom in the household and outside, while many Latinas have traditionally been forced into babysitting/ surrogate motherhood roles, along with looking after older relatives, decreasing the amount of time they might devote to athletic pursuits or other extracurricular activities. The upshot was that the old-fashioned communalism — and *machismo* — of the Latino family was one of the factors responsible for the low participation of girls in sports, suggesting that male dominance in the family unit was also a problem. Machismo is characterized by aggression and often violence on the part of Latino males against women, illustrating the patriarchal structure of gendered relations.[2]

A number of insightful writers have tackled the concept of machismo, most notably Gloria Anzaldúa, in several books and articles. In "This Bridge Called My Back," she and co-editor Cherrie Moraga suggested the difficulty that Latinas have in overcoming the male authority figure in the family.[3] Her classic work, *Borderlands/La Frontera*, exposed the gendered expectations of behavior in such families, where deference by females to dominant males is normalized; she called for a new higher consciousness to break down barriers Latinas face from male family members who expect them to be subservient. This obstacle often causes them to miss out on opportunities outside the stifling home environment.[4]

As well, practical problems, such as lack of money or transportation, have played a role in the scarcity of Latinas in sports around the country. Their 2005 participation rate of 36 percent was far behind the 52 percent of other ethnic groups, despite the fact that a 1986 Women's Sports Foundation report had shown that athletics can help lessen the recurrence of such health problems as obesity and diabetes.[5]

In Texas, the state with the second largest population of Latinos in the United States, girls of Mexican American descent have also struggled with the issue. Although their sports participation rate through time has risen — especially in the decades following the passage of the historic equity bill Title IX in 1972 — there are still relatively few Latinas involved in sports.

In 1971, before Title IX, fewer than 295,000 girls of any minority ethnicity participated in varsity high school athletics, accounting for 7 percent of the total number of players. By 2001 that number had increased to 2.8 million, or 41.5 percent of all participation.[6] This revolution has made its presence felt in Texas. Places where the Latino ethnic group has made significant strides are generally on the US border with Mexico, including most prominently El Paso, Laredo, and the Rio Grande Valley (RGV).

WHAT'S AT STAKE

In focusing on high school basketball in particular, this chapter seeks to do several things. The first is to discuss the historical case of participation by South Texas Latinas in athletics and entertain the theories put forth by Sylwester's 2005 *USA Today* article. The second objective of this chapter is to show various examples of excellence achieved by Latinas in the sport, outlining the trajectory and timeline, which reflect slow but steady progress in opportunity and eventually rough equity, through time. With this in mind, the chapter lists the major contributors to the sport since the modern era of girls' basketball began in 1979, including individual All-State honorees and competitors in the state's Final Four, where the four best teams in each enrollment classification compete each March for the Texas high school championship.

In looking at the Rio Grande Valley's history, both political and athletic, one can note the fact that there have been multiple reasons for the paucity of young women in the game of hoops. Now that the Valley's girls' basketball scene is dominated by girls with Hispanic surnames — in 2015–16, they accounted for more than 95 percent of the players on teams in an area with a population of 1.5 million people — it would be well to speculate as to factors that explain this emergence, beyond the obvious one of demographics: the area is 91 percent Latino.[7]

The fact is, Latinas have never been a dominant force in the game of basketball, for many reasons. But in select schools around the state, and at a handful of universities in demographically diverse areas, they have made inroads over the past three generations. Their participation rates remain lower than those of other ethnic groups, again for reasons to be discussed.

But the rates, whatever they may be, are a far cry from what they were in the old days in the Valley, when schools were almost all Anglo and sports teams were lily white with but a few exceptions, despite the presence of hundreds of thousands of Mexican American families. And there are role models out there who paved the way for the successes that may come in the future, as efforts to bolster opportunities continue to be made in the wake of resurgent interest and implementation of Title IX.

EXPLANATIONS FOR THE ISSUE

In the Rio Grande Valley of Texas, an area that lies on the US-Mexico border, the rate of participation of Latinas in basketball relative to their percentage of the ethnic group's population has illustrated this paradox. For generations, the participation of Anglo, or white, girls in the area dwarfed that of their Latina counterparts. Meanwhile, the population of the Mexican American ethnic group in the Valley has traditionally been dominant numbers-wise, rising from 60 to 70 percent of the total population from the 1920s to the 1950s, to 91 percent by 2010. But participation by Latinas in the game has always lagged well behind the population figures. Only in the period from 1990 to 2015 did the number of Latina athletes in the sport surpass that of the Anglo girls.[8]

In the earliest days of high school basketball for girls in this region, for example, Pharr-San Juan-Alamo won seven straight Valley titles from the late 1920s into the early 1930s; all starters were Anglo. A study of the rosters of teams from the 1920s into the 1950s reveals that a minuscule number of Latinas were involved in basketball; most years there were zero on most of the Valley teams, except for in the majority-Mexican areas such as Brownsville, Rio Grande City, and La Joya. In the heartland of the Valley, reaching from Mission and McAllen in the west to Weslaco, Donna, and Elsa in the Mid-Valley, and on to La Feria, Harlingen, and areas in the eastern section, most seasons were played with all-Anglo basketball rosters and coaches.[9]

Historically there has been a number of factors that determined the wide discrepancy between population and participation, as was originally outlined in this author's *Border Ball* (2009), a history of high school football in the RGV. The foremost reason seems to have been time, or lack thereof, because most Mexican American families lived at or below the poverty level and many were on the migrant trail for months at a time. Once back in the area, the females of these families generally held jobs and/or helped out as babysitters, leaving them unable to take time out to participate in extracurricular activities such as sports.[10]

A related phenomenon that contributed to this situation is the attitude of family heads toward athletic competition. As the *USA Today* article suggested, this is a recurring theme among Latino families even today, and in the early era it was even more prevalent. Family heads, generally fathers, carried over the concept of *machismo* — or gender bias, sometimes aggressive, from males toward females in traditional Latino culture — into the treatment of daughters. Females at the time struggled against a pervasive notion that sweating, competing, and otherwise doing "male" things such as athletics was unbecoming for a female.[11]

Another factor in the disparate numbers regarding population and participation was the consistent discrimination faced by the majority of Mexican American families in the Valley during the 1920s through the 1940s. Many schools were segregated in those days, either by rule or custom, including districts in Donna, Weslaco, and Harlingen. At Harlingen High, which opened in 1914, no Latina graduated from the school until 1922 and in 1921, the Ku Klux Klan marched through the downtown area to protest the fact that the female student in question was on the verge of completing her education.[12]

In Donna and Weslaco, the percentage of Latino enrollment in school in the late 1920s and early 1930s was less than 10 percent, as most of the students of Mexican American descent either went to special "Mexican schools" or had trouble making it through four years of high school, due to the language barrier on one hand and persistent discrimination on the other.

So with few of the youth able to stay in school, the chances of many Latinas playing basketball — or any sport — were slim. At some schools, the girls did take part in volleyball, and in Weslaco in particular, the percentage of Latinas in that sport reached the 50 percent mark as early as the late 1940s.[13] The other factor relating to discrimination that may account for the paucity of Latinas in basketball has to do with peer pressure. Oral histories from the era suggest that Mexican American students, male and female, were basically "not wanted" or were not encouraged to go out for teams.[14]

In academics, most South Texas school districts practiced to some degree the process of "tracking," which ostensibly selected students to be part of certain scholastic programs on the basis of their skill sets and potential but was eventually generally perceived as a way of funneling the Mexican American students into labor-based activities such as wood or metal shop and mechanics, or home economics for girls.[15] This practice, which some scholars insist continued into the 1970s in the Valley, was also applied in athletics, where Latinas were encouraged to go into volleyball or softball but not basketball. At the time, basketball was the most popular girls' sport and it remained almost entirely Anglo until the 1980s in most schools.

This might be part of the reason that later generations of Mexican American girls on the border showed less interest in the sport than in others, a carryover from decades of being excluded, shuttled into other sports, or discouraged from participating in athletics at all.

The final factor that has a bearing on the participation situation has to do with genetics, or physical ability. Nationwide the average Latina is two to three inches shorter than her African American and Anglo counterparts and in basketball, size is one of the most important elements to the game. Nonetheless, there have been a certain number of trailblazers who defied the odds to become excellent basketball players.

LATINA HIGH SCHOOL HOOPSTERS: CHANGES IN THE GAME AND PLAYERS

From the earliest era until the end of the 1970s, girls' basketball was a different animal altogether, a six-player, half-court affair in which guards and forwards (there were three of each) were hamstrung by rules that kept them limited to a specific area on the court. The old-fashioned version was a case of a couple of forwards, the position players who were stationed under the basket more or less, dueling back and forth in a sort of one-on-one game within the larger game. The guards brought the ball up to midcourt, passed it off, and were then eliminated from the action.

HONORED AS ALL-STATE

The first All-State Latina from the modern era came six years before the game transitioned into the five-player full-court variety fans are familiar with today. She was Kim Benavides of Donna, a 5'10" junior who made the grade in 1973. A year later, Sandy Luna of Poolville began a three-year run as an All-State performer, and her award on first team in 1974 was a rarity for a Latina.

The other Latinas who were honored by the state of Texas before 1979 included Mary Casillas of Southlake Carroll in the Dallas area and Midland Greenwood's Rae García of West Texas (1975); the trio of Amanda Aguilar (Victoria), Lucinda Aguirre (Friona), and Irene

García (El Dorado) in 1976, joined by Poolville's Luna. In 1977, the Donna Bravettes of the Rio Grande Valley landed their second All-Stater in the decade in Irma Avila, a fiery 5'4" guard who later became a winning hoops coach in her home area. Belinda Flores of Austwell-Tivoli was named to the prestigious team in 1978 as a 5'8" forward.

The interesting fact from the 1970s was that the majority of the players of Mexican American descent who were All-State winners came from areas of Texas where the population was plentiful in Latinos, mainly West and South Texas. After the passage of Title ix, participation in girls' athletics spiked over the next several seasons, doubling from 1972 to 1979. Although the bill was originally focused on correcting generations-long hiring practices of a discriminatory nature — e.g., in government business contracts — it quickly made its presence felt in ancillary areas: high school and college athletics, for example.

With the advent of the law and the transformation of girls' basketball into a version identical to that of the boys' game, then, interest and participation in the hardwood sport increased across the board. However, the number of Latinas reaching the highest achievement level did not see a similar spike, for various reasons. The first is physical and technical. The average Latina was just not as tall or heavy as her counterparts from the other ethnic and racial groups, particularly lagging behind the average African American athlete in these respects. This meant that one could generally find more girls of Mexican American descent in sports other than basketball, specifically track and field, cross country running, and volleyball.

For example, a research project analyzing the makeup of the high school sports teams at Weslaco High, in the Rio Grande Valley, reveals that annually, five times as many Latinas were involved in volleyball as were in basketball. When Mexican American attendance at the school rose from less than 10 percent (1920s and 1930s) to more than 40 percent of the enrollment by 1950, the Pantherette squads seldom had any Latinas on the roster. There were only three starters on the unit in the 1950s; however, in volleyball, the rosters from the 1940s into the 1950s consistently contained a Latina majority. During one season, of the seventeen players on the volleyball team, fourteen were Latina, including four starters.[16]

This scenario repeated itself across the Valley, from Harlingen to McAllen and in other places: into the 1960s, basketball remained the preserve of girls from what was rapidly becoming a minority White, or Anglo, population. Volleyball and track/cross country began to more evenly reflect the area's demographic transformation and by the 1970s, most of the outstanding runners competing at the highest levels were Latinas. The same was true for volleyball, but not for basketball.

ALL-STATE IN THE MODERN ERA

On the All-State basketball front statewide, there were ten Latinas on the honor unit from 1980 to 1988, but 1989 produced a banner yield, with no fewer than six making the list. Perhaps the best of the decade was Jeannie Conde of Troy, in Central Texas, who made All-State three times (1983–85) and was Class 2A Player of the Year as a senior in 1985, as a 5'8" front-court player. Tina Gutierrez of Grandview was a two-time winner of All-State honors (1986 and 1987) while Layra Ortiz of Freer made the squad in 1988, on an All-State unit that also included the great Sheryl Swoopes of Brownfield, the future Texas Tech superstar who ultimately became a six-time All-Star in the WNBA, winning four championships with the Houston Comets.

The bumper crop of 1989 had Ruth García of McAllen High and Monica Ramirez of Midland Lee for the bigger schools, in Class 5A. Sandra Chapa of Benavides, Becky Hinojosa of Lorenzo, Rosie Llanas of Wolfforth Frenship, and Denise Moya of Bloomington were the others. Hinojosa would also be named All-State in 1990, one of five Latinas that season. The leading Latina player in the state for 1990 and 1991 was probably Lori Calzade of Sanderson in West Texas, who made the All-State crew twice as a 5'10" post player.

The back-to-back yield of eleven players of Mexican American lineage in 1989 and 1990 was a high point in honor winners, as from 1991 to 1997 there was not a season in which more than three earned this distinction. The Valley's Most Valuable Player for 1991, Imelda Rubio of Edcouch-Elsa, led her team to thirty-one wins that season under Coach Fernando Livas, and the 5'10" post was awarded the highest honor in the state. She would later become, like Avila of Donna, a successful basketball coach in the RGV.

The Latina girls who earned All-State during the 1990s were predominantly from South Texas, starting with Uvalde's Liz Santos and Bruni's Veronica Herrera, in 1992, and extending to 1994 when Delmar Reyna of tiny Lyford won the prize after leading her team four rounds deep in the playoffs. Reyna, also a superb athlete in track and field, later became an NBA cheerleader.

Out in West Texas, Canyon always had fine teams and came up with a dominant force in Valerie Valdez, All-State in both 1997 and 1998, while back down south, little Agua Dulce won many games with two-time honoree Yajaira Uribe (1998–1999). Two-time winners were the drill at that stage, as next it was Diana Martinez of Comanche and Janina Lopez of San Antonio Taft who turned the trick.

In the twenty-first century, the number of Latinas reaching the highest milestone has increased, with five making All-State in 2001, seven in 2002, and seven in 2004. Among that excellent group was Stephanie Gonzalez of Witharral, a 5'9" star who was to attain the award three times from 2001 to 2003. Following Lopez at Taft was Natalie Mireles in 2001. The best female athlete of 2004 was Diandra Marquez of Andrews, All-State for the first of three seasons, as a sophomore, which is a rarity.

But 2005 was a year of distinction for Mexican American girls in Texas basketball as a record ten made the team, including Marah Guzman of Edinburg, a 5'2" power pack who later became a two-year starter at University of Texas–Pan American (UTPA) in her hometown. Three players from that squad would make it again as repeaters in 2006: Taalee Cisneros of Nixon-Smiley, Erica Rodriguez of Sterling City, and Guzman, while Katherine Bazan (Gonzalez) was eventually a three-time winner.

By now the performance and recognition of Latinas were consistent, as after eight in 2006, six more made the list a year later. Harlingen South legend Bianca Torre, considered by most to be the greatest girls' basketball player in Valley history, was on the team in 2007 and later would become the all-time leader in scoring, assists, and steals at UTPA, now the University of Texas Rio Grande Valley. The five kids on the 2008 All-State team included Hidalgo's 6-footer Victoria Gonzalez, who would repeat in '09 and move on to play college ball at Texas A&M-Kingsville. Gonzalez, Guzman of Edinburg, and Torre of South would make up three-fifths of a mythical RGV all-time basketball unit.

A record eleven Latinas were voted for the honor in 2012 with Zuly Martinez of Lipan and Erica Fernandez (Floresville) repeating from the year before. Laura Castillo of Plainview and Mila Ochoa of Witharrall were also multiple-year honorees. In 2013 there were eight superstars on the list.

IN THE BIG DANCE: LATINAS AT THE STATE FINAL FOUR

Although the number of Latinas gaining statewide recognition in hoops increased as decades passed, there have been only a handful who were able to play on a team that made the rare air of the state tournament. Mary Gutierrez was among the first, in 1962, as part of the Devine Arabians, who defeated Tulia 38–37 for the Class 2A title, having knocked off Valley power Mercedes in the regional round.

The Valley sent Weslaco all the way to the tourney in 1965 without any Latinas on the roster and Raymondville went the next season, again with an all-White club that lost at regionals. That season, Lyford rose from the Valley to the regionals before losing to Edna; none of the Valley teams, from towns that were by now at least 50 percent Hispanic, had any players of Mexican American lineage. Raymondville was back again at the state tourney in 1967 with superstars Dianne Gilliland and Judy Bartell, but no Latinas.

In 1966, though, 5'4" senior Nora Cisneros and 5'6" junior Frances Navejar made the trip with the Jourdanton Squaws, the winners of the Class 1A title who had one of the most amazing high school players not just statewide but in the nation. Carolyn Dornak scored 44 points in the final after canning 50 in the semis, and her career numbers still rank her among the top 100 scorers in the USA. She was a two-time college All-American at Wayland Baptist College and eventually a member of the Texas High School Basketball Hall of Fame.

When Waco Midway took the state title in 1969 — on two free throws with no time remaining — 5'5" Patty Ochoa was a member of the roster. Sandy Luna of Poolville, mentioned earlier, had the chance to go to state with her team in 1973 and, although just 5'4", led her team in rebounding during the tourney...as a freshman! The next season the Monarchs, from near Weatherford in unincorporated Parker County, made it back to Austin and this time achieved the ultimate, winning a state title over Klondike, 60–54. They went 32–5 for the season with Luna leading the way alongside Deborah Canafox and Norma Jo Steph.

In 1975, Southlake Carroll won the Class 1A crown with a three-OT win over Vega, with 5'3" senior Mary Casillas, mentioned earlier as an All-Stater, making the All-Tournament team for the victorious Lady Dragons. Victoria sent a great team to state in 1976, ultimately being derailed in the finals by Duncanville. The Lady Stingarees beat Weslaco in the semis to reach the peak, with speedy 5'3" senior

Amanda Aguilar making the All-Tourney squad.

These girls were all playing under the old "sextet" rules, in the half-court game. But as stated, in 1979 the rules changed and opened up the action: full-court, five-on-five basketball, with no movement restrictions for the players.

LATINA STATE COMPETITORS IN THE MODERN ERA

In 1982, Coach Mario Acosta's Del Valle team won the first state title in the history of Travis County, girls or boys, when the Lady Cardinals — with 5'3" junior Stella Castro and future University of Texas star Beverly Williams — aced the field at the Final Four.

Abernathy, near Lubbock, attended the state event in 1984 and 1986, winning each time. On the Lady Antelope roster were sophomore Liz Lopez in 1984, 5'2" senior Sandy García, and 5'2" junior Gina Salinas, marking one of the first times that a state championship team had claimed three players of Latina ethnicity.

In 1987, Texas Panhandle teams swept to all four state crowns, from Class 4A down to 1A, and two of the champs had Mexican Americans on the team. Levelland's Josephine Longoria (5'4" junior) would win All-State in 1988, capping a fine career. Morton, the Class 2A queen of '87, had a healthy contingent of four Latinas: 5'4" senior Imelda Burciaga, 5'6" junior Estefani Arteaga, 5'9" freshman Rosemary Franco, and 5'4" sophomore Alma Salinas.

Levelland was back for more in 1988, taking another trophy with Longoria now joined by 5'4" sophomore Becky Corrales, who scored ten points in two games at state and was named All-Tourney. She would be back in the state tourney the next season.

There was no stopping Brownfield in 1988, not with Sheryl Swoopes on the roster, and she led her team to an easy Class 3A state title with Sandra Morin and Leslie García as teammates.

In the 1990s, Klara Nava (1990) helped her Edna team to state, where it lost to Wylie in the finals, Nava scoring eleven in the defeat. Marion's Jessica Ybarra, a 5'7" star, made the All-Tourney team the next year, although her team lost in the 2A title game.

Levelland had traditionally been a team of multi-ethnic make-up and again had a standout Latina, 5'8" Cynthia Lopez, off the 1991 state tourney club. The same applied to Abernathy, which won the school's sixth Texas championship in 1991, Eva Dominguez (5'5" senior) and Priscilla Salinas (5'4" junior) getting to raise the trophy with their teammates at tourney's end.

The big gun for San Marcos in 1992 was Pat Luckey, one of the greatest players in state history; the 6'1" legend, who made Parade All-American in 1993 and later was one of the first females to dunk a ball (for the University of Houston). Luckey had Patricia Castillejas (5'2" senior) and Laura Rodriguez (5'4" junior) as teammates.

While Corpus Christi King has never been a powerhouse, the team did go to state in 1993 led by Marie Ramos, whose All-Tourney performance came despite the Lady Mustangs' defeat in the finals against Amarillo.

One of the finest programs in state history comes from Dimmitt, in Castro County, about sixty miles southwest of Amarillo. The Bobbies have long been a competitive giant in the sport and in 1993 took the whole ball of wax, capping a 33–3 season with a victory over Dripping Springs in the 3A title match. Senior Rosa Cruz, a 5'8" inside player, ranks as one of the best Latina high school players of all time. She had sixteen points and sixteen rebounds in the semifinal against Winnsboro and then snatched ten boards in the finals. Castro County may be considered the center of the universe in girls' hoops, as Dimmitt and Nazareth have won thirty-five combined state crowns (girls and boys).

On the western edge of the Hill Country, Ozona has not been as successful as Castro County, but in 1995 the girls' team there shot for the heights with no fewer than four Latinas on the squad: Julie Perez (5'2" sophomore), Megan Tambunga (5'5" sophomore), Jessica Avila (5'5" freshman), and standout Gloria Pena Alfaro. Pena Alfaro led the charge to the 2A title with thirteen points against Cooper in the championship game, after getting twelve (with eight rebounds) against Poth in the semis.

The next season Canyon claimed the eighth of what ended up being thirteen state titles, as 5'9" junior forward Valerie Valdez (All-Stater, noted earlier) produced twenty-five points in two games for All-Tourney honors. She later played at West Texas State (now West Texas A&M) in her hometown and now coaches at her high school alma mater.

That '96 tourney also marked the return of Ozona, as the Lady Lions won back-to-back titles with Perez, Jessica Avila, and Tumbunga as returners, Leslie Avila (5'4" sophomore) now on the varsity quintet. Levelland was back in the Dance for 1997 with 5'3" Melissa Hernandez at guard, and the team won its seventh state title that season. Lisa Serna (5'6" sophomore) of Poth and C.C. Cano (5'4" junior) of Whiteface helped their teams win it all in '97 in 2A and IA, respectively.

It seemed that every season at least one of the Texas winners had a Latina in the fold; in 1998 it was Randall, with Melissa Trevino as a 5'4" senior knocking in six points in the final. Diana Martinez of Comanche also competed in the tourney, scoring ten points in her final outing.

From 1999 to 2001, there were a handful in the game, including Crystal Herrera of Winnsboro (5'8" post) who managed six points in the final of 2001, the team's third straight appearance in the Final Four. Plainview's Mystie Ortega (2001) and the Calallen pair of senior Mary Montez and junior Monica Pena toiled for the Lady Wildcats that season at state.

In 2002, San Antonio Taft lost in the finals to Mansfield, but Natalie Mireles was on the All-Tourney team. Shallowater captured the 2004 2A crown with two Latinas, and Archer City won in IA with, 5'7" sophomore Brittany Martinez, a great player who scored six in the final and then had thirteen points and six boards as the team defeated Muenster by one for the Texas Cup; that new competition matched the champs of divisions I and II from the Class IA level.

The next spring, Canyon won its twelfth state title, with Sasha Monreal, a 5'9" junior, and 5'8" sophomore Noni Valdez playing. That weekend, Seagraves earned the Class IA ring with Judy Rodriguez (5'7" sophomore), Tori Bueno (5'8" junior), Vanessa Jacuinde (5'9" sophomore), Tiffany Hernandez (5'6" senior), and Patricia Rodriguez (5'8" senior) on a team with the most Latinas on a title winner in history. Judy Rodriguez was an all-around star: she had nine points, six rebounds, five assists, and seven steals in the final. In the Texas Cup, the Rodriguez girls combined for eighteen points as the team defeated perennial power, Nazareth, 56–51.

Cy Fair was the 5A winner in 2008, paced by the memorable Ogwumike sisters, Chiney and Nneka; a sophomore on the trophy unit, 5'5" Aarika Reyna, was learning from the best. When the team returned to state in 2010, Reyna was instrumental, having averaged 13.8 points per game (PPG) for the year. Now a senior, she helped the Lady Bobcats win, making All-Tournament alongside senior Chiney Ogwumike, a McDonald's All-American who later played at Stanford.

The keynote from 2009 was the title won at the 3A level by Waco Robinson, whose coach was Brenda Gomez, the first Latina mentor to win state.

The team from the tiny town of Smyer was to win back-to-back crowns in 2010 and 2011 with Cassi Hernandez (5'2" freshman), Marissa

García (5'7" sophomore), and Ashley Escobedo (5'2" junior) on the roster in 2010. The next season Escobedo and García were back for more as the Lady Bobcats repeated.

Canyon took the 2011 4A title with twins Shayla and Shawna Monreal, both 5'6" juniors. Shayla scored eight in the final with four rebounds in a tournament that saw Millie Rivera of Lucas Lovejoy make the All-Tourney team, although her squad lost to Abilene Wylie in the 3A final.

For the 2012 state event, Zuly Martinez of Lipan, a 5'7" senior, was awarded All-Tourney along with Mia Ochoa, a 5'1" junior, of Witharrall. The next season, Ochoa scored a dozen points in the final as her squad won it all, over Class 1A foe Saltillo. She had gone for twelve points and handed out seven assists in the semis versus Leakey. That year, Ochoa made All-Tourney and All-State, as one of the best Latina guards in some time.

MAKING IT AT THE NEXT LEVEL: UTEP

If there have not been many Latinas playing basketball at the high-school level through the years, it stands to reason that there have been even fewer on the college scene. And this is the case, but there are programs in which they have made their presence felt. One school that is particularly notable here is The University of Texas–El Paso, which due to its geographical location and enrollment makeup has been a leader in putting Latinas on the NCAA court. The city has been at or near 80 percent Hispanic for decades.

The program began Division I basketball in 1975 and for the first thirty-one seasons was a veritable backwater, regardless of the ethnic makeup of the roster. The UTEP Miners posted just six winning seasons through 2006 and did not achieve their first NCAA Tourney bid until 2008. However, from 2007 to the current time, UTEP has been very competitive, recording seven winning campaigns during that stretch with tourney trips in 2008 and 2012, taking twenty or more victories five different times. In 2014 the Miners rolled through the Women's National Invitation Tournament (NIT) for five triumphs, losing by two in the championship to Rutgers.

In its history, UTEP has enlisted thirty-four athletes of Mexican American extraction, and some of them are among the program's best, statistically. Gloria Estrada was the first outstanding example, as the 5'5" native of Fabens averaged 14 PPG in 1977 and scored a high of thirty-one points against New Mexico State in January 1977. She also has the distinction of having played for the first winning team in program history, as the Miners went 13–12 under her direction in 1976–1977.

The next Latina star for UTEP was Marcella Lopez in 1986. A hometown product, the 5'5" guard was a four-year letter winner from 1982 to 1986, leading the team in steals, free throw percentage, and field goal accuracy as a senior. Lopez was the first Latina to make All-Conference for the school, an honorable mention in '86.

Following on her heels was Martha Contreras, a 5'4" El Paso guard from 1986 to 1988 who paced the attack in steals and assists and ranks No. 13 all time in steals. Her best assist night was twelve against Southern Colorado on 1988, and she came up with eight steals against UT-San Antonio as a junior in 1987.

Then there was Veronica Rosas, a long-range shooting threat out of Killeen who knocked in twenty-seven three-pointers for the 1990 Miners.

Perhaps the finest Latina of all to play basketball for UTEP was Monica Ramirez, a 6-footer from Midland who played from 1990 to 1994. In her final two seasons with the Miners, she led the team in rebounding (8.5 in 1994) while scoring 14.5 PPG as a senior. Ramirez, a two-time first team All-Western Athletic Conference selection, recorded a career best of eighteen boards versus Colorado State in 1994 and is still in the program's top twenty in career scoring and rebounding. UTEP won eighteen games during Ramirez's sophomore season to set what was then a program record for success.

Norma Sierra can rival Ramirez in a statistical sense, as from 1988 to 1992 she passed for 248 assists. She finished her tenure with the Miners ranked seventh in steals and eighth in assists and is one of four Latinas in the top thirteen for steals, all time. She later became a high-school coach, at Hutto and then Pflugerville Hendrickson.

Not to be overlooked is Terri Pedregon, who came to the UTEP campus from tiny Clint and at 5'7" was a four-year letter earner on the wing. She collected 286 assists during her career, twice leading the Miners in steals, placing first in free throw accuracy in 1995.

The school has had some effective Mexican American guards; in the latter stages of the 1990s, Michelle Montoya certainly fit that bill. The El Paso native played from 1995 to 1998, and in her senior year led in assists with sixty-seven for a solid 16–11 club. The next season it was Christine Mata at the helm, as she was No. 1 in assists; also from El Paso, she is tenth in steals all time, capping her 1997–2001 career by being named to the conference All-Defensive Team in 2001. As a senior, Mata also paced the team in free throw percentage and passed for eleven assists in a single game.

In 2000, one of the team's deadliest shooting powers was April Garza, a California transplant who was first on the team in three-pointers made.

By 2003, the Latina stars were Romie de Anda and Ana Valtierra. De Anda was a 6'1" forward who could shoot, connecting on 40 three-pointers in 2003, while New Mexican Valtierra ranks fourth all time in assists, with 324, and fourth also in steals. That tandem helped the Miners to a 16–13 record in 2004.

THE HEART OF THE VALLEY

Located near the US-Mexico border in Edinburg, The University of Texas Rio Grande Valley (UTRGV), which was known as University of Texas–Pan American from 1989 to 2015, has had a women's basketball team since the 1970s, when it was called Pan American University. In a region that is approximately 90 percent Hispanic according to census data, it would figure that the prominent university would have had its share of Latinas on the basketball team — and this is indeed the case.

After its birth as a quasi-intramural outfit in the mid-1970s, the Lady Broncs (now Vaqueros) joined the National Association of Intercollegiate Athletics (NAIA) ranks in 1984 and by 1986 had an NCAA program playing as an independent.

Through the years, the program has been known for two things, one being its peripatetic nature (four different conference affiliations, ten years as an NCAA independent) and the other being its inability to succeed. The program has posted just two winning seasons in thirty-eight years, and these have both come under Coach Larry Tidwell. The Lady Broncs went 14–14 in 2005 under DeAnn Craft; but for their history, headed into the 2016–2017 season with 303 wins and 628 losses, the .325 percentage ranked them in the bottom ten across the country in success rate.

The NAIA Lady Broncs of 1973 to 1976 were a credible crew, winning twenty-nine games and losing twenty-eight. The coach of the team in those days was John McDowell, who had been an excellent forward with the men's team.

Once they hit the NCAA, however, times got rough, with consecutive 0–27 seasons in 1988 and 1989. The second season carries a significant footnote, however, as the coach was Becky De Los Santos, one of the first Latina head coaches in NCAA history.

Looking at the roster of the school's basketball program through time reveals that there have been eighty women of Mexican American lineage to suit up for the squad. Fifty-two of those can be placed in the early years, 1970s and 1980s, and most of them were natives of the Rio Grande Valley.

Nelda Billescas was the first Latina standout, from 1981 to 1985, and she was also a member of the NAIA Lady Bronc volleyball team during her career. She was a hard-nosed athlete who as a senior was honored with the Ann LaMantia Award as top student-athlete on campus.

Sofia de Alva, a Valley native from McAllen, was another top-flight performer. She lettered from 1983 to 1986, bridging the NAIA and NCAA days, and was an expert passer at point guard. De Alva achieved ten assists in two games, against Southwestern Louisiana in 1985 and Texas Southern in 1984, and ranks in the top ten all time in field goals made and field goal percentage. Her total of 119 assists in 1986 is sixth all time. Feeding the nation's leading scorer, McAllen's Becky Dube, was de Alva's predilection, but she also scored well when needed: in February 1986 she tossed in seventeen points at Abilene Christian, with Dube sending in twenty-seven.

MENTOR PROVING GROUND

Although the Lady Broncs generally remained near the bottom of their conference, they did produce a number of future coaches.

Rachel Juarez is among the single-game program leaders for rebounds, having corralled seventeen against Texas A&I (now Texas A&M University–Kingsville) in December 1984; she played from 1985 to 1986 and in time would become one of the Valley's great coaches. At Hidalgo, then Edinburg High and eventually Laredo United in her hometown, Rachel Juarez Carmona was to win more than 500 lifetime games and was still active and hard to beat in 2016.

Iris Garza is another Lady Bronc who went on to fame as a coach, mainly at Pharr-San Juan-Alamo High and later Robert Vela High in Edinburg. She was a speedy little guard for the university quintet from 1988 to 1992 and ranks in the top ten in games played (108), free throws made, assists (225), and steals (161). She knocked down all seven of her free throw tries against Southwestern Louisiana in March 1992.

Garza's teammate on the Lady Broncs for two seasons was Araceli Rios, an All-Valley point guard from Edcouch-Elsa High School who played from 1990 to 1994; she was to transition into volleyball and coach in Edinburg. There, she led Economedes High to the playoffs in nine of twelve seasons and left to become the first coach at new Robert Vela High in 2012; that team has made the postseason in each of her five seasons at the helm. Coach Rios, now Ortega, is the sister of four-year UTPA Bronc starter Lalo Rios, boys' basketball coach at Vela from 2012 to 2017.

At one time in the mid-2010s, the city of Edinburg had a real brawl every time the high school teams got together. Along with Carmona at Edinburg High, there was Jenny Rae Gaytan at Edinburg North and Kelly Garrett coaching at Economedes. Gaytan, now García, was a Lady Bronc guard from 1995 to 1999 while Garrett — now at Harlingen South High — was a battling backcourt star for Pan American in the 1990s. Garrett played in 108 NCAA games and ranks fourth all time in assists.

Other Lady Broncs who have become coaches include Monica Cardoza, now Rodriguez (played 1993–1994) and Clarisse Arredondo (2001–2003).

A DROUGHT ENSUES

Out of La Feria High in the Valley, Angela Casas (1994 to 1998) is on the career stat chart with 458 rebounds during her career, a total that ranks No. 7 in team annals. Veronica Guerra was a defensive special-ist who came up with seven steals against Southwestern Louisiana in December 1999.

In the 2000s, the Lady Broncs had few Latinas, but a couple carved out a niche as lettermen and spot players. Jennifer Arriola (2001–2003) was a rangy shot-blocker while Joanna Fuentes (2002–2006), Cynthia Ramirez (2004–2008), and Andrea Garza (2008–2010) were role play-ers who saw sporadic minutes on court.

HOMEGROWN HEROES

The quality of girls' basketball in the Valley improved steadily as the new century continued. Back in the 1960s and 1970s, Weslaco, Raymondville, and Lyford had all been to the state tournament, and standouts such as Harlingen's Stacy Siebert (among the top rebounders in Texas Tech history) gave the area some headlines beyond the border in the 1980s. In the first decade of the 2000s, Harlingen South was a consistent force at the regional tournament while the legendary Teresa Casso of McAllen always had her Lady Bulldogs in the hunt for the Sweet 16. And two of the Valley's greatest hoopsters went from incredible high-school careers to the local university.

Marah Guzman of Edinburg paced her team to the Sweet 16 as a senior in 2006, having been the Valley MVP twice and averaging more than 20 PPG over a stellar four-year career that included All-State honors twice. As a senior she led the area in scoring at 28 PPG and took five steals a night with eight assists and six rebounds per.

After playing two seasons at Western Texas College in Snyder, the 5'2" speedster came home to play for the Lady Broncs. She started her career in style with a 16-point outing against Texas A&M International in January 2009 (made seven of eight free throws) and would become a starter in the backcourt midway through her junior year. Over two seasons with the club, Guzman was among the team leaders in assists. Always a tremendous shooter, she made ten of ten free throws against South Dakota as a senior and was able to make the grade as the program's shortest starter since the 1970s.

Guzman wrapped up her college career and coached at Juan Diego Academy in Mission, along with McAllen ex Casas, before taking a similar role at Memorial High in McAllen.

When Guzman was a standout at Edinburg High, the Lady Hawks of Harlingen South were about to unveil a force of nature named Bianca Torre. From the first time she stepped on the court for Coach Dawn Engelman, the 5'4" guard was the best. She played four seasons for South, making All-State like Guzman and leading her team to the Sweet 16, and gained national headlines for a game in which she scored twenty points but also made twenty steals. "B" hit for 24.9 PPG as a junior with 10.9 steals, 7 rebounds, and 8.2 assists. Her senior year she averaged 24.3 PPG, 11.1 steals, 4.7 boards, and 9.9 assists. No one has ever been better in the Valley.

Torre had grown up playing against the boys at the Boys and Girls Club in Harlingen and attributed her success in the sport to the hard knocks given on a nightly basis on the club courts. That is why she was known as a hard-nosed competitor whose hustle and endurance became legendary in the Valley.[17]

Once on the college campus in Edinburg, Torre immediately entered the starting lineup and never left, and by the time she was done at UTPA she was the holder of more records than any player, Latina or otherwise, in women's basketball.

Torre, now coaching at Edinburg High, played 115 games, scored 1,439 points, made 277 free throws, recorded 393 assists, and pilfered 226 steals. All of these totals are No. 1 in program history. She is third in field goals, second in three-pointers, and second in free throw percentage (.780).

She was the only player in the Great West Conference to make All-Conference four times, was Newcomer of the Year as a freshman, and rebounded from a severe knee injury late in her junior year; one point away from tying the program record for points at that stage, Torre defied the odds and made it back on to the court as a senior, eclipsing the record and then some.

As for single-season prowess, Torre's 525 points in 2011 ranks fourth, and she has two of the most productive three-point seasons, making 73 in 2011 and 64 in 2010. Her .814 mark at the free throw line in 2010 is fourth all time, with her .785 showing in 2011 at No. 9. Three of the top ten single-season performances in steals came from the pride of South High, and she contributed 34 and 32 points for her best-scoring games, two nights apart in December 2010, against Texas State and nationally ranked Oklahoma State, respectively.

Guzman and Torre were teammates with the Lady Broncs in 2009 and 2010, allowing Valley basketball fans to see two of the best ever to run the court in high school, getting their chance to perform at the next level. Those two greats paved the way for Latinas in the Valley, showing that nothing can stop an athlete if she has what it takes to compete and thrive.

By 2015–2016, Coach Tidwell had made program history with back-to-back 19-win seasons — netting the first two postseason appearances in school history — and the Vaqueros counted four Latinas on the roster, two from Weslaco, one from Los Fresnos, and one from El Paso. Athletic Weslaco Pantherette Angela Villarreal, like Guzman and Torre a high school MVP of the Valley, joined the UTRGV squad as a freshman.

LADY JAVELINAS' NO. 1

It is not difficult to determine the top Latina basketball player in the history of Texas A&M–Kingsville, because few would argue against Lorie Martinez.

The sharpshooter appeared on campus out of Incarnate Word Academy in Corpus Christi in 1998 and in four scintillating seasons became one of the university's most accomplished stars. Starting off with a bang, Martinez averaged 18.1 PPG as a freshman and was named Newcomer of the Year in the Lone Star Conference and freshman All-American. She served notice of what was to come in February 1998, hitting a game-winning hoop at the buzzer to beat Eastern New Mexico.

Over four years with the Lady Javelinas, Martinez was to set a national Division II record for career three-pointers (385), post the best program free throw percentage by season (.911) and career (.852), score a best of 36 points one night against St. Edward's, and lead her team to the NCAA Division II tourney. The 2001 team (27–7 for the year) that went to the Dance did so with a Latina as its star and a Latina, Debbie Robledo, as its coach.

Martinez was the only Lady Javelina ever named All-Lone Star Conference (LSC) four times and ranks first all time in games, minutes, points, assists, steals, and three-pointers. Elected to the university's Hall of Honor in 2006, Martinez, now Ruiz, can lay claim to being the best basketball player in Lady Javelina history, Latina or otherwise.

The program has had other Latina standouts, such as Dina Flores, who collected 220 assists from 1982 to 1986: this number places her in the top ten lifetime. Janie Jimenez was on the All-Region team in 1983 as the school made its first postseason appearance.

The first great one had been Sandra Jimenez (1977–1978), who is one of thirteen players to reach 1,000 points for a career, although she only played two seasons in Kingsville. Her team also defeated rival Pan American twice during that span in the Battle of South Texas. In the mid-1990s, Claudia Castillo was a solid hand for the squad, making second team ALL-LSC in 1994, her only season with the school.

The other outstanding Latina in hoops at Kingsville was Felicia Soza (2007–2010), who rang up 59 three-pointers in 2008, scored 436 points in 2010, and ranks fifth all time in games, second in three-point percentage, seventh in free throw percentage, and sixth in defensive rebounds. For a time, Soza played alongside Victoria Gonzalez, who is in the record books as one of the program leaders in blocked shots. In high school, Gonzalez led her Hidalgo Lady Pirates squad to the state Final Four in 2009, where she made All-Tourney, also winning All-State honors.

CONCLUSION

In sum, it can be noted that the participation of Latinas in high school basketball, particularly in places where demographic trends would suggest it, is far more frequent in today's game than in the early era of the sport.

As girls continue to deal with family traditions militating against extracurricular activities, they have nonetheless increased their numbers by the decade, along with accolades and honors on the hardwood. The specter of machismo still exists in many households, but its effects seem to have greatly abated in terms of limiting participation.

As this survey of Latinas in Texas hoops has suggested, areas with higher concentrations of Mexican Americans such as West and South Texas have been the leaders in participation, developing standout players at both the high school and college levels.

Discrimination suffered in past times has been effectively mitigated by a number of civil rights acts as well as the memorable Title IX decision of the early 1970s. These days, Latinas are as welcome as any racial or ethnic group in high school sports, and thus there have emerged trailblazers seeking to outdistance the genetic factors that have always made it difficult for a physically smaller ethnic group to make other than the occasional inroads. Judging from the high participation rates in predominantly Latino areas such as the Rio Grande Valley of Texas, this trend should continue in the future.

QUESTIONS:

1. Why did Mexican American athletes in general tend not to play for their schools in the early decades of the twentieth century and continuing until around the 1970s? How did this trend impact males? Females? Why was there a difference?

2. Why did the participation of Latinas in basketball not change significantly, even after the passage of Title IX?

3. Given that opportunities have improved, why are Latinas still so underrepresented in hoops at the collegiate level?

NOTES

1. MaryJo Sylwester, "Hispanic Girls in Sports Held Back By Tradition," USA *Today*, March 29, 2005, A1–2.

2. R. P. Resnick and Yolanda Quiñones Mayo, "The Impact of Machismo on Hispanic Women," *Affilia* 11:3 (1996): 257–77.

3. Cherrie Moraga and Gloria Anzaldúa, eds., *This Bridge Called My Back: Writings by Radical Women of Color*, 4th ed. (Albany, NY: SUNY Press, 2015).

4. Gloria E. Anzaldúa, *Borderlands/La Frontera: The New Mestiza* (Austin: University of Texas Press, 1987).

5. The Women's Sports Foundation Report, "Addressing the Health and Physical Activity Needs of Girls in the Boston Metropolitan Area," November 2007.

6. Erin Irick, "NCAA Sports Sponsorship and Participation Rates Report: 1981–82 to 2010–11," *Indianapolis:* NCAA (2011): 69.

7. Gregory Selber, "Hardwood Heroes: A History of High School Basketball in the Rio Grande Valley," Vol. 1, McAllen: Rio Grande Valley Sports Hall of Fame, 2017.

8. Ibid.

9. Ibid.

10. Gregory Selber, *Border Ball: A History of High School Football in the Rio Grande Valley* (New York: Linus Publications, 2009).

11. Ibid.

12. Selber, "Hardwood Heroes," 2017.

13. Ibid.

14. Selber, *Border Ball*, 2009.

15. Pedro A. Noguera, "Educational Rights and Latinos: Tracking as a Form of Second-Generation Discrimination," Berkeley *La Raza Law Journal* 8:1 (1995).

16. Selber, "Hardwood Heroes," 2017.

17. From author's personal interviews with Bianca Torre, 2016.

EL TRI VERSUS THE STARS AND STRIPES:

On the History of the US-Mexico Soccer Rivalry

Luis Alvarez
University of California, San Diego

IN JUNE 2011, MEXICO DEFEATED the United States 4–2 in the final of the Gold Cup at the Rose Bowl in Los Angeles. The match was another in the fierce rivalry between the two countries and crowned Mexico champions of the biannual tournament involving North American, Central American, and Caribbean nations. It was a sensational game that saw the Americans leap to an early 2–0 lead, only for the Mexicans to equalize just before halftime, and eventually cap their comeback with a dazzling goal from the left foot of Giovani dos Santos that brought the overwhelmingly pro-Mexico crowd to delirium. This was neither the first nor last time the US faced boos, jeers, and flying cups of beer (or worse) from a hostile crowd while playing Mexico on the former's home ground. Afterwards, in his trademark stoic fashion, American coach Bob Bradley said resignedly, "Obviously...the support that Mexico has on a night like tonight makes it a home game for them."[1]

US goalkeeper Tim Howard wasn't as measured. He vented in a post-game interview, "It was a fucking disgrace that the entire post-match ceremony was in Spanish. You can bet your ass if we were in Mexico City it wouldn't be all in English."[2] Off the pitch, fan behavior ranged from Mexican Americans demonstrating split allegiance by wearing jerseys that were half red, white, and blue and half red, green, and white to supporters from both sides clashing in the stands and via social media and hurling the worst of racial epithets and stereotypes. To most observers, all of this came as no surprise. Similar scenarios had unfolded surrounding every US-Mexico match since the mid-1990s, including Mexico's 1–0 victory in the 1998 Gold Cup final also played in LA, the US's (in)famous win in the round of 16 knock-out stages of the 2002 Korea-Japan World Cup, and more than a dozen so-called "friendly" matches.

This chapter charts the recent history of the US-Mexico soccer rivalry. I argue that this rivalry is a product, literally, of neoliberal globalization and a site where the players, fans, and media that cover the games (re)negotiate citizenship, belonging, and race.[3] The intensification of the rivalry since the mid-1990s has revealed competing conceptions of citizenship, belonging, and race at the same time it has produced transnational practices of civic belonging conditioned by the contingency of hemispheric economics and politics. More to the point, I discuss how the rivalry has enflamed anti-immigrant racism and generated practices of citizenship that simultaneously blur and harden the line between the two nations. Rather than frame the rivalry in the "us versus them" terms it is played on the field, I explore how those who play, organize, advertise, cheer, and broadcast the games illuminate competing experiences of globalization and locate fútbol as a site that sparks politics, cultural contestation, and transnational identities.[4]

MARKETING RIVALRY: EL TRI IN THE US

The US and Mexico first confronted one another in a qualification match for the 1934 World Cup in Italy. In front of a sold-out crowd in Rome that included Benito Mussolini, Italian American striker Aldo "Buff" Donelli scored four times to lead the US to a 4–2 victory. Until 1990, the two sides clashed just twenty-six times, only seven times on US soil. Since then, however, they have played thirty-seven times, including twenty-six matches in the US. Ten of the eleven "friend-lies" since 1990 — games whose location is not dictated by a host tournament — have been in the US. Only eight times in the last twenty-four years have the two played in Mexico. Since 2007, moreover, Mexico has played a staggering forty-five of their sixty-six "friendlies" on American soil, usually in front of sold-out crowds. In the same time frame, El Tri has played only fourteen friendlies in Mexico. One sportswriter has observed that in the last quarter century it is easy to see that "the best supported team in America was Mexico."[5]

Why has the Mexican national team had such a remarkable presence in the US over the last two-and-a-half decades? The short answer is globalization and the emergence of El Tri as a hemispheric marketing brand worth millions to the Federación Mexicana de Fútbol Asociación (FMF), the United States Soccer Federation (U.S. Soccer), television media conglomerates like Televisa and Univision, and the companies that sponsor them, including Coca-Cola, Anheuser-Busch, and Home Depot. The rapidly growing market for Mexican national team soccer in the US reflects the dramatic rise of the ethnic Mexican population in the United States since the 1980s. While there were roughly 4.4 million Mexican immigrants and 15 million total Mexican-origin folks in the US in 1990, those numbers grew to 11.7 million and nearly 35 million, respectively, by 2011.[6] Not unrelated was soccer's growth in the US — including hosting the 1994 World Cup, the establishment of Major League Soccer (MLS) in 1996, and the growth in adult community leagues beyond the "pay to play" youth leagues so popular in suburban areas across the country.

Seismic demographic shifts combined with the untapped potential of fútbol as moneymaker made El Tri a lucrative commodity, and there was a long line to cash in. When the TV station Spanish International Network was renamed Univision after it was acquired by a partnership between the Mexican-owned Televisa and Hallmark in 1986, the network leaned on Televisa's successful formula of soccer and telenovelas to grow into a thirteen-billion-dollar empire by 2010.[7] While soccer was largely ignored by US television until the mid-2000s, Univision made it a staple of its programming, including showing World Cup matches live in 1986 and 1990 when the only other option for fans of the global game was to attend closed-circuit viewings. Convinced soccer could sell, Univision executives launched a grassroots campaign that included fans calling their local cable companies to demand the network be added to their channel lineups.

The execs were right, and viewer numbers went through the roof. By the 2011 Gold Cup it was no surprise that Univision topped all of

US TV ratings during peak Saturday night viewing for the length of the tournament, including eight million viewers alone during Mexico's victory over the United States in the final — numbers equal to that year's Game 7 of the Stanley Cup and final round of the U.S. Open golf tournament on NBC.

Advertising partnerships boomed in kind. Companies like Budweiser and Allstate have long sponsored both the US and Mexican national teams on Univision, recognizing that the network and soccer are, in the words of an Allstate executive, "a great way to communicate to a Hispanic audience."[8] El Tri, echoed another ad exec, "are selling out stadiums, selling jerseys, selling sodas, selling beers — any way you look at it they are a money-making machine because the fans are so passionate."[9] Another noted, "Put your latest advert inside a Mexico versus 'anyone' World Cup match and you are guaranteed to reach a prime advertising market and lots of them."[10]

Soccer-specific interests benefited from the branding of El Tri in the US, too. In 2006, for instance, Soccer United Marketing (SUM), the marketing wing of MLS, struck a deal with the FMF that guaranteed the Mexican national team would play twenty-two games in the US for twenty million dollars. When NAPA Auto Parts and BEHR paints renewed seven-figure deals with SUM in 2013 to sponsor El Tri in the US, they cited ESPN's agreement to air Mexico matches in English as a key factor. NAPA's vice-president for marketing noted that "the partnership delivers a great deal of visibility for Mexican and Mexican American consumers, especially among our target market of men 18 to 49." He continued, "It's a centerpiece of our entire Hispanic marketing program."[11]

All of this points to El Tri being one of the top sports brands in the United States. Their popularity north of the border is an example of advertising that taps into culture-specific characteristics of race, ethnicity, and national markets. While market outreach to Latino communities was a mixed bag of success and failure for many MLS franchises, corporate interests were able to tap into Mexican purchasing power in the US by effectively targeting Spanish language, income, and educational levels to understand the unique power of El Tri to mediate ties to Mexico and life in the US for many immigrants.[12] The reconstitution of US-based Mexican soccer fans into a consumer market, to borrow from Arlene Dávila, "reverberate(s) within public understanding of people's place, and hence of their rights and entitlements."[13] The rivalry as commercial culture is constitutive of people's identities and belonging. Combined with migration patterns and diasporic allegiances, the emergence of El Tri as hemispheric marketing brand helped give rise to a fierce US-Mexico rivalry. More than just a result of unbridled commodification, however, it illuminated competing narratives of race, belonging, and citizenship.

VITRIOLIC DEBATE: THE (SOCIAL) MEDIA

If a US-Mexico association prompted partnership in the boardroom, it hasn't always done so elsewhere off the pitch. The intense competition, verging on hatred, among both players and fans has prompted a discourse that mirrors popular debate over immigration and the presence of Mexicans and other Latinos in the US since the 1986 Immigration Reform and Control Act (IRCA) that provided a path to citizenship for millions of undocumented immigrants. The backdrop to El Tri's branding in the US and rivalry with the US men's national team (USMNT) included what George Lipsitz described as "a brand of economic fundamentalism favoring free markets," the intensification of deregulation and global flow of capital, ideas, and labor, along with the growth of mass technology and communications, that has resulted in "low wages, high unemployment, slow growth, high interest rates, and devastating social spending on health, housing, and education" all over the map.[14]

If the 1994 North American Free Trade Agreement (NAFTA) ushered in the latest stage of neoliberalism, it was accompanied by intensified militarization of the US-Mexico border. Mexican and US authorities have deployed low-intensity warfare against undocumented immigrants, including military-inspired technology and enforcement techniques, all aimed to control human traffic across the border. The result was government initiatives like Operation Blockade in El Paso (1993), Operation Gatekeeper in San Diego (1994), Operation Safeguard in Nogales, Arizona (1994), and Operation Rio Grande in South Texas (1997), each accompanied by additional resources and authority for the border patrol, Immigration and Naturalization Service (INS), and, more recently, Immigration and Customs Enforcement (ICE).

The angry outcry over undocumented immigration and shifting demographics toward "majority-minority" status and "Latinoization" led to a number of anti-immigrant legislations and campaigns. Examples include California's Proposition 187 in 1994, which sought to limit access by undocumented immigrants to health care and education; late 1990s anti-affirmative action campaigns in Texas and

California; the anti-bilingual education Proposition 227 in California; the 2000 anti-gang Proposition 21 in California; the federal passing of House Resolution 4437 in 2005 that imposed stiff legal sanctions for "aiding" undocumented immigrants; and Arizona's passing of Senate bill 1070 criminalizing undocumented immigrants in 2010 (followed by similar bills in several other states). All served to stir an anti-immigrant, racially tense political climate.

In this context, it is not surprising that the USA's increasing soccer success against Mexico resonated beyond the pitch. Prior to 1991, the US beat Mexico only twice in twenty-seven matches since "Buff" Donelli's heroics in 1934. When the US upset Mexico 2–0 in the semi-finals of the 1991 Gold Cup, few fans on either side would have imagined that the United States would win sixteen, lose ten, and draw nine of the next thirty-five matches, including a 12–5–5 record since 2000 and taking into account the "dos a cero" classic in the 2002 World Cup.

Results on the pitch and politics off it have made the US-Mexico soccer rivalry a flashpoint for vitriolic debate. The 1998 and 2011 Gold Cup finals in Los Angeles (both won by Mexico), for example, sparked heated discussion over whether immigrants should root against and boo the USMNT. *Soccer America*'s report of the 1998 final noted, "Any remaining doubts about the identity of the home team were dispelled when the two teams took the field. The fans came, saw, booed and threw things — at the United States. Whistles greeted the US national team when it took the field and during its national anthem."[15]

The range of opinions was evident in letters submitted to the *Los Angeles Times* after the '98 match. Printed under the headline, "What's Needed is some Civility," letters included charges of "anti-Americanism," the "sub-human" character of Mexican team supporters and immigrants, and not so subtle calls to "go back to Mexico."[16] A letter from USMNT supporter Frank Rodriguez underscored the complex perspective of many Mexican Americans, in particular. Rodriguez wrote, "Never had I been so ashamed to be a Mexican American. My son and I were pelted with beer, soda, and God knows what else for having had the temerity to display an American flag and cheer for our team. I watched with dread as I saw my son's eyes filled with confusion at the disrespect displayed while our national anthem was played."[17] Such views were echoed following the 2011 final, including by CNN's Ruben Navarrette Jr., who labeled the spectacle of Mexican fans booing the US as "misplaced" loyalty and "ugly nationalism" that "turn my stomach."[18] As online comments in response to Navarrette Jr. indicated, much of this debate was shrouded in hyper-masculine terms. In confrontations in the stands and on anonymous message boards, gender was often the terrain for casting and experiencing class, national, or racial insults.

Response to US–Mexico matches also included backlash from conservative political pundits like Patrick Buchanan and Samuel Huntington. Buchanan summed up his view of the 1998 Gold Cup final by stating, "What took place in the LA Coliseum was a two-hour orgy of anti-Americanism, an explosion of hatred against the United States."[19] Conservative websites and blogs like Libertarian Today and the Southern Nationalist Network also got in on the action. In its coverage of the 2011 Gold Cup final, for instance, the latter argued:

> As events surrounding a recent soccer match in Los Angeles show, much of the Southwest is already ethnically and culturally Mexican. And the people living there for the most part have no desire and no incentive to assimilate into the lifestyle of the US Anglo minority. As their numbers continue to explode, Mexicans living in California will expect to impose their politics, their language, their religion, etc. on the State. And the next generation of them, which will include many millions who were born in the States and therefore are entitled to vote, hold office and receive government benefits, will not sit idly by as a disenfranchised majority — they will expect *and insist on* running the show. And the US Federal Government will be unable to deal harshly with these Mexican nationalists because Hispanics will make up a huge percentage of the population in many states, tying the hands of the politicians. This could be how the US Empire dies — if the dollar hasn't been completely destroyed by that time.[20]

Amidst fears over the "browning" of the US, such commentary was likely driven in part by a desire to defend white racial privilege and class interests. The uproar over the rivalry revealed the diminished overrepresentation of those who have historically benefitted from what David Roediger called "the wages of whiteness."[21] The often offensive political banter surrounding the rivalry was, to be sure, a two-way street. This was evident, for instance, at an under-23 US-Mexico Olympic qualifier in 2004 at Estadio Jalisco in Guadalajara when Mexican fans chanted "Osama," in reference to the 9/11 terrorist attacks, in attempts to rattle US players. Yet, the racially tinged commentary against El Tri and Mexican-origin communities in the US was inextricable from the broader context and debate over immigration reform, border security, and related economic concerns north of the border. With nearly 100,000 flag-waving fans, many of them Mexicans in support of El Tri, the Gold Cup finals played in 1998 and 2011 were a powerful reminder of the demographic, economic, and political changes wrought by globalization in Los Angeles and elsewhere.

Since the 1990s, the rivalry has blurred the line between sport and politics. The rivalry shows how the symbolic rhetoric of race, citizenship, and belonging was deployed to advocate for inclusion and exclusion in the United States, underscoring the heterogeneous narratives and experiences of globalization.

CHOOSING SIDES: THE PLAYERS

The athletes enmeshed in the rivalry also reveal its cultural politics. In a time when the security and stability of the nation-state are uncertain, players on both sides generated new strategies for dealing with such contingencies. They have practiced forms of citizenship and belonging oriented toward multiple and transnational social configurations rather than homogenization.

Since its inception, the USMNT included players with immigrant backgrounds, in part because immigrant communities fueled the popularity of soccer in the US. Italian, Spanish, and Portuguese-heritage players dotted early US rosters; Mexican-born Hugo Salcedo played for the US in the 1970s. Salcedo was part of the 1972 Munich Olympic team and played in the Pan American games the year before. While he grew up in East LA and attended University of California, Riverside, Salcedo was born in Jalisco. Following his playing career, he became a social worker, a sports agent, and, eventually, a U.S. Soccer and CONCACAF executive (the governing body for North American, Central American, and Caribbean soccer), devoted to developing young Latino talent and improving the sport's limited reach into Latino communities. Young Latino stars of the sort Salcedo identified often had to be steered away from baseball, basketball, and gridiron football, only to face a choice of whether to play for the US or Mexico based on dual citizenship available through their Mexican immigrant parents.

In recent years, a number of US-born players of Mexican descent have charted a complicated rendering of the rivalry and national affiliation. The national teams themselves have consisted of players with connections on both sides of the border. Mexican Americans Hérculez Gómez, Luis Gil, and Joe Corona, among others, chose to represent the US despite playing professionally in Mexico's top-flight domestic league, Liga MX. Gómez, who was born in LA of immigrant parents and grew up in Las Vegas, summarized the relationship between the United States and Mexico for himself and many others: "Sometimes you do feel like you're stuck in the middle."[22] Defender Edgar Castillo from Las Cruces, New Mexico underscored Gómez's point. Castillo initially played for Mexico's under-23 squad before switching to the US and the senior USMNT.[23]

There are examples in the reverse, too. Richard Sánchez, born and raised in Mission Hills, California, played for FC Dallas of the MLS but has been on the under-17 and under-20 Mexican national teams. Sánchez was the starting goalkeeper for the 2011 El Tri side that won the under-17 World Cup played in Mexico. Isaác Brizuela and Miguel Ponce were both born of immigrant parents in Northern California and played for Mexico. Ponce, who won a gold medal with El Tri at the 2012 London Olympics and was part of Mexico's Brazil World Cup team, was born in Sacramento. He moved to Guadalajara when he was an infant and eventually to Tijuana at age ten to be closer to his father who worked in California. Ponce commuted across the border to San Ysidro, California for high school every day. Thinking back over his decision to declare for El Tri, he said, "In my case, I feel more Mexican because almost all my life I've been living in Mexico. But in a certain moment, it doesn't matter. I could have played for the U.S. too."[24]

In recent years, Mexico's women's team, Las Tri, has made Mexican American players their anchor. Mexican American college soccer stars were recruited so heavily for the 1999 Women's World Cup that the team was actually conceived as a Mexican American squad during qualifying and based their training in San Diego, not Mexico. The team even conducted Spanish lessons for its US-born athletes.[25]

The decision to play for Mexico or the US was different for each player. Desire for playing time may have factored as much as generational or national affiliation. While they might be labeled commodified bodies embedded in the rivalry's commercialism — "bought and sold," to borrow the parlance of professional soccer personnel — they were also public figures performing hybrid belonging and citizenship in a transnational era. In doing so, players challenged the borders of us versus them on and off the pitch, how the civic imaginary might be (re)bordered to include a broader range of citizenship and belonging.

PANCHO VILLA'S ARMY VERSUS THE AMERICAN OUTLAWS: THE FANS

Like the players they cheer for, fans on both sides exemplified the contested nature of the rivalry. This was evident in 2013, when supporter groups for the US and Mexican teams entered litigation. Pancho Villa's Army (PVA), the US-based fan club for El Tri, charged that the American Outlaws (AO), the primary US national team club, interfered with their plans to attend the 2014 World Cup in Brazil because of racial motivations. The suit alleged that AO leadership threatened to cut ties with a Nebraska-based travel agency, where AO originated, if the company continued to work with PVA in designing travel packages. PVA sought up to one million dollars in damages, sued the company, TenDot, for breach of contract, and accused the AO of interference for influencing the termination of the contract.[26]

PVA was organized by Sergio Tristan, a Texas–born attorney and decorated Iraq War veteran, in Austin in 2012. He wanted to do what AO did for US fans but for Mexican American fans of El Tri. The name Pancho Villa's Army derived from the iconic Mexican revolutionary who fought US and Mexican forces along the border during the Mexican Revolution. PVA held special meaning as a name because, as the organization noted, Villa was known for invading Columbus, New Mexico, in 1916. It was not unnoticed by PVA that U.S. Soccer often scheduled home World Cup qualifiers against Mexico in Columbus, Ohio, because there were fewer Mexicans in the stands there than in sites in the Southwest and it was often bitter cold in winter months, making for uncomfortable and unfamiliar playing conditions for El Tri. PVA is organized via "battalions," with factions in cities across the US. Its activities, conducted in English, include fostering community, organizing match-watching parties, and travelling to matches in and outside of the US.[27]

When the group was launched in 2012 it faced racist backlash. Tristan noted, "At the very beginning, we experienced a lot of it. We tried to make a huge push to inform US fans that we aren't here to do an anti-US campaign. The racism has gone away as we've tried to maintain a respectful tone on and off the site, but that first month we had a lot of people from different organizations telling us that we needed to go back to our country and stuff like 'wetbacks don't belong [in the US].'"[28] PVA's initial difficulties fit with the longer narrative of US-Mexico soccer, including internet "flame" wars between fans, insulting chants from both sides in the stands, and the politicization of the rivalry as a proxy for who is deserving of full citizenship.

The fan experience also reveals that national belonging and citizenship practices were inseparable from the same globalizing economic forces that helped generate the rivalry in the first place. The PVA-AO legal battle is one example, but so is the actual match-day experience. One needed only to scan El Tri supporter sections at the 2010 South African or 2014 Brazilian World Cups to see that FIFA's global commercialism was unavoidable. Inundated by beer commercials and corporate advertising in the stadiums, El Tri supporters made the wearing of Mexican *lucha libre* wrestling masks and *sombreros* made in China mainstays of their fan identity, not to mention the high cost of traveling to and attending international tournaments.[29]

Just as supporters feed the hyper-commercialization of the rivalry and global game, so too do they create alternate public spheres in support of their teams. Like the players they follow or even worship, fans in the stadiums and online adopt multiple identities. As PVA demonstrates, this includes a kind of hybrid citizenship that enacts inclusion into the US civic imaginary at the same time they magnify differences that would normally exclude them from belonging.

"EL AZTECAZO"

Michael Orozco Fiscal, the Mexican American center back born in Orange, California, scored the lone goal in the USA's 1–0 victory over Mexico in a friendly at Estadio Azteca in Mexico City in 2012. It was the first-ever win for the US on Mexican soil, despite twenty-four previous tries, and was viewed as a major breakthrough for the USMNT because it shattered the vaunted Azteca curse. Orozco's goal came late in the match and saddled him with *persona non grata* status in Mexico, even though he had played professionally in Liga MX. Just a year later, in October 2013, he scored a goal for the US that tied Panama in a World Cup qualifier and kept Mexico's hopes of qualification alive. In an interview with Univision, he said he thought he'd redeemed himself in the eyes of Mexican fans. "Not even a year ago I was one of the most hated players because of 'El Aztecazo' [as his 2012 goal has become known] but I think the tides have turned and now I am one of the most loved for the goal for the tie [against Panama]. It is close to my heart because Mexico has to get to the World Cup....I wish them luck and I will continue to support them." He continued, "Here [in Mexico] the doors were opened for me to start my career and I enjoyed it very much. My parents are Mexican, I am Mexican. I ended up defending another jersey but I continue to be Mexican."[30]

As with others involved in the US-Mexico rivalry, Orozco's experience encompassed complex national affiliations and identities. The athletes, fans, and media who play, follow, and cover El Tri versus the Stars and Stripes navigated the social, political, and economic contingencies of globalization to reveal new possibilities and practices of race, citizenship, and belonging. For Orozco and many others, the rivalry meant crafting Mexican, American, or Mexican American experiences that radiated in multiple directions, including the cross (ethnic and racial), intra (fissured on lines of gender, class, generation), and trans (as in transnational).[31] The recent history of the US-Mexico soccer rivalry tells two interrelated stories of fútbol in North America: one centering on the lucrative marketing of El Tri and their rivalry with the USMNT and another on the cultural politics of sport as they unfold on and off the pitch. Rather than reduce the rivalry to sheer commercialism or, simply, a game that unfolds on the field, it may also have much to teach us about race, belonging, and citizenship in the era of neoliberal globalization.

QUESTIONS:

I. Why have the media and sponsors become so interested in US-versus-Mexico matches? What is the significance of this trend?

2. Some of the athletes mentioned were born in Mexico, raised in the US, and play for the US. Others were born in the US, raised in the US or Mexico, and play for Mexico. Do you agree or disagree with the reasons stated by the various athletes concerning their decisions to play for the US or Mexican side? Why or why not?

3. Can you think of other examples of how cultural politics play out in US sports today?

NOTES

1. Bill Plaschke, "Again, It's Red, White and Boo: Mexico Rallies behind Overwhelming Support at Rose Bowl," *Los Angeles Times*, June 26, 2011.

2. Rich Chandler, "Tim Howard: 'It's a F***** Disgrace That Entire Gold Cup Post-match Ceremony Conducted in Spanish,'" Off the Bench, NBC Sports, http://offthebench.nbcsports.com/2011/Q6/28/tim-howard-its-a-f-disgrace-that-entire-gold-cup-post-match-ceremonv-conducted-in-spanish/.

3. José M. Alamillo, "Beyond the Latino Sports Hero: The Role of Sports in Creating Communities, Networks, and Identities," *American Latinos and The Making of the United States: A Theme Study*, National Park Service (2013): 161–183.

4. Juan Javier Pescador, "¡VamosTaximaroa! Mexican/Chicano Soccer Associations and Transnational/Translocal Communities, 1967–2002," *Latino Studies* 2, no. 3 (December 2004), 352–376.

5. Gary Hopkins, *Star-Spangled Soccer: The Selling, Marketing and Management of Soccer in the* USA (New York: Palgrave McMillan, 2010), 157.

6. Ana Gonzalez-Barrera and Mark Hugo Lopez, "A Demographic Portrait of Mexican-Origin Hispanics in the United States," Pew Research: Hispanic Trends Project, http://www.pewhispanic.org/2013/05/01/a-demo-graphic-portrait-of-mexican-origin-hispanics- in-the-united-states, May 1, 2013.

7. Hopkins, *Star-Spangled Soccer*, 265–266.

8. Simon Evans, "Triumphant Mexico Soccer Team Becoming Major Brand in the U.S.," Reuters, January 28, 2011.

9. Ibid. The ad exec is Michael Hitchcock of Texas–based Playbook Management International, who specialize in soccer business in North America.

10. Hopkins, *Star-Spangled Soccer*, 270.

11. Christopher Botta, "NAPA, BEHR Renew Deals with Mexican Team," *Street and Smith's Sports Business Journal*, http://m.sportsbusinessdaily.com/Journal/lssues/2013/02/ll/Marketing-and-Sponsorship/SUM.aspx, February 11, 2013 .

12. Jorge Iber, "Sports and Consumerism," *Oxford Bibliographies, Latino Studies*, April 28, 2014.

13. Arlene Davila, *Latinos, Inc.: The Marketing and Making of a People* (Berkeley: University of California Press, 2012), 2.

14. George Lipsitz, *Footsteps in the Dark: The Hidden Histories of Popular*

Music (Minneapolis: University of Minnesota Press, 2007), 70.

15. Duncan Irving, "Coliseum Rocks as Tricolores Three-Peat," *Soccer America* 53, no. 7 (March 2, 1998): 8.

16. "What's Needed Is Some Civility," *Los Angeles Times*, February 21, 1998.

17. Ibid.

18. Ruben Navarrette Jr., "Immigrants, Don't Boo U.S. Teams," July 21, 2011, http://www.cnn.com/2011/OPINIQN/07/21/navarrette.soccerA,.

19. Patrick Buchanan, "Anti-Americanism in LA," http://library.flaw-lesslogic.com/la.htm.

20. "Soccer, Mexico & the US Empire's Breakup," June 29, 2011, Southern Nationalist Network, http://southernnationalist.com/blog/2011/06/29/soccer-mexico-the-us-empires-breakup/.

21. David Roediger, *Wages of Whiteness: Race and the Making of the American Working Class* (London: Verso, 2007).

22. Interview with Hérculez Gómez by Michael Davies and Roger Bennett, *Men in Blazers,* Grantland Network Podcasts, March 19, 2013, http://espn.go.com/espnradio/grantiand/plaver?id=9073010,.

23. Dan Frosch, "Born in United States but Playing for Mexico," *The New York Times*, July 23, 2008.

24. Mark Zeigler, "Miguel Ponce: From San Ysidro to Brazil," *San Diego Union-Tribune*, June 8, 2014.

25. Mike Jensen, "Mexican Soccer Team Has American Accent, Half of the Improbable Women's World Cup Squad Comes from North of the Border," *Philadelphia Inquirer*, June 17, 1999; Grahame Jones, "Mexico Imports a U.S. Product," *Los Angeles Times*, August 28, 1998.

26. "USMNT, Mexico Supporters Groups Could Head to Court over World Cup Travel Plans," mlssoccer.com, http://www.mlssoccer.com/news/article/2013/10/18/usmnt-mexico- supporters-groups-could-head-court-over-world-cup-travel-plans.

27. www.panchovillasarmy.com.

28. Noah Davis, "Pancho Villa's Army," http://www.sportsonearth.com/article/54475946/, July 24, 2013.

29. Varela Hernandez, account of Mexico game at South Africa World Cup 2010, in Peter Alegi and Chris Bolsmann, eds., *Africa's World Cup: Critical Reflections on Play, Patriotism, Spectatorship, and Space* (Ann Arbor: University of Michigan Press, 2013).

30. "Michael Orozco Rooting for Mexico," espnfc.com, October 17, 2013, http://espnfc.com/news/story/ /id/1585876/ us-michael-orozco-savs-rooting-mexico?cc=5901,.

31. Juan Flores, "Reclaiming Left Baggage: Some Early Sources for Minority Studies," *Cultural Critique* 59 (Winter 2005): 187–206.

"MUST I BE A PATRIOT TO PLAY BALL?"

Latinas/os, Muslims, and Showing "Respect" for America

Roberto Sirvent
Hope International University

IN 2004, WHEN PUERTO RICAN baseball player Carlos Delgado refused to stand during the playing of "God Bless America," he was met with two especially notable, and similar, responses. One came from Major League Baseball commissioner Bud Selig. The other arose from Jeff Wilpon, son of Fred Wilpon, CEO and owner of the New York Mets, the team for which Delgado played at the time. Delgado had been protesting the hymn for quite some time, choosing to sit in the dugout quietly during the seventh-inning ritual. His dissent had gone largely unnoticed. Delgado was a critic of the Iraq War, calling it "the stupidest war ever," and had earlier objected to the USA's turning the small Puerto Rican island of Vieques into a bomb-testing ground. "They lived in that target practice area for 60 years," Delgado said, referring to accounts from island residents. "They tell you stories of how, in the middle of the night, a bomb blew up. I never experienced it, but I can imagine it. I can see why you might be a little hostile from time to time."[1]

Selig, who had required all teams to play "God Bless America" after the 9/11 attacks, responded cautiously. "I'm in the process of getting more information, but eventually I would like to sit down and discuss it with Carlos," he said. "I am very sensitive to this kind of issue, both as a matter of respect for our country and for one's right to express his opinion."[2] Selig was not the only one who framed this protest in terms of "respect" for the United States. The New York Mets organization followed suit, with Jeff Wilpon relaying a message from his father: "Fred has asked and I've asked him to respect what the country wants to do."[3] Here, both Selig and Wilpon interpret Delgado's refusal to stand for the playing of "God Bless America" as a sign of disrespect towards his nation. While neither of them claim that participating in such rituals is the *only* or *best* way to honor America, they are clear about two things: participating in the ritual is a matter of *respect*, and refusal to participate is a matter of *disrespect*.

Delgado's protest — and the reaction that followed — is reminiscent of another story of anti-militaristism dissent enacted by a black athlete. During the 1995–1996 NBA basketball season, Mahmoud Abdul-Rauf refused to participate in the acknowledgment of the pre-game national anthem.[4] Rather than stand and salute the American flag, he instead spent the time stretching or placing his hands on his side. He would even avoid looking at the flag, later saying he found a contradiction between being Muslim on the one hand and venerating the American flag on the other. It should come as no surprise that many people saw this as a tremendous sign of disrespect to America. Terrell Stokes, a Muslim and freshman point guard at the University of Maryland, was quick to condemn Abdul-Rauf's actions. "I think he should stand up for the flag, to respect the flag because we live in this country," he said. "The flag doesn't have anything to do with religion."[5] In the midst of this uproar, a reporter directly confronted Abdul-Rauf about his actions: "How can you do this? Don't you realize the flag is a symbol for freedom and democracy throughout the world?" Abdul-Rauf swiftly responded. "It may be a symbol of freedom and democracy to some," he said, "but it's a symbol of tyranny and oppression to others."[6]

After receiving a short suspension, Abdul-Rauf reached an agreement with the NBA where he would be required to stand for the national anthem but could bow his head and recite a Muslim prayer to himself. A statement read on his behalf by one of his representatives indicates the NBA's central concern with Abdul-Rauf's actions: "My intentions were not in any way to be *disrespectful* to those who regard the national anthem as a sacred ceremony. I am an African American, a citizen of this country and one who respects freedom of speech and freedom of expression."[7] But to conclude that this matter was (somehow) resolved is to ignore the myriad ways that dissenting actions are regularly policed and punished in professional sport leagues. According to sportswriter Dave Zirin, despite the apparent reconciliation between Abdul-Rauf and the NBA, "the clock was on for him to be drummed out of the league."[8]

In this chapter, I examine the rhetoric of "respect" used when criticizing athletes who refuse to participate in their sport's patriotic and militaristic rituals. Because non-patriotic athletes and fans are often scolded for not showing "respect" for America or its flag, it is worth questioning — or at least complicating — how the term functions. By analyzing the Delgado and Abdul-Rauf controversies alongside each other, I argue that the rhetoric of respect not only serves to condemn someone as un-American (or not a *true* American) but also obscures the deceptive nature of US imperial and militaristic propaganda.[9] In other words, to demand "respect" for America and its flag is to overlook questions such as: "Are America, its flag, and its anthem even *worthy* of respect?" and "What is the line between respect and worship?"

I address and respond to each question below. First, I attempt to demonstrate that the United States may not in fact be worthy of the kind of respect demanded by its patriots. By contesting claims that "who we are" as a nation is a beacon of freedom, equality, and democracy, I suggest that the reality is a bit darker. More to the point, I argue that "respecting" the American flag simultaneously entails *disrespecting* all the victims of state-inflicted violence done in its name. Second, I draw on political theorists and religious studies scholars to show how the language of respect is actually a secularized rhetorical attempt to claim that a particular athlete or fan is not only refusing to "respect" the nation-state, s/he is refusing to *worship* it. I conclude by using the story of Sebastien De La Cruz, the eleven-year-old Mexican American who gained fame by singing the national anthem at a San Antonio Spurs game, to explain why the Latina/o sport community should not celebrate this kind of "inclusion" and "diversifying" at pre- and in-game militaristic rituals. Rather, what should be embraced, anticipated, and fought for is the end of American militarism itself.

As the reader will note, this chapter could not be timelier. Because of the events that have transpired since Colin Kaepernick's anthem protest in 2016, I make it a point throughout to connect the Delgado and Abdul-Rauf controversies to debates around the NFL player protests.

As we engage the complex intersections of race, nationality, and even religion, I offer a quick note of clarity. In no way do I suggest that Latinas/os, Muslims, and African Americans deal with the exact same tensions and struggles in navigating what "American-ness" looks like for them. After all, each group has its own histories and narratives of oppression inflicted upon them by the "land of the free." Moreover, there is a large number of Afro-Latinas/os, black Muslims, and Latina/o Muslims, so none of these groups are mutually exclusive of one another. And while many people of color in this country find it repugnant to salute the American flag or ask for God's unique blessing when attending sporting events, I do not claim that *all* people of a particular racial group resist the state's imperial propaganda. As I will discuss in this chapter, it is equally important to observe and analyze the diversity of thought and practice *within* these communities, especially when some of its members see no irreconcilable conflict between their racial or religious identity (e.g., black or Muslim) and their American one. In Carlos Delgado's case, for example, we will see that one of his harshest critics was fellow Latino Ozzie Guillén.

Last, and briefly, it is important to place these acts of resistance in their proper context. Many of us are familiar with the courageous actions of African American athletes John Carlos and Tommie Smith at the 1968 Olympics (on the podium, both raised black-gloved fists as the national anthem played during the medal ceremony). Fewer people are familiar with the words written by Jackie Robinson in his autobiography: "I cannot stand and sing the anthem. I cannot salute the flag; I know that I am a black man in a white world. In 1972, in 1947, at my birth in 1919, I know that I never had it made."[10] And even fewer fans are aware that the history of anthem protests by athletes begins with track star Eroseanna Robinson in 1959.[11] Ever since then — consciously or not — athletes engaged in anti-war and anti-imperial activism have just been following her lead.

IS AMERICA WORTHY OF RESPECT?

When the NFL passed a policy in May 2018 threatening to fine teams if their players refused to stand and show "respect" for the American flag, critics of the policy approached the controversy from many angles. Some commentators claimed that even though players were allowed to remain in the locker room during the singing of the anthem, it was nonetheless another instance of the NFL engaging in "forced patriotism." Other critics claimed that *true* patriotism involves the right to protest injustices that controvert the perceived "ideals" of America. Still others claimed that the protests never had anything to do with patriotism, the flag, the military, or the anthem, despite the fact that Colin Kaepernick clearly stated otherwise: "I am not going to stand up to *show pride in a flag for a country* that oppresses black people and people of color," he said. "To me, this is bigger than football and it would be selfish on my part to look the other way. There are bodies in the street and people getting paid leave and getting away with murder."[12] Finally, and not surprisingly, critics of the NFL's new rule claimed that the US military fought to protect the very right the NFL protesters are trying to exercise.

One of the most perceptive yet underreported criticisms of the NFL policy pointed to the U.S. Flag Code to show that the league actually does not care at all about showing "respect" to the flag. According to this code, the NFL, its teams, and its fans have been showing "disrespect" for the flag for years. For example, the code clearly states that "the flag should never be used as wearing apparel, bedding, or drapery" and "the flag should never be used for advertising purposes in any way whatsoever."[13] This might come as a shock to NFL teams that print the American flag on its team jerseys, and for team executives who exploit their fans' jingoism to maximize profit. Interestingly, while such practices might be good for a business's bottom line, they are strictly condemned as a sign of disrespect in the U.S. Flag Code. What the code does *not* consider disrespectful, however, is kneeling.

Framing the debate in terms of "respecting" or "disrespecting" is a common reaction to player protests. In 2005, in what was largely considered a direct response to the "unpatriotic" actions of Carlos Delgado, Venezuela-born manager (and former player) Ozzie Guillén imposed a $500 fine on any one of his players who failed to acknowledge the national anthem. In an interview with *Sports Illustrated*, he explained, "If you're not from this country, you should respect the anthem even more than Americans because you should feel pleased you're here. And if you're from this country, you should have respect for people who are dying for it."[14] The same rhetoric is often employed against Muslim Americans. Consider journalist Jason DeWitt, who wrote an article about fans being "outraged" at Dion Waiters, a Muslim ballplayer for the Miami Heat and formerly for the Cleveland Cavaliers. Waiters had caused uproar when he chose to sit in the locker room while the national anthem played. "One would think Waiters would have some respect for a nation that has made his success possible," DeWitt writes. "That was clearly not the case — due to his 'Islamic faith,' which for some reason apparently supersedes respect for America."[15]

The rhetoric of "respect" too quickly assumes that "America," its flag, and its anthem are in fact worthy of respect. But why is America worthy of respect? If we concur with Guillén, DeWitt, and the millions of others who share their patriotic sensibilities, it is probably for a whole host of reasons. Kevin Scholla, a journalist for *Breitbart*, hits on some of the most common reasons in a single article, conveniently titled, "Sports Fans Must Show More Respect for National Anthem." Fed up with fans who leave their hats on, talk, or remain seated for the national anthem, Scholla writes, "[F]or whatever reason some people just can't stand still and shut their mouths for 120 seconds to honor the greatest nation ever known to man."[16]

Scholla appreciates the fact that most people at sporting events will salute the flag and have their hands on their hearts. But, he laments, "there will be the disrespectful sprinkled throughout each and every section, no matter the event, state, or venue." He continues:

> It's bad enough when people refuse to stand for "religious reasons." You can live and work in this country and reap all of its incredible benefits, but rising for a couple of minutes would be outrageous apparently. Then you have the Occupy Wall Street types. They're not usually at the ball park, but they are very often at political events. They don't stand because America to them is evil or oppressing or some other manufactured nonsense designed to give them something to think about other than what sheets to use in mom's basement later that night. Perhaps the worst offenders though are those who deep down are ordinary Americans. The disrespect for our flag, our veterans, and our country as a whole, seems to come not from malice but from laziness.[17]

Scholla is not finished yet. He doubles down on his claim that refusing to participate in the national anthem is a sign of disrespect to our troops. He says that "brave veterans" can spot fans who refuse to properly honor their nation and that someone "who selflessly fought for us and likely lost friends overseas is met with complete disregard from those who are oh so spoiled." Scholla later praises Sarah Palin's remarks about the chills that run down her spine whenever she hears the Star-Spangled Banner. He then holds her up as a model of someone who has "a healthy appreciation for our exceptionalism." Eager to end on a high note, Scholla leaves his readers with some helpful advice: "Stand up, put your hand on your heart, look at our beautiful flag for two minutes, and remember all of those who sacrificed for our precious freedom."[18]

But showing "respect" for the national anthem is problematic for many Americans, especially given that the anthem, written by slave owner Francis Scott Key, celebrates slavery and US militarism.[19] It is also troubling when team managers, coaches, media pundits, and even President Donald Trump equate showing "respect" for America with showing *gratitude* for America. In their estimation, players should be "grateful" for living in a country that pays them millions of dollars for playing with a ball. But as comedian Samantha Bee observes, rhetoric of "gratefulness" has a haunting history. "Hey, wow, and what a conversation we're having," she quipped. "Talking about black people and their owners and how they should be grateful for the privilege of working on a field. Who says Trump is taking us backward?"[20]

Delgado and Abdul-Rauf strongly objected to claims that the US is a beacon of freedom or, as Scholla put it, "the greatest nation ever known to man." If Delgado is right about the "stupidity" of the Iraq War and the destruction caused by the American military involvement in Vieques, then the United States is probably *not* the greatest nation ever known. At least not to Iraqis or Puerto Ricans. Similarly, when Abdul-Rauf asserted that the American flag might be a symbol of freedom and democracy to some privileged white Americans but that it is a symbol of tyranny and oppression to others, he was contesting any notion that the United States can possibly deliver freedom with bombs and military occupation.

Delgado and Abdul-Rauf are neither naive, deceived, nor historically ignorant. Nor are they alone in their critiques. Noam Chomsky, for example, one of the fiercest critics of American foreign policy, was interviewed about US immigration policy. "People in Central America and Mexico, people are fleeing to the United States," he says. "Why? Because we destroyed their societies. They don't want to live in the United States. They want to live at home."[21] Another vocal critic of US imperialism, Glenn Greenwald, has written extensively on the USA's militaristic campaigns and policy against Muslims. Citing an article by Andrew Bacevich, Greenwald examines how the United States has invaded, occupied, or bombed *fourteen* Muslim countries since 1980. Greenwald is quick to point out that this "count excludes the bombing and occupation of still other predominantly Muslim countries by key US allies such as Israel and Saudi Arabia, carried out with crucial American support." Also excluded, he adds, are the "coups against democratically elected governments, torture, and imprisonment of people with no charges."[22] If these charges are taken seriously, it is hard to argue why the United States — the country that an international Gallup poll found to be the number one greatest threat to world peace — is so worthy of our salutes, songs, and cheers.[23]

To be clear, I am not attempting to *prove* that America, its flag, and its anthem are unworthy of respect. Such a daunting task does very little to persuade the "true believer" that America is far from a force for good in this world. Moreover, the term "America" is itself a contested concept, so its meaning and symbolic import vary across different segments of the US population. My goals are much more modest. What I hope to do instead is show (albeit briefly) why the United States is seen by many (domestically and internationally) as a nation unworthy of the type of respect and veneration demanded by Delgado's and Abdul-Rauf's critics. More important, I hope to show that athletes like Delgado and Abdul-Rauf have *good reason* to protest the veneration of the United States and its flag. Public criticism of Delgado's and Abdul-Rauf's actions reveals the many contradictions and ideological blind spots that undergird the American patriotic imagination.

Moreover, this is not an attempt to demonstrate that American patriots are somehow stupid for not knowing about America's history of slavery, Indigenous genocide, or terrorizing Latin America and the Middle East but to show that ideology is crafty, and that many forces are at play to form in American professional sport what Lisa Lowe calls "the politics of our lack of knowledge."[24] In other words, it is not that Ivy League graduates who run the White House and State Department are *dumb*; rather, these highly educated people interpret histories through various ideological lenses, with American nationalism, exceptionalism, and innocence being just a few examples. These ideologies play a significant role in distorting how America's military actions around the world are remembered, ignored, or justified.

Obviously, not *all* Americans know about US foreign policy in Latin America and the Middle East. There are plenty of people who do not have the slightest idea of the US doing any real harm to other countries, or that the West's most reputable polling agency found that the United States — not Iran, North Korea, or Russia — is the greatest threat to world peace. Part of this might be ignorance, but much of it is also due to the success of American propaganda (aided, of course, by the US corporate media). After all, the nation-state's project of cultivating patriotic citizens involves the selecting, deselecting, hiding, and eliding of histories — what Lisa Lowe calls "the economy of affirmation and forgetting."[25] For those who *are* unaware of, say, US foreign policy in Latin America and the Middle East, settler colonialism, slavery and its afterlives, America's use of torture and terror around the globe, its massive income inequality and criminalization of the poor, and its policing and caging of black and brown bodies, then perhaps this chapter might be helpful to the open-minded sports fan. But an open mind is not the only thing necessary to begin resisting the state's use of professional sporting events to support its militaristic goals. Narratives of progress, along with claims to the exceptional moral stature of the United States, are as seductive as they are crafty. And to most Americans, they are nearly impossible to let go.

Patriots who dismiss these actions as mistakes and aberrations, or who refuse to see them as accurate representations of what America *really* stands for — that is, liberty, equality, and democracy — run against a host of scholars who view such violence and oppression as *constitutive* of American identity, not a radical departure from it.[26] "The patriotic narrative delivered at school," writes legal scholar Dean Spade, "tells us a few key lies of US law and politics." Among them are:

> that the United States is a democracy in which law and policy derive from what a majority of people think is best, that the United States used to be racist and sexist but is now fair and neutral thanks to changes in the law, and that if particular groups experience harm, they can appeal to the law for protection. Social movements have challenged this narrative, identifying the United States as a settler colony and a racial project, founded and built through genocide and enslavement.[27]

Contrary to how critics of Delgado and Abdul-Rauf view the American narrative of social progress, cultural theorists and students of social movements notice the violence deeply embedded within the structure of the state. Such theorists, Spade argues, have "been essential for exposing the central harms faced by native people, women, people of color, people with disabilities, and immigrants." Moreover, he adds, they expose "that state programs and law enforcement are not the arbiters of justice, protection, and safety but are instead sponsors and sites of violence."[28]

So what of the "freedom" that so many sports commentators claim is represented in our anthems and flag? Not only do many scholars complicate the USA's reputation as a "land of the free" and offer a counter-narrative of the supposed "freedoms" that it spreads around the nation and globe, they also question anyone who responds to America's "misdeeds" by saying, "Well, I'm not respecting what the United States *does*; I'm respecting what the United States *stands for*." The assumption here is that any alleged injustice by the United States is tragic and maybe even wrong, but that it is not who we *really* are. This is, no doubt, an expedient way to interpret and understand US actions around the world. It is also a convenient way to look at the violence that the state brings to its own communities every day. Writing about the American prison regime, for example, Dylan Rodriguez observes, "Brutality, torture, and excess should be understood as an essential element of American statecraft, not its corruption or deviation."[29]

State violence does not grant us our freedoms nor, as many Americans believe, do our troops fight for our rights.[30] But these are myths we are told. And these myths are recited in our national hymns. This practice fuels many accusations towards resisters of US militarism that in refusing to pledge allegiance to the flag, they are essentially *dis*respecting the troops. The most obvious reply is that refusing to sing the national anthem is not a sign of disrespect; what *is* disrespectful to the troops is sending them to die and kill for the narrow strategic and economic interests of the elite few. The narrative that the US fights wars for humanitarian reasons, or to protect our rights and security, is quite problematic.[31] "The fundamental reason why countries invade other countries, or seek forcibly to depose their governments, has not changed over the course of history," Steven Kinzer writes. "It is the same reason children fight in schoolyards. The stronger one wants what the weaker one has."[32]

The US wants us to imagine that our wars are fought for the causes of rights and liberty, that *those* are the ideals for which its soldiers are risking their lives. But soldiers do not die and kill for our rights.

And they do not die and kill for our freedom. They fight to pursue the goals of American foreign policy, which are strictly strategic, economic, and imperial in nature. As Charles Tilly writes,

> [A] portrait of war makers and state makers as coercive and self-seeking entrepreneurs bears a far greater resemblance to the facts than do its chief alternatives: the idea of a social contract, the idea of an open market in which operators of armies and states offer services to willing customers, the idea of a society whose shared norms and expectations call forth a certain kind of government.[33]

Of course, the state could not garner any kind of support, allegiance, or "respect" if it was candid and forthright about its true military objectives. It understands, cleverly, that a different narrative must be told to get its citizens on board.

This shrewd ideological sleight of hand is captured perfectly in a *House of Cards* episode where First Lady Claire Underwood is attempting to negotiate with an Islamist detainee from Guantanamo:

CLAIRE: "You're a well-educated man, Yusuf, and you don't care about Islam or the caliphate. You're just using that to radicalize soldiers."

YUSUF: "Just as you use democracy and freedom."

CLAIRE: "So now we understand each other."[34]

Contrary to what the corporate media would have us believe, it is the *state* that disrespects the troops, not those who refuse to stand for the national anthem. Thankfully, many US veterans are aware of the state's true motives, which explains the rise of the anti-war group Veterans for Peace. After all, it makes sense that some of the most vocal and insightful critics of US foreign policy come from within the military ranks. To give one example, Iraq War veteran Vincent Emanuele describes Veterans Day as "one of the most hollow and absurd holidays in American society." He writes, "Unless you have stock in Lockheed Martin or Goldman Sachs, there's really no reason to thank me for my 'service.' We destroyed Iraq and killed innocent people. We mutilated dead bodies and tortured prisoners. And we did it all for geopolitical and corporate interests."[35] Thus, the country's ruling class attempts to deceive soldiers — and us — about its true military aims. Professional sporting events are therefore more than just sites for radicalizing fans to root and purchase jerseys for their home team. They have also become a prime place for the US to radicalize its citizens to fight and die for it.[36]

The debates raised above aim to trouble certain assumptions that America, its flag, and its anthem are actually worthy of respect. Critics of people like Delgado and Abdul-Rauf claim that Americans should respect the benefits offered by the state, the values it represents, and the freedoms that our soldiers die and kill for. In short, athletes and fans should respect *who we are as a country*. But what if *who we are* is *not* a nation grounded in liberty, equality, and democracy? What if our *true* values, as evidenced not by what the US says but actually *does*, are settler colonialism, oppression, imperialism, and anti-black racism? As Keisha Blain so masterfully chronicles in her book *Set the World on Fire*, many Black nationalists of the early twentieth century viewed the US as "irredeemably racist" and therefore held little hope that the American concept of "freedom" would ever apply to them.[37] So what if *who we are* as a nation is not what we have been told at our public schools and professional ball games? What if the truth about who we are is much darker and more sinister? What if our state is *not* worthy of a salute?

I close this section by sharing Dave Zirin's reaction to Ozzie Guillén's policy of fining his players $500 for refusing to stand for the national anthem. After reading Guillén's interview with *Sports Illustrated*, Zirin reflected on his time as a public school teacher:

> When I taught in DC public schools, I made sure my class knew that they had a choice when it came to saying the Pledge of Allegiance. It seemed obscene to require my students to stand and salute the flag, when many of them came here as refugees from El Salvador, Guatemala, and Colombia, precisely to escape the dirty wars brought to them by Great Flag Waving Americans like John Negroponte, Oliver North, and Ronald Reagan....For me, the national anthem belongs at sporting events about as much as Trent Lott belongs at the Million Man March. The US is alone in the world in regularly asking its sports fans to stand as one and salute a flag. This is garbage. Sports should be a patriotism-free zone. We are watching players from the US, Latin America, and increasingly Asia, hit baseballs made in Costa Rica and field in gloves made in

Taiwan. The only purpose served by the national anthem is to remind the many nationalities in the stands and on the field exactly whose foot stands internationally on their collective neck.[38]

RESPECT OR WORSHIP?

But let us assume for a moment that America, its flag, and its anthem *are* worthy of respect. What makes a nation-state worthy of *this kind of* respect: the singing of songs, the hand over the heart, the saluting of troops, the dying and killing? Do these not seem like rather odd ways of showing mere *respect* towards something? When we think of showing respect towards the grocery store attendant, we think of making pleasant conversation, looking her in the eye, perhaps even shaking her hand. When we talk of paying respect towards our telephone company, we think of paying our bills on time and refraining from using expletives when voicing complaints to customer "service" attendants. But equating a telephone company to the nation-state seems like an unfair comparison, right? Not according to political theorist Alasdair MacIntyre, who makes this exact comparison:

> The modern nation-state, in whatever guise, is a dangerous and unmanageable institution, presenting itself on the one hand as a bureaucratic supplier of goods and services, which is always about to, but never actually does, give its clients value for money, and on the other hand as a repository of sacred values, which from time to time invites one to lay down one's life on its behalf....[I]t is like being asked to die for the telephone company.[39]

To die or kill for the telephone company seems quite preposterous on its face. But such acts are regarded as entirely appropriate when performed for the nation-state. So what explains this attachment? How did we come to regard the nation-state as something that demands and deserves our sacrifice?

Legal theorist Paul Kahn argues that a unique theology has captured the imaginations, hearts, and bodies of American citizens. "The serious claim of political theology," he writes, "is not that that the secular should yield to the church — whatever church that might be — but rather that the state is not the secular arrangement it purports to be."[40] Kahn joins a host of scholars who expose the theological concepts and power plays involved in what Elizabeth Shakman Hurd calls "the politics of secularism."[41] If Kahn is right that state allegiance is not just a matter of theory but *theology*, then what exactly is being demanded of fans at professional sporting events: respect or *worship*? Before patriots too quickly dismiss this as an unfair accusation — that they are involved in something more than respect — it is worth consulting Francis Bellamy's original intent behind writing the Pledge of Allegiance. Explaining how, in the words of William Cavanaugh, "The pledge was meant to sink into schoolchildren through ritual repetition," Bellamy admitted: "It's the same way with the catechism, or the Lord's Prayer."[42]

The rhetoric of respect, then, is best seen as a secularized attempt to disguise what's really going on — worship.[43] Hymns, songs, flags, B-2 bombers, more songs, more flags, *bigger* flags. The presence of all these serves to further the American theological project, all in the language of paying "respect" to it. "In a crisis, it remains true today that the secular state does not hesitate to speak of sacrifice, patriotism, nationalism and homeland in the language of the sacred," Kahn writes. "The state's territory becomes consecrated ground, its history a sacred duty to maintain, its flag something to die for."[44] Indeed, this is not a matter of *mere* respect to a *mere* country or a *mere* flag. It is *not*, as many patriots claim when they scold those sitting out the anthem, *just a song*.

Obviously it is *not* just a song. If "God Bless America" or the national anthem were *just* songs, then refusing to respect them would not cause such uproar and calls for athletes to leave the country. This "love it or leave it" attitude is easier to understand if we consider that the object or concept at hand (e.g., nation, flag, freedom) is no mundane thing; it is a god. The same offense and threats would hardly result from someone refusing to stand for "Take Me Out to the Ballgame." Baseball is not one's god (at least we hope not), so refusing to sing its time-honored tune is not akin to dishonoring a deity. If anything, the fan who refuses to sing along to "Take Me Out to the Ballgame" might be accused of being a buzzkill or a party-pooper, but not a heretic.

Former NBA great Hakeem Olajuwon knew perfectly well that a fine line existed between respect and worship. During the Abdul-Rauf controversy, he urged Muslim athletes to distinguish between the two. Claiming that singing the national anthem *does not* go against the teaching of the Koran, Olajuwon said, "It's so important that people understand that there is a difference between respect and worship." He added, "People who worship the flag should also understand that there is a difference."[45] So while Olajuwon argues that he does not see any inherent conflict between Islam and singing the national anthem, he does admit that it *is* possible to worship the flag. It just appears that Olajuwon has found a way to pay respect to the flag without crossing the line to worship. While I do not attempt to contest Olajuwon's claim that allegiance to America and Islam are compatible (being insufficiently familiar with Islamic theology to properly address this issue), I do wish to contest his notion that these rituals are not fundamentally (or usually) about worship.

A common response to this accusation might come from an atheist sports fan who responds, "All I'm doing is singing a song and removing my hat. I don't really believe the United States is God. What nonsense! I don't have a god; I'm an atheist!" A similar response might come from a Christian sports fan who says, "I'm not worshipping the flag. I'm a Christian! But God gave me this country and it's part of God's mission on this earth to spread freedom!" But such reactions, according to theologian William Cavanaugh, hang on a substantivist view of religion, one that sees religion as the substance of one's *beliefs* (i.e., "I don't really *believe* that money, reason, my country, or the flag is really a god"). But, Cavanaugh argues, if you are going to assess whether something is being worshipped, a functionalist approach — how something might *function* as a god — might be more appropriate:

> A functionalist says it makes no difference if he thinks it is a metaphor or not; what matters is the way he behaves, that is, the way free market ideology actually functions in his life. If it walks like a duck and quacks like a duck, it is a duck. If it acts like a religion, it is a religion. If people pledge allegiance to a flag, salute it, ritually raise and lower it and are willing to kill and die for it, it does not much matter if they acknowledge it is only a piece of cloth and not a god.

To paint a more complete picture and critique of idolatry, Cavanaugh refers to the Bible:

> [T]he problem of idolatry is not one of belief but of behavior. Idolatry is not so much a metaphysical error as misplaced

loyalty, a lack of trust in the one true God. In the First Book of Samuel the Lord equates the Israelites' request for a king with serving other gods, for they have rejected the Lord from being king over them (8:7–8). Isaiah accuses the Israelites of putting their trust in horses and chariots — military might, in other words — rather than the Lord (31:1–3). Jesus says we must choose between two masters, God and wealth (Mt 6:24). Paul warns the Philippians of those for whom "their god is their bellies" (3:19). Such people presumably do not believe that a deity resides in their breadbasket....[I]dolatry is not mistakenly believing that something mundane is a god, but rather devoting one's resources and energies and life to serving something that is not God. Whether or not one claims to believe in the biblical God is not the crucial point.[46]

In other words, the nation-state does not really care if it can get us to assent to a particular *belief* about it. It wants our heart, our allegiances. The state's goal is not to get us to *believe* that the US or Freedom or Democracy is an actual god. It just wants us to *treat it* as such.

Of course, this is not to say that *everyone* who sings along to the national anthem at a sporting event is worshipping the state. I remain confident that some people, like Olajuwon, have found ways to stand yet still resist its worship. I even had a friend recently tell me that he is as anti-patriotic as anyone could be, but he still stands and removes his cap while the anthem is played at a baseball game. When I asked him why, he said, "So I don't get beat up in the parking lot afterward." This approach seems rather justifiable. What I do argue, however, is that many of us deceive ourselves into thinking that *all* we are doing in these rituals is merely "respecting" the country we live in, that we do not really believe that the United States or its flag is a god. But if Cavanaugh is right — that what truly matters is not what we *believe* but what we *do* — and if we are willing to give our bodies *to* and *for* it, then, in the words of George W. Bush, Mission Accomplished.

CONCLUSION

In June 2013 the San Antonio Spurs invited 11-year-old Mexican American Sebastien De La Cruz to sing the national anthem at their NBA Finals game against the Miami Heat. His performance was met with various racial slurs and accusations from people around the

United States that he was here illegally. The racist attacks were rightly condemned. Later, in 2016, De La Cruz was invited by Univision and *The Washington Post* to sing the national anthem at a Democratic Primary Debate.[47]

When addressing why this chapter should be of interest to scholars of Latinas/os in sport, perhaps the first implication is that the Latina/o community be more cautious in what they choose to celebrate, even if it is an uncommonly talented 11-year-old singing the national anthem. Yes, the racist slurs leveled against De La Cruz are inexcusable. They should be condemned. But so should the USA's militarism and imperialism that depends on these rituals to foster allegiance in its citizens. It is not "progress" when a Latina or Latino is included in the cast of those singing the national anthem at professional sporting events around the country. This inclusion or diversifying may seem like a step in the right direction for racial progress, but it simply adds, expands, and further glorifies US imperial actions at home and abroad. Thus, it should worry us even more when Sebastien De La Cruz is used and exploited by a political organization like the Democratic Party. We might recall that in response to Donald Trump's motto that we "Make America Great Again," Democratic presidential nominee Hillary Clinton could come up with nothing better (or more historically accurate) than "America has always been great." Is *this* the narrative that Latinas/os want to be "included" in? Is *this* the narrative we wish to tell?

To deepen our awareness of what Lisa Lowe calls the "violence of inclusion," it is equally important for Latinas/os to resist narratives of assimilation that accompany immigration debates.[48] Stories like De La Cruz's reinforce narratives of "good" immigrants and "bad" immigrants, even if De La Cruz is not an immigrant at all — he was born in Texas. Still, De La Cruz is deemed the ideal poster boy for the immigration rights movement since he can sing, he's light-skinned, his father served in the military, and he loves America. *This* is the kind of "immigrant" the Democratic Party wants. Hence the popular slogan used by immigration rights activists, many of whom are Latina/o: "We Are Not Criminals." But as Martha Escobar argues, "when we claim that immigrants are not criminals, the fundamental message is that immigrants are not black, or at least, that immigrants will not be 'another black problem.'"[49]

When Latinas/os instead are able to rally around the slogan "No One is Criminal," we will be forced to reappraise the values of citizenship itself, an institution that, as Raúl Al-qaraz Ochoa writes, "legitimizes the global capitalist order, as well as their borders and their nation states." He continues, "So when we talk about citizenship today, we should ask who/what benefits from the exploitation of an illegal class."[50] Thus, the goal is not to fight for "inclusion" in an imperial state but to fight for a world without borders at all.[51] At the very least, immigration rights activists should be careful not to be seduced by narratives of American exceptionalism, American innocence, and the ideologies with which they are associated.[52] As Tamara K. Nopper reminds us, "those committed to social justice have a formidable task: articulating the value and rights of the immigrant without relying on anti-black and pro-capitalist tropes."[53]

The attempt to use Sebastien De La Cruz to assimilate Latinas/os into the US imperial project is similar to the controversy that erupted around a photo that went viral depicting a woman wearing an American flag as her hijab, made from the same artwork as Barack Obama's "hope" poster. While liberals praised this photo as depicting the idea that "Muslim Americans are Americans too!" many Muslim Americans wanted nothing to do with it. In her article, "Please Keep Your American Flags Off My Hijab," fashion blogger Hoda Katebi writes, "The American flag represents oppression, torture, sexual violence, slavery, patriarchy, and military & cultural hegemony for people of color around the world whose homes and families have been destroyed and drone-striked by the very person/former president whose campaign images this one seeks to replicate."[54] It is no accident that Katebi's words echo how Abdul-Rauf perceived the American flag as a symbol of tyranny and oppression. Ultimately — and courageously — both reject any notion that America's so-called "values" are compatible with what Islam teaches them about justice, equality, and true liberation.

One last implication has to do with another way that athletes are exploited for nationalistic propaganda and the effects this has on the communities they represent.[55] The United States has a vested interest in making its outsiders (or its "others") think it is perfectly reasonable to stay true to their identities while also offering their public and lethal loyalty to America. In other words, when a high-profile Latina/o, Muslim, African American, Native American, or Asian American athlete stands up to honor and salute the American flag, it gives the state something — someone — to point to as the normative model of assimilating identities. "Hey, Puerto Rican community! If Carlos Delgado can pledge his allegiance to America, then maybe it's time you get over what we did to your island!" Or "Hey, Muslim Americans! If Mahmoud Abdul-Rauf can learn to see the American flag as a symbol of freedom and democracy — not tyranny and oppression — then you should too!" We might also imagine the patriotic practices of African American, Native American, or Asian American athletes being used to pressure other members of those groups to "let go of" the state-inflicted genocide, exploitation, and oppression that haunt their communities. "If *they* can bow down to the Red, White, and Blue," it is urged, "then surely *you* can too."

This chapter has not been an attempt to point the finger at one person, institution, league commissioner, politician, or even the state itself. As Dean Spade notes, referencing Michel Foucault, the most nuanced accounts of state violence understand "power is decentralized and that certain practices, ways of knowing, norms, and technologies of power are distributed in myriad ways rather than only a single person or institution."[56] The problems outlined above will not be solved if we all stopped paying homage to the American flag at professional sporting events. They will not be solved if one commissioner decides that forced patriotism should not be part of the seventh inning stretch. And they will not be solved if a basketball team stopped inviting 11-year-old Mexican American boys to sing the national anthem. The complicated path forward involves questioning our attachments to the nation-state; listening to those who refuse allegiance to it; examining the many ways in which we are complicit in US militarism and imperialism; and, perhaps most important of all, imagining and creating transnational solidarities with both victims and critics of US state violence. Only then will we be better positioned to dismantle oppressive ideologies that, in the words of Lisa Lowe, significantly shape "the limits of what can be thought and imagined."[57]

QUESTIONS:

1. Do you believe the national anthem should be played at professional sporting events? Why or why not?

2. In what ways do Afro-Latino athletes like Carlos Delgado face harsher criticism of their political protests than do non-Black Latinos?

3. In what ways do narratives of American exceptionalism and American innocence influence one's patriotic attitudes?

NOTES

1. William C. Rhoden, "Delgado Makes a Stand by Taking a Seat," Sports of the Times column, *New York Times*, July 21, 2004. http://www.nytimes.com/2004/07/21/sports/sports-of-the-times-delgado-makes-a-stand-by-taking-a-seat.html?_r=0

2. Ibid.

3. Dave Zirin, "The Silencing of Carlos Delgado," *The Nation*, December 7, 2005, https://www.thenation.com/article/silencing-carlos-delgado/

4. For an excellent overview of the Mahmoud Abdul-Rauf controversy, including how the politics of patriotism intersected with Islamophobia, US militarism, anti-Blackness, and ideologies of secularism, see Zareena Grewal, "Lights, Camera, Suspension: Freezing the Frame on the Mahmoud Abdul-Rauf-Anthem Controversy," *Souls: A Critical Journal of Black Politics, Culture, and Society* (2007) 9:2: 109–122.

5. Ken Denlinger, "Abdul-Rauf to Stand for National Anthem," *The Washington Post*, March 15, 1996, https://www.washingtonpost.com/archive/sports/1996/03/15/abdul-rauf-to-stand-for-anthem/c9bbaec8-792f-479d-ac64-394040b65089/

6. Kevin Patrick Kelly, "Dave Zirin on Muhammad Ali & How Athletes Raise Political Consciousness," MintPress News, June 28, 2016, https://www.mintpressnews.com/MyMPN/dave-zirin-muhammad-ali-athletes-raise-political-consciousness/

7. Jason Diamos, "Pro Basketball; Abdul-Rauf Vows Not to Back Down From NBA," *New York Times*, March 14, 1996. http://www.nytimes.com/1996/03/14/sports/pro-basketball-abdul-rauf-vows-not-to-back-down-from-nba.html (italics in text added).

8. Kelly, "Dave Zirin on Muhammad Ali."

9. Although Abdul-Rauf is not from the Middle East, it is worth reviewing Christopher Rivera's work on representation of Latinas/os and Middle Eastern Muslims as "Brown threats": Christopher Rivera, "The Brown Threat: Post-9/11 conflations of Latina/os and Middle Eastern Muslims in the US American Imagination," *Latino Studies* (2014), Vol. 12, 1: 44–64.

10. Evan F. Moore, "Baseball Historians Are Reminding Everyone of How Jackie Robinson Was Treated," *Chicago Sun-Times*, April 15, 2018, retrieved from: https://chicago.suntimes.com/sports/baseball-histori-ans-are-reminding-everyone-how-jackie-robinson-was-treated/. See Jackie Robinson, *I Never Had It Made: An Autobiography of Jackie Robinson* (New

York: Harper Collins, 1995).

11. Ashley Farmer, "Black Women Athletes, Protest, and Politics: An Interview with Amira Rose Davis," *Black Perspectives*, 14 (October 2016), retrieved from: https://www.aaihs.org/black-women-athletes-protest-and-politics-an-interview-with-amira-rose-davis/. See Amira Davis's forthcoming book, *"Can't Eat a Medal": The Lives and Labors of Black Women Athletes in the Age of Jim Crow*.

12. Steve Wyche, "Colin Kaepernick Explains Why He Sat during National Anthem," NFL *News*, August 27, 2016, retrieved from: http://www.nfl.com/news/story/0ap3000000691077/article/colin-kaepernick-explains-protest-of-national-anthem (emphasis in text added).

13. Sidra Javed, "Hey NFL, Selling Jerseys With US Flag Is Disrespectful. Kneeling Isn't," *Carbonated*.TV, May 24, 2018, retrieved from: https://www.carbonated.tv/viral/ex-nfl-player-jersey-american-flag-numbers-disrespect-code

14. Michael Farber, "The Wisdom of Ozzie," *Sports Illustrated*, May 16, 2005, http://www.si.com/vault/2005/05/16/8260839/the-wisdom-of-ozzie

15. Jason DeWitt, "NBA Player Refuses to Stand for the National Anthem – The Reason Why Has People Outraged," *Top Right News*, November 8, 2014. http://toprightnews.com/nba-player-refuses-to-stand-for-the-national-anthem-the-reason-why-has-people-outraged/

16. Kevin Scholla, "Sports Fans Must Show More Respect for National Anthem," *Breitbart*, May 20, 2013, http://www.breitbart.com/sports/2013/05/20/scholla-column-national-anthem/

17. Ibid.

18. Ibid.

19. Jon Schwarz, "Colin Kaepernick Is Righter Than You Know: The National Anthem Is a Celebration of Slavery," *The Intercept*, August 28, 2016, retrieved from: https://theintercept.com/2016/08/28/colin-kaepernick-is-righter-than-you-know-the-national-anthem-is-a-celebration-of-slavery/. See also Imani Perry, *May We Forever Stand: A History of the Black National Anthem* (Chapel Hill: University of North Carolina Press, 2018).

20. Lee Moran, "Samantha Bee Skewers Fox News' Hypocrisy over NFL Protests," *Huffington Post*, September 28, 2017, https://www.huffingtonpost.com/entry/samantha-bee-nfl-protests-fox news_us_59cc9828e4b-05063fe0f2276. For a great discussion on the continuities between slavery and other forms of domination today, especially in the field of sports, see Steven W. Thrasher, "Super Slaves," *Radical History Review* (2016) 125: 168–178.

21. "Noam Chomsky on Organizing for a Next System," *Truthout*, April

19, 2016, http://www.truth-out.org/opinion/item/35691-noam-chomsky-on-organizing-for-a-next-system. For accounts of US policy in Latin America, see Cecilia Menjívar and Néstor Rodríguez, eds., *When States Kill: Latin America, the U.S. and Technologies of Terror* (Austin: University of Texas Press, 2005); Jean Franco, *Cruel Modernity* (Durham, NC: Duke University Press, 2013); Lars Shoultz, *Beneath the United States: A History of U.S. Policy toward Latin America* (Cambridge: Harvard University Press, 1998); and Stephen Kinzer, *Overthrow: America's Century of Regime Change from Hawaii to Iraq* (New York: Times Books, 2006).

22. Glenn Greenwald, "How Many Muslim Countries Has the U.S. Bombed or Occupied Since 1980?" *The Intercept*, November 6, 2014, https://theintercept.com/2014/11/06/many-countries-islamic-world-u-s-bombed-occupied-since-1980/; see Andrew J. Bacevich, "Even If We Defeat the Islamic State We'll Still Lose the Bigger War," *Washington Post*, October 3, 2014, https://www.washingtonpost.com/opinions/even-if-we-defeat-the-islamic-state-well-still-lose-the-bigger-war/2014/10/03/e8c0585e-4353-11e4-b47c-f5889e061e5f_story.html

23. "Noam Chomsky: Why America is the Gravest Threat to World Peace," *Alternet*, August 20, 2015, http://www.alternet.org/noam-chomsky-why-america-gravest-threat-world-peace

24. Lisa Lowe, *The Intimacies of Four Continents* (Durham, NC: Duke University Press, 2015), 39.

25. Ibid., 3.

26. See for example Saidiya Hartman, *Scenes of Subjection: Terror, Slavery, and Self-Making in Nineteenth Century America* (New York: Oxford University Press, 1997); Lowe, *The Intimacies of Four Continents*; Moon-Kie Jung, João H. Costa Vargas, Eduardo Bonilla-Silva, eds., *State of White Supremacy: Racism, Governance, and the United States* (Stanford: Stanford University Press, 2011); Patrick Wolfe, "Settler Colonialism and the Elimination of the Native," *Journal of Genocide Research* (December 2006), 8(4): 387–409; Randall Williams, *The Divided World: Human Rights and Its Violence* (Minneapolis: University of Minnesota Press, 2010); Aziz Rana, *The Two Faces of American Freedom* (Cambridge: Harvard University Press, 2010).

27. Dean Spade, *Normal Life: Administrative Violence, Critical Trans Politics, & the Limits of Law* (Durham, NC: Duke University Press, 2015), 2.

28. Ibid.

29. Dylan Rodriguez, *Forced Passages: Imprisoned Radical Intellectuals and the U.S. Prison Regime* (Minneapolis: University of Minnesota Press, 2006), 47.

30. See Charles W. Mills, *The Racial Contract* (Ithaca: Cornell University Press, 1997); Chandan Reddy, *Freedom With Violence: Race, Sexuality, and the US State* (Durham, NC: Duke University Press, 2011).

31. See Kinzer, *Overthrow*.

32. Ibid., 321.

33. Charles Tilly, "War Making and State Making as Organized Crime," in *Bringing the State Back In*, Peter B. Evans, Dietrich Rueschemeyer, and Theda Skocpol, eds., (Cambridge: Cambridge University Press, 1985), 169; quoted in William Cavanaugh, *The Myth of Religious Violence: Secular Ideology and the Roots of Modern Conflict* (Oxford: Oxford University Press, 2009), 177.

34. *House of Cards*, Season 4, Episode 13, Director: Jakob Verbruggen, Performers: Robin Wright, Farshad Farahat, Netflix, 2016.

35. Vincent Emanuele, "Veterans Day in Trump's America," *CounterPunch*, November 11, 2016, retrieved from: https://www.counter-punch.org/2016/11/11/veterans-day-in-trumps-america/. For a detailed study of "Lockheed Martin's campaign to scare us into spending more on defense," see William D. Hartung, *Prophets of War: Lockheed Martin and the Making of the Military-Industrial Complex* (New York: Nation Books, 2012), 270.

36. See Mia Fischer, "Commemorating 9/11 NFL-Style: Insights into America's Culture of Militarism," *Journal of Sport and Social Issues*, 38:1 (2014): 199–221; Michael Silk, *The Cultural Politics of Post-9/11 Sport: Power, Pedagogy, and the Popular* (New York: Routledge, 2012); M. Butterworth and S.D. Moskal, "American Football, Flags, and 'Fun': The Bell Helicopter Armed Forces Bowl and the Rhetorical Production of Militarism," *Communication, Culture & Critique* (2009), 2(4): 411–433; Tricia Jenkins, "The Militarization of American Professional Sports: How the Sports-War Intertext Influences Athletic Ritual and Sports Media," *Journal of Sport and Social Issues* 37:3 (2013): 245–260; Roberto Sirvent and Duncan Reyburn, "Uniforms and Unanimity: Reading the Rhetorical Entanglement of Militarism and Sport through Mimetic Realism," in Michael L. Butterworth, ed., *Sport and Militarism: Contemporary Global Perspectives* (New York: Routledge, 2017), 191–208.

37. Keisha N. Blain, *Set the World on Fire: Black Nationalist Women and the Global Struggle for Freedom* (Philadelphia: University of Pennsylvania Press, 2018), 106.

38. Dave Zirin, "American Anthem," *CounterPunch*, May 17, 2005. http://www.counterpunch.org/2005/05/17/american-anthem/

39. Alasdair MacIntyre, "A Partial Response to My Critics," in *After*

MacIntyre: Critical Perspectives on the Work of Alasdair MacIntyre, John Horton and Susan Mendus, eds. (Notre Dame, IN: University of Notre Dame Press, 1994), 303, cited in William T. Cavanaugh, *Migrations of the Holy: God, State, and the Political Meaning of the Church* (Grand Rapids: Eerdmans, 2011), 36–37.

40. Paul W. Kahn, *Political Theology: Four New Chapters on the Concept of Sovereignty* (New York: Columbia University Press, 2012), 18.

41. Elizabeth Shakman Hurd, *The Politics of Secularism in International Relations* (Princeton, NJ: Princeton University Press, 2008). See also Hussein Ali Agrama, *Questioning Secularism: Islam, Sovereignty, and the Rule of Law in Modern Egypt* (Chicago, University of Chicago Press, 2012); Mateo Taussig-Rubbo, "Sacrifice and Sovereignty," in Austin Sarat and Jennifer L. Culbert, eds., *States of Violence: War, Capital Punishment, and Letting Die*, (Cambridge: Cambridge University Press), 83–126; William T. Cavanaugh, *Myth of Religious Violence*; Talal Asad, *Formations of the Secular: Christianity, Islam, Modernity* (Palo Alto: Stanford University Press, 2003); Timothy Fitzgerald, ed., *Religion and the Secular: Historical and Colonial Formations* (New York: Routledge, 2016); Carolyn Marvin and David W. Ingle, *Blood Sacrifice and the Nation: Totem Rituals and the American Flag* (Cambridge: Cambridge University Press, 1999); Jonathon S. Kahn and Vincent W. Lloyd, *Race and Secularism in America* (New York: Columbia University Press, 2016).

42. Francis Bellamy, quoted in Cecilia O'Leary, *To Die For: The Paradox of American Patriotism* (Princeton, NJ: Princeton University Press, 1999), 178, quoted in Cavanaugh, *Myth of Religious Violence*, 117.

43. See Robert Bellah and Phillip E. Hammond, *Varieties of Civil Religion* (New York: Harper & Row, 1980).

44. Kahn, *Political Theology*, 23.

45. "BASKETBALL: A Puzzled Olajuwon Speaks Out on Citizenship," *New York Times*, March 14, 1996, retrieved from: https://www.nytimes.com/1996/03/14/sports/basketball-a-puzzled-olajuwon-speaks-out-on-citizenship.html

46. William T. Cavanaugh, "The Root of Evil," *America Magazine*, July 29–August 5, 2013, http://americamagazine.org/issue/root-evil

47. Colby Itkowitz, "He Endured Racist Attacks after Singing at NBA Game. Now He's the Opener for Democratic Debate," *Washington Post*, March 9, 2016, https://www.washingtonpost.com/news/inspired-life/wp/2016/03/09/he-endured-racist-attacks-after-singing-at-nba-game-now-hes-the-opener-for-democratic-debate/

48. Lowe, *The Intimacies of Four Continents*, 6.

49. Martha D. Escobar, "No One is Criminal," in *Abolition Now! Ten Years of Strategy and Struggle against the Prison Industrial Complex*, Critical Resistance, ed. (Oakland: AK Press, 2008), 57.

50. Raúl Al-qaraz Ochoa, "Legalization Kills Revolution: The Case Against Citizenship," *Un Pueblo Sin Fronteras*, December 27, 2010, retrieved from: https://antifronteras.wordpress.com/2010/12/27/legalization-kills-revolution-the-case-against-citizenship/

51. Harsha Walia, *Undoing Border Imperialism* (Oakland: AK Press, 2013).

52. See Tamara K. Nopper, "Strangers to the Economy: Black Work and the Wages of Non-Blackness," in P. Khalil Saucier and Tryon P. Woods, eds., *Conceptual Aphasia in Black: Displacing Racial Formation* (Lanham, MD: Lexington Books, 2016), 87–102; and Katie Walker Grimes, "Nonwhiteness Will Not Save Us: The Persistence of Antiblackness in the 'Brown' Twenty-First Century," chapter in *Christ Divided: Antiblackness as Corporate Vice* (Minneapolis: Fortress Press, 2017), 147–176.

53. Nopper, "Strangers to the Economy," 101.

54. Hoda Katebi, "Please Keep Your American Flags off my Hijab," *JooJoo Azad*, January 23, 2017, http://www.joojooazad.com/2017/01/keep-your-american-flags-off-my-hijab.html.

55. Notable examples include the stories of Ibtihaj Muhammad (United States fencer), Ben Johnson (Canadian sprinter), and Cathy Freeman (Australian runner). Thanks to Michael L. Silk for his insights on this complex phenomenon where "states can legitimise/normalise emblematic subjects in various ways so as to discursively construct/constitute a narrative of belonging/citizenship that masks over the various complexities of difference/being other(ed)."

56. Spade, *Normal Life*, 2. See Michel Foucault, "Governmentality," in *The Foucault Effect: Studies in Govermentality*, Graham Burchell, Colin Gordon, and Peter Miller, eds. (Chicago: University of Chicago Press, 1991), 103.

57. Lowe, *The Intimacies of Four Continents*, 137.

"FÚTBOL FEMENINO" COMES TO THE NEW SOUTH:
Latina Integration through Soccer

Paul Cuadros
University of North Carolina–Chapel Hill

JENNIFER MENDOZA BEASLEY GREW UP in Colorado playing soccer. Soccer and being an athlete were second nature to Jennifer. She played club soccer. She played on her high school team. She was a strong defender and an expert at breaking up plays and clearing the ball. When she graduated from high school and enrolled at Yale University she continued to play, eventually becoming the women's team captain her senior year. At Yale she met her husband, and after graduating the couple moved to North Carolina, where her husband was from. She became a mom with two kids. After so many years, soccer seemed no longer part of her life.

But then Jennifer moved close to Siler City, North Carolina, a poultry-processing town that had seen a large influx of Mexican and Central American immigrants that had transformed the town. Siler City had become *Soccer City* — at least for the men. On any given Sunday, the local parks were filled with men from the poultry plant playing in *La Liga* (The League), letting off steam from a hard work week. But as the *ligas* grew they opened up their game and field and began to form women's teams. The women's teams became so popular and lucrative they have exploded all over Siler City and the Piedmont area. Jennifer rediscovered soccer. She now plays in *La Liga* teams, including indoors, and coaches a girls' team for Chatham Soccer League, the local club team. She has seen the rise of *fútbol femenino* in the area and how it has changed itself and the women who participate in it. But perhaps more important, it has provided her with an outlet to keep playing the sport she loves.

The women's leagues in Siler City continue to grow but now include indoor teams, since an indoor facility opened in 2009. There are usually six indoor teams of up to ten players each, depending on the team. The outdoor teams struggle a bit in terms of numbers because they must field more than eleven players, but *La Liga* usually has four teams from Siler City that compete with teams from towns in the area. All the teams are predominately Latina. Jennifer plays on both outdoor and indoor teams depending on her availability. "Honestly, I think being in the US you have this sort of idea that women can do the same sort of things as the men," Jennifer says. "Here, I think women feel like they can play."

Many of the female players are playing to cope with their lives and responsibilities; sports is a way to deal with life's pressures. "Being a mother, working full time, you turn to soccer, you turn to sports," Jennifer continues. "I always turn to sports, and a lot of the women do, too. I think a lot of the women leave their stress on the field. That's what I see a lot of and it creates that family bonding too. It's not just about going to see the males play, but about the moms and females playing too."

One thing Jennifer has seen more recently is young Latinas getting involved in club play or playing for teams in *La Liga femenina* in Siler City. Like their suburban counterparts, many young Latinas are turning to clubs to develop their game and play more often. "I think I have been seeing a lot more youth playing," says Jennifer. "In Asheboro, there's been a couple of youth sprinkled in but I think in Siler City it's been more younger players playing."

Jennifer plays when she can but has been busy coaching a youth team of Latinas for Chatham Soccer League, the county's local soccer club. Her team struggles with maturity and playing in a league with rules and punishments for violating those rules compared to their experiences with *La Liga* teams, which have fewer consequences for out-of-bounds behavior. At a recent game with her teenage girls' team, a fight broke out between two players. "It was really just one player that was going back and forth with another player from the other team. She hasn't quite fully matured and understood what's acceptable," Jennifer says about her player who received a red card in the game.

Jennifer says there are more options now for young Latinas to play soccer and to become athletes like she was at their age. With teams in *La Liga* and teams from the local soccer club to develop skills, Latinas are choosing to get in the game in ways they have not before. "There are options now," Jennifer says. "I think part of when I was out there and playing in *La Liga* I was looking at some kids and thinking they must be coming through the middle school. There were a couple of girls that were pretty good. They were hitting seventh grade and they were phenomenal players."

It is early Sunday morning and the cars begin to pull into the Tienda Diana soccer fields in Siler City. The fields are located on the outskirts of the small poultry-processing town that was one of the inspirations for Mayberry, the quintessential Southern burg depicted on *The Andy Griffith Show*. These fields are in constant use on Sundays when the poultry workers unwind after a hard week. Soccer on Sundays is the one thing the men look forward to during long work days.

But the men are not the only ones who are showing up with their cleats on Sundays these days. This morning, it is women, Latinas dressed in bright uniforms, who step out of their vehicles. They are accompanied by their husbands, boyfriends, and fathers, and many have brought their own children. The "*futboleras*" are a mixed bunch of women who range from teenagers to women in their mid-thirties with families of their own. They come originally from all over Latin America, but the majority are from Mexico. The younger players were born in Siler City.

All over the Triangle (Raleigh, Durham, Chapel Hill) and Triad (Greensboro, Winston-Salem, High Point) regions of North Carolina, Latina women soccer leagues and teams are sprouting up. Hundreds of Latinas are playing soccer, expanding the limits of traditional female roles and perhaps transforming the norms of femininity in their own families and in their communities. This chapter examines how three Latina players, each with a different immigration status, broke through traditional roles in their families in order to become athletes, and how soccer has helped them to grow and become stronger and more independent.

I coached each of these players through high school, and even after graduating the women have continued to play in new adult women soccer leagues. These leagues, or *ligas*, were traditionally created for Latino men and represent a familiar cultural space, one that allows men to be free and reaffirm who they are within this society. These leagues and the cultural space they provide are well documented in the study, "Soccer and Latino Cultural Space: Metropolitan Washington Fútbol Leagues."[1]

The women's leagues represent a new space alongside and within this existing one among Latinos in the US, one where Latinas can also find greater freedom, crush cultural stereotypes, and define a new dynamic in the Latino family. The impact of these athletic pioneers remains to be seen, but the daughters of these players are seeing that Latinas can be determined, physical, and winners. The soccer field becomes the first and perhaps the only place where many young Latinas can step away from the kitchen and the home and related responsibilities.

SOCCER CITY

Today, Siler City, North Carolina, is more than 50 percent Hispanic, according to the 2010 census. Siler City has been at the forefront of Latino migration and demographic change in the Southeast for more than 20 years. In 1990, there were only 184 Hispanics out of a total population of 4,808. By 2008, that number had risen to 2,740 out of a population of 8,564, or 39.3 percent of the population, according to the U.S. Census Bureau. The majority of Latinos in Siler City come from Mexico, but there are also many Central Americans, people from Guatemala, Honduras, and El Salvador. And there are a number of Latinos who are US citizens who have moved from such cities as Los Angeles and Chicago.

The explosive growth of the Hispanic population was due in large part to the recruiting practices of the poultry-processing factories. Siler City was home to two processing plants, and the county is home to some 300 chicken farmers. Manufacturing is the major employer in Siler City, with sales, shipments, and receipts in excess of $400 million and an annual payroll of $69 million for employing 2,684 employees, according to the U.S. Census Bureau's 2007 Economic Census of the town. The poultry-processing industry became a gateway for Latino immigrant workers to come and work in the South.[2]

Like many small rural communities in the South, Siler City has had a difficult time adjusting to the influx of newcomers. That tension between long-time residents and the newcomers resulted in a series of confrontations with regard to Latinos in Siler City. The first was a letter the county commissioners sent in 1999 to the Immigration and Naturalization Service, asking that they send agents to deport Latino immigrants who had no papers. The second incident was a contentious school board meeting in Siler City where it was proposed that Spanish-speaking Latino children be moved out of the elementary school to their own school where they could learn English. And, in February 2000, the town endured an anti-immigrant rally at its City Hall that featured David Duke, a former grand wizard of the Ku Klux Klan.

I wrote about these struggles in my book, *A Home on the Field: How One Championship Team Inspires Hope for the Revival of Small Town America* (2006). I helped to lead the fight to create a varsity soccer program at Jordan-Matthews High School, the only high school in Siler City. In 2002, the school formed the first women's varsity soccer program. This team was predominantly Latina and remains so today. I coached the team for more than nine years. The high school team was the first organized women's soccer team in Siler City. A middle school girls' team soon followed.

In 2006, Carlos Gumucio, a local Latino businessman who owned the Tienda Diana, a Latino food store, bought land outside the town and created three soccer fields for Latino leagues to use. These soccer leagues were male leagues and are the best organized competitive sports for Latinos in town. On any given Sunday, hundreds of Latino families go to the "Diana Fields" to watch the men play all day. But there were no women's teams.

In 2010, Gumucio created a league for Latinas. He charged each team a registration fee of $150 for the season. In addition, the teams must pay $50 to the referees directly for each game. This is also the traditional way in which the male leagues are organized. "I created the league because I saw that women were playing fútbol in other places like Sanford, Greensboro, and my daughter said, 'We could do the same here with our fields and the league here,'" Gumucio said. Gumucio is originally from Bolivia but lived in the US for many years. He is a naturalized citizen and his wife is Peruvian.

The women's league in Siler City has only five teams, with about 100 women. Each team plays the others during the season and the champion is eventually awarded with a trophy.

"YOU HAVE TO BE STRONG"

The players are neatly dressed in blue jerseys and white shorts with matching white socks. They look impeccable. To say this women's soccer team is well organized is an understatement. Every player knows her position on the team, and they all arrive on time. They know better than to show up late for a game.

All the Latina players know about Amelia or have heard of the pint-sized Guatemalan with the uncanny ability to clear balls from the backfield. Amelia is fearless, tough as nails, determined to win at all times, and as demanding of her players as she is of herself. She is quick to anger, opinionated, bright, and supremely confident.

I first met Amelia when she tried out for the Jordan-Matthews women's soccer team in 2006. She did not make the team her freshman year. Undeterred, Amelia tried out again the following year and made the team. By her junior year she was a starter and a stalwart in the defense. She was a captain of the team by her senior year.

On this Sunday, Amelia is off the field and on the sideline. She is sitting out due to a red card suspension she received the previous week. She stands on the sidelines shouting instructions and admonishing her teammates if they flinch when the ball comes at them. Amelia does not flinch at anything. "I love it," she says, not taking her eyes off the game. "Sometimes I think of not playing, but I keep playing. I tell my sisters to do sports, to not to get into trouble." The "trouble" that Amelia speaks about is what many young Latinas find themselves in when they turn fifteen and begin dating. I have coached several girls who have gotten pregnant during their freshman year only to return to the team as mothers the following season.

Amelia graduated from high school in 2010. Today she works at a printing plant, inserting subscription cards into magazines that are distributed all over the country. She works with other Latina women on her line. They are considered the lowest of the workers at the plant. She makes $8.75 an hour.

Amelia had plans to go to community college, but those plans fell through right before her high school graduation. In May 2008, the North Carolina community college system barred access to undocumented students, based on the recommendation of the state Attorney General, according to the system's office of public affairs. The system had previously allowed individual colleges to determine themselves whether to admit these students. A clarification by the Department of

Homeland Security upheld the ban. In 2010, the system's board of governors changed its position and recommended admission for these students. Meanwhile, students like Amelia wait for a final ruling so they can go to school.

Now Amelia works all day making sure people get those ads that slip out of their magazines. But soccer is never far from Amelia's mind. She knows that soccer has helped her become a stronger person and given her more confidence. "I do feel empowered sometimes," she says. "I think you learn to express yourself better. All that I learned from fútbol is it helps to defend myself at work."

Amelia explains that the company provides food for workers but the Latinas are always forced to take their turn last, after everyone else has picked through the food. "That was not just. I told the manager they should rotate the order so everyone got a chance to be first. We'll see what happens. You have to defend yourself. You have to be strong."

Being strong is what Amelia's young life has been all about. Her family is from the little town of Aldea Nueva Candelaria, near Retalhuleu, Guatemala, where they raised corn and rice on a small farm. The family consisted of six children. When Amelia was ten, her parents left to come to the US to seek a better life for their family and found their way to North Carolina. The family was separated for three years. "We missed them terribly," she recalls. "They called every Saturday and we had to travel thirty minutes to talk to them by phone."

When Amelia's parents saved enough money they brought her and her siblings across the border through Arizona. She was then twelve. "We were in a big group of people, maybe thirty people. Walking all day and night. It was hard. It was hot and we were afraid the *migra* might get you."

From Arizona, the group piled into a van and made their way across the country to North Carolina. "We stopped in a lot of states. It was like it would never end," she says. At last, the van stopped in Fayetteville, North Carolina, where her father had arranged to pick her up. "At first I didn't recognize him, but when he came up to us a lady said it was him. My mom recognized me and I recognized her right away."

Siler City was a strange place for Amelia. "At first it was very hard for me," she says. "I didn't know English, I was frustrated all the time; I wasn't angry, just sad." Amelia was happy to be reunited with her family, but she missed Guatemala and her family and friends there. "I didn't know any people. So I started to play with my cousins and I started to make friends and so I played more."

For many migrant children, the one familiar thing they can do when they come to the US is play soccer with other kids. Soccer becomes that little piece of home they find here. For many of the kids, the school teams become their first experience with organized soccer. "It helped me," Amelia says, recalling her days on the high school team. "It helped me to organize my time and to get to know more people. My style of playing was better too."

In Guatemala her parents had not encouraged her to play soccer. They were afraid that she might get hurt. But in the US, they did not stand in her way. She could play on the high school team as long as she met her obligations at home and at school. "At first they didn't want me to play because they thought it would affect my studies, but then they learned it was a positive thing."

But Amelia missed practices because she had to take care of her little brother. I have found many Latina girls often miss out on extra-curricular activities for the same reason. They feel tethered to the house, frustrated because they want to participate in activities or just hang out with their girlfriends. "My mom told me to decide which days I could practice and which days I needed to be home to take care of my little brother. I wanted to play, so I would always fight with my mom, more with her than my dad, but they had to get used to the idea," she says.

Coaches have to be flexible when it comes to Latina girls' schedules. Allowing them to stay home some days to accommodate their responsibilities meant they could still participate with the team. This leeway was important in providing that connection to their school and a space where they could be with their girlfriends, sharing an experience and relieving the pressure of growing up in a strange country. "Soccer is a place to get away from the routine," Amelia says. "Sometimes a team is the best place to get rid of feelings that bother us."

Amelia had a stellar career in high school, making All Conference, a distinction granted to only a select few players. She was equally excellent in the classroom, but her plans to attend community college ended when the system barred the doors to students without papers. So Amelia stayed home for a while, taking care of her younger siblings and helping out. With each year of not being able to study, Amelia's choices diminished. She decided she needed to get a job and start contributing to her family. She found the factory job. "My life is not complicated," she says. "I go to work and I play soccer on Sundays. I have been going to a new church. Everyone in my family goes. My mom said, 'Do you want to go to church on Sundays or play soccer?' So we picked a church where we could go on Saturdays." Amelia's life now reflects the lives of the men in Siler City. They work hard all week at a menial job and then let off steam on Sundays, playing soccer all day.

It is Sunday and Amelia is dressed to play. She has her dark hair pulled back tightly and her fingernails are painted crimson. She formed a team for the new Siler City women's league. Amelia finds the new Siler City women's league more convenient than some of the other leagues. There is a league for women in Sanford, one in High Point, and another in Raleigh.

Amelia has carefully selected her new team. She has included several family members, four white women from Sanford, two African American women, and the rest a mix of Guatemalan and Mexican players. There are twenty-two players in total, with the majority coming from Siler City. Six of the players are in high school, but the rest are women who work nearby. Some are single, and some have husbands and children. "Everyone speaks in English, sometimes a mix of English and Spanglish," she says. The team meets one day a week to practice and work on conditioning.

On game days, the team has tremendous support from the men in their lives: boyfriends, husbands, fathers, and brothers. The women's games are more of a family affair. Amelia has seen little machismo as regards their playing soccer. "I hear about some mothers and fathers who say only men have the right to play, but then I hear many say it's a good thing because it's healthy," she says. "Maybe if we were back in our home countries it would be different because I don't remember ever women playing like this there. But here it's different. It's more liberal and free."

Amelia does hear some men run them down. She admits the support is halfway there. "I hear it sometimes. The guys say, 'Hey, you kick the ball like a woman.' That's bad. They feel superior playing fútbol. They have the tendency to look at who is stronger, but some of the girls can really play equal to them."

The Latina women's game has also been helpful to the families, says Iris Moreno, who owns and runs the *Federación de Fútbol de Sanford* and the women's league there. She says it has helped some relationships and marriages. Conversely, Moreno says, there are a lot of breakups because of soccer, because the men spend their one day off playing all day long. "The women resent it. So this is a way for families to come together and do something together as a family," she says.

In 2011, Amelia and two of her friends decided to try coaching kids in the Siler City parks league. She coached kids between seven and ten years old. Female coaches in sports are rare, and for these Latinas to volunteer to coach was a big step toward taking a leadership role in the community. In contrast, none of the boys who played for the school have ever coached youth sports. "The first day? A few obeyed, some were rebellious, but after a while they got to know me and what I wanted," Amelia says. "I learned a lot, how to understand kids more, how to form a team, to have harmony. It was a nice experience for me."

Amelia took that experience and incorporates it into her new team. Soccer is the one place where she can be herself more fully, where she can express herself and feelings more openly. "With the women you have to be more strict," she says. "If you motivate someone you can get them to progress. In the game, I let it all hang out, all those things in life I don't let out. I am nice off the field, but in the game I am not. I am there to win."

BETWEEN HOPE AND FEAR

Rachel was resplendent in white and sequins. She took a turn around the smoke-covered dance floor as the *caballeros* lined up to pin five- and ten-dollar bills to her veil and have a chance to waltz with her before someone else tapped them on the shoulder. She was beautiful, her makeup simple and tasteful, her strapless wedding gown elegant. Rachel took turns dancing with the men, chatting and nodding her head before someone else stepped in with a bill and a pin.

Rachel's wedding was vastly different from many of the Latina marriages in Siler City. First, having a wedding at all was a bit of a novelty. Many Latinas get "married" by simply hooking up, or getting "*juntada*" (joined), with a man in a common-law marriage. Fancy weddings are rare because of the cost. And it was unprecedented that Rachel would have her wedding at the Siler City Country Club, a place that once upon a time saw no Latinos or African Americans celebrating in its clubhouse. The Country Club is the top of the pyramid for Siler City society, and for Latinos to rent it out and use it was a rarity. But that was Rachel. She had broken a lot of ground growing up and playing soccer. In fact, Rachel would rather wear a pair of cleats than high heels.

I have known Rachel for five years, since she tried out for the high school women's soccer team. After every practice her father would show up, and the two of them would spend an extra hour working on shots and dribbling. Rachel was her own toughest critic. Even when she excelled in the game her senior year and became a captain and a top goal scorer, she would criticize herself and her game. No amount of praise would motivate Rachel. She had to be challenged. By the end of her high school career she was All Conference and All State — one of only two Latinas at the school to become All State.

Dressed in a sky-blue jersey with white piping and dark blue shorts and white socks, Rachel is getting her team ready to play a team from Asheboro, North Carolina, about thirty miles west of Siler City. The latter team is known as "*las Borrachas*" (the Drunkards) because two of the women always show up after drinking or hung over. Rachel is the manager of her team, known as *Alemania*, or Germany, despite not being German or having any connection to Germany. Rachel said the team chose the name Germany because they admired the style of game the Germans played. The team is a mix of Honduran and Mexican women.

The women all love Rachel. They know Rachel can play. Her new husband, José, walks up and down the sideline meeting and talking with the other men. Her father sits quietly on the sideline.

The game begins, and Rachel is a bit sluggish. But as the game progresses, she picks up her pace and has excellent chances to score a goal. At the final whistle, she has kicked two goals past the *Borrachas'* goalkeeper to win the game. Rachel says that she would never have scored a goal in her life if she and her family had stayed in Honduras.

Hurricane Mitch forever changed the lives of many people in Honduras, including Rachel's family, in 1998. Rachel's family lived in the capital, Tegucigalpa, in a little neighborhood called Bella Vista. From her house she could look out the window and see the tall Jesu Cristo statue with his arms held out low in El Picacho Park. Rachel's house was a two-story structure made of bricks and stones with a dirt floor and a *pupuseria* on the bottom floor where the family sold *pupusas* (a cornmeal flatbread with various fillings) to customers. Multiple families lived in the house. "We had a dining room, a *sala*, and a kitchen," Rachel says. "We all slept in one big room, mom and dad and me and my brother." After the hurricane struck, Rachel's family moved to the United States. Her parents left the ravaged city first, leaving her and her brother behind with an aunt. Later, the family brought Rachel and her brother by plane. "This all happened right after Mitch. The school was closed and I never finished the second grade," she says.

Hurricane Mitch caused the deaths of nearly 6,500 Hondurans and displaced 1.5 million, due to heavy flooding and mudslides. Tens of thousands of homes were destroyed, with an estimated five billion dollars in damage incurred, according to the 1998 report, "Mitch: The Deadliest Atlantic Hurricane Since 1780."[3] Rachel's house survived the storm, but the city had been devastated. When she arrived in Siler City, Rachel was struck by how everything was neat and clean. "Where I lived, if you reached fourteen you were married and with a kid, and by eighteen you had two kids. I never saw anyone that age with a high school diploma."

And Rachel never saw any young girls kick a ball or play soccer. But in Siler City she could play, and she wanted to play. Rachel is defined by a fierce sense of equality, of wanting the same opportunities that men or anyone else has. But playing soccer has not been easy. She has had to take on the one person in her family on whom she models herself: her mother. "It has been like World War III," she says. "It's not just your family though, but your friends, everybody. I know if I was in Honduras I would not even touch the ball. It's the culture. Here it's more liberal and parents get over it, not allowing you to play, too."

But getting her mom to accept her desire to play and to keep on playing has not been easy. Rachel says her mother was raised in the "old way" and her values reflect that. She wanted Rachel to be at home. "She said I shouldn't be playing outside because I'm a girl," Rachel asserts. "She said that I would get kidnapped, raped, or hurt. She said that by playing with boys it was like putting myself in danger. She thinks that girls are not capable of playing soccer to that level."

Rachel remembers coming home from playing at Chatham Middle School when she injured her ankle and couldn't walk well. When she got home she didn't dare tell her mom. She went straight to bed and covered her swollen ankle. When her mother came into the room and asked her to do something the ruse was up and Rachel had to explain she was injured. "She said, 'You see what happens when you play that sport! I told you! I hope you learned your lesson,'" Rachel recalls. Despite her ankle swelling to the size of a softball, Rachel kept playing.

Rachel explains that her mom barely made it to the sixth grade. She had to work. She was not treated well by her family and married young. She says her mother looks at everything that could go bad, instead of the potential of things. "*Ella es muy cerrada*, she is very closed off. She's even closed-minded to me going to college. She was not in agreement with that. She wanted me to work. But I want more."

Many young Latinas have to fight with their mothers against the traditional values and roles for girls. It's the mothers who generally do not want their daughters to stay after school and participate in clubs or sports. They want them home helping to take care of the little ones and staying in the house for their own safety.

Rachel has succeeded on the field and off because of the unwavering support of her father, who taught her how to kick a ball and practiced with her for hours. Her father always supported what she wanted to do. She did very well on her high school team and also excelled in the classroom.

Rachel is studying to become a nurse. She has a special immigration status called Temporary Protective Status (TPS), which the federal government bestowed on Honduran survivors of Hurricane Mitch. She has to get the status renewed every eighteen months, but she has a driver's license and a social security number and she can study and work in the country.

Temporary Protective Status is granted to eligible nationals from designated countries following a natural disaster like Mitch or certain wars. People with TPS cannot leave the country but can travel freely in the US. They can obtain work authorization but cannot attain permanent residency status through TPS, according to the U.S. Bureau of Citizenship and Immigration Services, a division of the U.S. Department of Homeland Security. There are currently 70,000 Hondurans with TPS status in the US due to Mitch. Other nationals accorded TPS are from other Central American countries: El Salvador, Guatemala, and Nicaragua.

But many people and schools do not understand what TPS status is. And so when Rachel applied to the University of North Carolina at Greensboro she was incorrectly rejected as being undocumented, when she is not. She is also not eligible for federal financial aid, said Marty Rosenbluth, staff attorney for the Southern Coalition for Social Justice and an immigration attorney.

Rachel, thus, decided to attend Sand Hills Community College and work toward her nursing degree there. But that was also a struggle because the admissions staff at Sand Hills didn't know what to do with her TPS status. With some legal help, Rachel was able to make the school understand that she was lawfully in the country and the community college had to admit her at the in-state tuition rate. But dealing with the school's ignorance regarding her status has been difficult. At one point, she was unable to sign up for her classes because she was waiting on her renewed TPS status to come through. "Every time I try to stay positive something bad happens," she says through tears. "But at least I can go to college. I killed myself in high school so I could go to college."

Rachel is finding that working and going to school are difficult, but her main problem is convincing her school that she is a lawful resident. She doesn't want to drop out because of her immigration status. "If I flunk out of nursing school, okay, I can accept that because it was me, it was my fault — but not because of this, not because of them and my papers."

But this is not the only thing weighing heavily on Rachel's mind. Several months ago, José, her new husband, was arrested for a DWI in Alamance County. Alamance is one of several North Carolina counties that run a special federal program called 287g, which allows local law enforcement to check someone's immigration status. José was found to be undocumented by the Immigration Customs and Enforcement division of the Department of Homeland Security. He is now facing deportation to Mexico.

The 287g program allows local and state law enforcement officials to partner with ICE and authorizes them to detect, detain, and deport unauthorized immigrants. There are sixty-seven such partnerships between local law enforcement and ICE across the country, according to DHS. North Carolina has the most jurisdictions, eight, of any state in the country. The program was created in 1996 but was little used until recently. It was meant to help local authorities catch violent felons who were undocumented, but in practice it has been implemented most often after minor traffic violations. A study of the program found that most of the people caught under the program were not dangerous or violent criminals.[4]

Rachel does not know what she will do if José is forced to leave the country, but her feelings about the United States have soured. "I don't want to live here anymore in the US, but I don't want to live in Mexico or Honduras either. I was thinking we could live in Canada," she says wistfully. Rachel and José have been thinking of moving north because they have heard you can become a citizen of Canada more easily. "I left my family in Honduras so I have done it before," she says. "My parents made a tough decision for their family. I can make one too."

For now, Rachel says, she lives in the moment, in a frozen piece of time bookended by hope and fear. "It's having hopes, that's what you live on."

But there is one place where all these problems are chased away. The soccer field is a refuge from all her problems, the one place where she can be who she wants to be based on her own guts and talent, a place where the field is level for everyone, where papers don't matter. "It's something I have fought for all my life. I'm still up for it. It's where I can express myself and improve myself," she says. "It's like a career. Most of my friends are not as passionate about it as I am. They take it as a hobby. I take it as part of my life. I would have chosen this as a career. It's all about fútbol."

"LA GRINGA"

Javiera still remembers the moment when the Latina girls started calling her "la Gringa." They were all gathered around the middle school soccer coach who had asked the girls to return tryout forms in order to play. All the white girls had their forms filled out. None of the Latina girls had brought theirs — except Javiera. One of the Latina girls said, "Oh, see, she's a *gringa*," and they laughed. The name stuck.

I heard about Javiera — a short, stocky player with a wide smile and enormous dark eyes — before I met her. There was a lot of talk by the Latina soccer players on the high school team about la Gringa and how good she was. Javiera was so good, she started as a freshman.

During her first game with the high school team, she collided with another player and ended up with a black eye. I thought for a moment that would be the last time we would see la Gringa. It was a test to see how much she loved the sport and whether she wanted to play at this level. She showed up to practice the next day with a nice shiner.

Javiera was born into a family of six in Santa Barbara, California. But jobs were scarce there and families were doubled up in homes, sharing rooms and trying to get by. Her father picked up the family and moved to Siler City because he had friends and relatives who told him there were jobs in North Carolina. "When I came I had all white friends," she says smiling. "I hardly had any Latino friends. Back then in Siler City there weren't that many Latino families."

Javiera grew up very differently from Amelia and Rachel. She mixed and hung out with white kids, learning their culture. But she was never invited into their homes. She spoke mostly English and her Spanish was fading.

The one constant that Javiera had in her life was soccer. Soccer became her life because her dad loved the sport. Her father formed a youth team for kids and Javiera played there. "My dad taught me the basics of soccer," she says. "He was very laid back. He made us feel like even if we didn't win it was okay. I think that's why we had so much fun."

Javiera got better and soon she was dribbling circles around the boys and other players in middle school. "I would practice on my own, dribbling, tricks. I would say to my dad, 'Let's go and head the ball,' and we would kick together. That's why I became so close to my dad. I was not a typical Latina, I was not at home. Most of the time it was me and him."

As Javiera grew up her world began to change. Her friends, most of whom had been white, now tended to be Latina. She played on the middle school team and dominated the games. In high school, Javiera continued her athletic career, becoming All Conference three years in a row and All State in her senior year. When she graduated, she had become the top female goal scorer in Jordan-Matthews' High School history.

But in Javiera's senior year, tragedy struck. She was driving to school one morning with her father when ICE agents stopped their car. They told her to get out and searched her father and her. They had an order for deportation for her father. The agents then drove to her house and arrested her brother. A month later her mother and brother moved back to Mexico, leaving her to live with a sister and her husband and child. That senior year, Javiera lived with no support other than her sister, and she missed her dad terribly. Many Latino immigrant families in the United States live in mixed-status households, where some members of the family are US citizens or lawfully in the country and others are not. "That was hard. I lost my dad. He was my rock. We did everything together," she said.

After graduation, Javiera was accepted to a nearby college where she is studying criminal justice. She wants to be an FBI agent. But putting herself through school alone has been hard. Because her parents still have assets in the US, Javiera receives little financial aid for school. She works full time as the manager of a local fast food restaurant, to pay for books and make ends meet. She took a semester off from school to save money for tuition and other costs. She then returned to school, looking forward to the challenges of academia.

While Javiera faces obstacles with her education, she is in better shape than Rachel and Amelia. Her US citizen status allows her to pay tuition at the in-state rate and she is eligible to pursue financial aid. Her future is more unfettered than that of the other women. Rachel has a tougher road. She can go to school, but she has to find a way to pay for it and she has to educate school administrators about her special status. And there is the added cost of paying tuition at a four-year university without financial aid. Amelia, on the other hand, has little chance of receiving a four-year degree. She can't afford to pay the out-of-state tuition cost at a community college, let alone pay to earn a degree at a four-year school.

Javiera continues to play soccer on a women's team in Raleigh. The level of play is more competitive than that in the new Siler City league.

"I feel alive when I play," she says. "It boosted my confidence and I learned how to be more social with the other girls, how to connect with them. I learned how to be strong and be able to overcome barriers. Even though you're a woman, we can play the sport as good as the guys. It doesn't matter what sex you are, you can achieve great things."

CONCLUSION

While all three of the players described above are very different from one another and face different challenges in life, they are all united by their love of soccer and their struggle to find acceptance as athletes. Their love of sport clashes with the model of what a young Latina woman should be. This is a prime example of their personal struggle to transcend cultural constraints in the US and in their home countries. It has helped them cope with the political and legal issues they face due to their uncertain and temporary status.

I believe we are just beginning to appreciate how the Latina identity will be transformed by women like these. They are strong, athletic, skillful, fast, and champions. These are uncharacteristic expressions with which to describe Latina women. We know from various studies that girls who participate in sports during adolescence have greater self-esteem, do better academically, and are healthier.[5] Their status as athletes elevates these women beyond their traditional role in the home. In addition, this new status in their communities is a powerful indicator of sociocultural integration in the United States. Women's soccer in the US is big, with large numbers of young girls playing in youth leagues, women playing in college, and even a professional women's league — not to mention the US women's national team, a perennial power in world soccer. Latinas are now taking steps to get on the field. What is interesting is that they are taking these steps first in their own cultural spaces, in their own leagues and fields.

Soccer has taught them to overcome adversity. This resilient attitude plays out in their lives and everyday interactions. Amelia could not have challenged her boss without the leadership skills she learned from the pitch. Rachel would not have had the perseverance to go to school without the discipline obtained from soccer. And Javiera would not have had the independence to live her life deprived of her parents so young without her experience on the field.

One of the things to consider about each player is how prominent they are among their people. Soccer and its fields are an important cultural space for the Latino community. But fútbol has been a man's game until now. The men have been the heroes, the women spectators. Now the roles are reversed. This cultural space, this space where the community can come together and express itself freely in its own way with its own rules and organization, is becoming more equal and inclusive.

Perhaps as important is that women are finding a place in their lives where everything is equal. Where their achievement is based solely on their own work and performance. There is no language barrier on the field. There are no papers required to play. You don't have to be a man to play soccer. Women can play, too. "It says, not only do good players come out of the guys, but that girls are capable of competing with the guys; that way the guys will have respect for the girls," Rachel says. "They will consider you an equal. It feels good: you expect me to be bad because I am a girl, you expect me to suck, but then they find out I am good."

QUESTIONS:

1. Why is playing soccer perceived as an attractive option for some of the Latinas in the region of North Carolina referred to above?

2. How does the circumstance of these women playing soccer impact the dynamic in the Latino family? Do you believe this is for the better? Why or why not?

3. What are some of the key impediments for these young women to play, and continue playing, soccer?

NOTES

1. M. Price and C. Whitworth, "Soccer and Latino Cultural Space: Metropolitan Washington Fútbol Leagues," in D. Arreola (ed.), *Hispanic Spaces, Latino Places* (Austin: University of Texas Press, 2004), 167–188.

2. A. J. Cravey, "Latino Labor and Poultry Production in Rural North Carolina," *Southeastern Geographer*, 1997, 37(2): 295–300.

3. National Climatic Data Center, National Oceanic and Atmospheric Administration, "Mitch: The Deadliest Atlantic Hurricane since 1780," 1998.

4. H. Gill and M. Nguyen, *The 287 (g) Program: The Costs and Consequences of Local Immigration Enforcement in North Carolina Communities* (Chapel Hill: University of North Carolina Press, 2010).

5. J. Zimmerman, *Raising Our Athletic Daughters: How Sports Can Build Self-Esteem and Save Girls' Lives* (New York: Doubleday, 1998).

CONCLUSION:

"Are Any of These Guys/Gals Latino/a?": Moving the Sport History of Latinos/as into the Mainstream of Academics and Popular Literature

Jorge Iber
Texas Tech University

A FITTING WAY TO BEGIN the conclusion to this anthology comes from the work of noted scholar of African American athletics, David K. Wiggins. In a collection focusing on important teams, events, and organizations of segregated sports in the US, Wiggins summarized how such entities helped to challenge notions of African American inferiority. His focus is on another racial group but, as readers no doubt have noticed in reading the preceding essays, much of what he indicates below also applies to the Latino/a experience. For, as Wiggins notes, athletic competition demonstrates

> ...the lengths to which people will go to achieve victory as well as how closely connected it is to business, education, politics, economics, religion, law, family, and other social institutions. Sport is, moreover, partly about identity development and how individuals and groups, irrespective of race, gender, ethnicity, or socioeconomic class, have sought to elevate their status and realize material success and social mobility.[1]

On October 14, 2016, teacher and blogger Eric Cortes produced an essay for Latinorebels.com that mirrors much of what Wiggins argues here, but in an "unusual" setting. Cortes discusses how, whenever he sits down to watch any athletic event, "you turn on the TV, you flip on a sport and a little radar detector goes off in you searching for the person who shares your heritage."[2] Obviously, this is a relatively simple task for when Latinos are viewing Major League Baseball (MLB), but it becomes a bit more difficult when the contests are from the National Football League (NFL) or the National Basketball Association (NBA). Cortes's "problem" in this regard is that he is a huge fan of what he calls "the greatest spectator sport in the world," the National Hockey League (NHL). Aficionados of the rink are not likely to find many Latinos on the ice, as the number of Spanish-surnamed athletes in this sport is quite limited.[3]

On the evening of the start of the 2016–2017 NHL campaign, however, something of note occurred as far as the role of Latinos in US-based sports is concerned. On October 12, the Toronto Maple Leafs skated against one of their main rivals, the Ottawa Senators. The result of the game was, not surprisingly, a loss for the seemingly ever rebuilding squad from Canada's largest metropolis. That is where the "ordinary" aspect of this evening ended. The four goals scored by Toronto all came off of the stick of a new "savior" for the franchise, a young man named Auston Matthews. After Matthews netted his first NHL goal, the camera panned around the arena and settled on the parents of the first overall pick in the 2016 draft. Justifiably, dad Brian and mom Ema Matthews beamed with pride. Cortes, however, focused on something beyond the pale. Ema Matthews looked Latina, and a quick review of internet websites confirmed that she was indeed (a native of Hermosillo in the state of Sonora, Mexico).

Brian and Ema raised their son in that "hotbed" of hockey history and tradition, Scottsdale, Arizona. Like other moms of elite athletes, Ema went out of her way to help her son make it to the "bigs." She even moved with Auston to Switzerland so that he could spend one season in a league there while preparing to move on to the NHL. While overseas, she plied her boy with all of the "traditional" favorites that all hockey moms whip up, including tortilla soup! As Matthews' career progresses with the Leafs, it will be of interest to see how Latino/a writers present his story to their co-ethnics, as well as to the broader population. Perhaps Auston might even get more Spanish-surnamed youths interested in putting on skates and hitting the rink![4]

The story of Auston Matthews is but a very recent manifestation of the growing awareness of the role of sport in the daily and historical experiences of the Spanish-speaking population in the US. Almost everywhere one looks on the web and other media, it is possible to find individuals of this background making their mark in athletic competition (at all levels). An overview of a Hispanictrending.net page in late

2016 (a site compiled by marketing expert Juan Tornoe) document-ed anecdotes such as the following: how Texas A&M University and Louisiana State University (LSU) now broadcast their Southeastern Conference (SEC) football games in Spanish; the launching of a new show specifically targeting Hispanic/Latino fans on ESPN; the first game broadcast in Spanish by the St. Louis Cardinals; and the estab-lishment of an all-Hispanic basketball league (and the concerns raised thereby — in line with Chappell's piece) in Richmond, California.

All of these accounts bring up to date many of the issues articu-lated in a historical context by the stories presented in this antholo-gy. Lest we present too upbeat a perspective (as noted in our essays), Tornoe also draws attention to less positive stories in his listings. For example, one essay (by Michael Sayonara) points to a very important trend hinted at by Cortes's article: if the number of Latinos/as in the country (and thus, in high school sports) is growing so rapidly, why is it that there are not many more individuals of this background on the gridiron, courts, and diamonds of large American universities? Latinos/as are certainly making progress in their representation in politics, business, and elsewhere; why does their incorporation into collegiate athletics (and hence, at the professional level as well) lag?[5]

Likewise, a story by Juan Vidal in *Rolling Stone* builds upon the Sayonara essay by noting, "It's no secret that Latinos consistently dom-inate in sports like boxing and MMA (mixed martial arts), where college participation is not a requirement. Generally...and especially in immi-grant households...sports are not viewed as something to seriously pur-sue." Vidal's work also goes beyond this point to feature accounts on how Latino/a athletes are sometimes harassed for not being "American enough," as happened in high school basketball games in Maryland and Iowa. It is doubtful that such insolence would take place in an MLB or NFL stadium, or in an NBA or NHL arena. Still, it seems, it is perfectly acceptable to behave in this manner in places such as Maryland, Iowa, and elsewhere, where Latino/a athletes are forming a larger and larger percentage of the local population (and hence, members of local scho-lastic teams).[6]

A final example from current events that ties to what is discussed in the historical literature presented in this anthology can be seen in the highly acclaimed article and segment on the football team from Mendota (California) High School (Aztecs) and their coach, Robert "Beto" Mejia.[7] As noted in these items, the MHS squad has been successful on the field and has been a source of great pride to the predominantly Latino (and immigrant) populace of this struggling farming community. More recent stories, however, have focused on legal troubles for Coach Mejia, which led to a heated discussion about his status with the school and team. Is this the type of role model that kids in Mendota need? Early in 2016, there was even uncertainty about whether Mejia would be allowed to return. In the end, he was allowed to guide his charges, and they responded with an excellent season, finishing 13–1 and making it all the way to the Division 6AA regional finals before bowing to Amador High, 21–14, on December 9.[8]

In summary, this work has sought to present a look at aspects of the sporting precedent and a glimpse into the present and future significance of Latino/a participation in US athletics. Men and women of skill and courage have broken down barriers in the past, and their descendants continue to do so in the early twenty-first century. A final quote from the Juan Vidal essay noted above well summarizes why studying this topic is of substance:

> The fact is, in a time of so much concentrated anti-immigrant and anti-Hispanic rhetoric, young Latinos need to see more relatable heroes that can model a path for them in the world of competitive sports. Ultimately, we need a more pronounced multicultural presence across the board so that our rosters can better reflect what America actually looks like now. Come to my neighborhood, or any neighborhood like it on any given Saturday, and you will see future superstars holding their own. And maybe one of them, if provided with the proper support from parents, coaches and mentors, could even be the first Latino NBA MVP in history. Nothing would be more American.[9]

May this anthology help spur even more discussion of the functions and implications of athletic competition regarding the lives of the Spanish-surnamed populace in the United States.

NOTES

1. David K. Wiggins and Ryan A. Swanson, eds., *Separate Games: African American Sport behind the Walls of Segregation* (Fayetteville: The University of Arkansas Press, 2016), ix.

2. Eric Cortes, "Auston Matthews Might Be the NHL's Great Brown Hope," http://www.latinorebels.com/2016/10/14/auston-matthews-might-be-the-nhls-great-brown-hope/.

3. Ken Woolums, "Auston Matthews Is a Rare Breed," http://www.espn.com/blog/statsinfo/post/_/id/120346/auston-matthews-is-a-rare-breed.

4. One Nacion, "Auston Matthews, Hockey's Newest Star, Has Latino Heritage," http://www.espn.com/blog/onenacion/post/_/id/5746/auston-mathews-hockeys-newest-star-has-latino-heritage.

5. Juan Tornoe, "Hispanic Trending: Documenting Latinos' Imprint in America," http://www.hispanictrending.net/sports/.

6. Juan Vidal, "Why Does American Sport Have a Latino Problem?" http://www.rollingstone.com/sports/news/why-does-american-sports-have-a-latino-problem-w440069.

7. Scott Harves, "Drive, Determination at Mendota High," http://www.espn.com/espn/story/_/id/10450321/from-farm-fields-football-fields-there-drive-determination-mendota-high.

8. Bryant-Jon Anteola, "Mendota High Football Coach Beto Mejia Pleads No Contest to Insurance Fraud," http://www.fresnobee.com/sports/high-school/prep-football/article53453955.html. For further information on the Mendota High School Aztecs 2016 season, see also: http://www.maxpreps.com/tournament/cqvwf5opEea-8KA2nzwbTA/football-fall-16/2016-cif-state-football-championship-bowl-games.htm; and http://www.maxpreps.com/high-schools/mendota-aztecs-(mendota,ca)/football/home.htm.

9. Juan Vidal, "Why Does American Sport Have a Latino Problem?"

CONTRIBUTOR BIOS

FREDERICK LUIS ALDAMA is University Distinguished Professor, Arts & Humanities Distinguished Professor of English, University Distinguished Scholar, and Alumni Distinguished Teacher at The Ohio State University. He is the 2018 recipient of the Rodica C. Botoman Award for Distinguished Teaching and Mentoring and the Susan M. Hartmann Mentoring and Leadership Award. He is the award-winning author, co-author, and editor of 39 books. In 2018, *Latinx Superheroes in Mainstream Comics* won the International Latino Book Award and the Eisner Award for Best Scholarly Work. He is editor and coeditor of eight academic press book series as well as editor of Latinographix, a trade-press series that publishes Latinx graphic fiction and nonfiction. He is creator of the first documentary on the history of Latinx superheroes in comics (Amazon Prime) and co-founder and director of SŌL-CON: Brown & Black Comix Expo. He is founder and director of the Obama White House award-winning LASER: Latinx Space for Enrichment & Research as well as founder and co-director of the Humanities & Cognitive Sciences High School Summer Institute. He has a joint appointment in Spanish & Portuguese as well as faculty affiliation in Film Studies and the Center for Cognitive and Brain Sciences. His children's book, *The Adventures of Chupacabra Charlie*, will be published by OSU Press in January 2020. For more on Aldama visit: www.professorlatinx.com

LUIS ALVAREZ is Associate Professor of History, Director of the Institute of Arts and Humanities, and Director of the Chicanx Latinx Arts and Humanities Program at University of California, San Diego. He is the author of *The Power of the Zoot: Youth Culture and Resistance during World War* II (University of California Press, American Crossroads Series) and co-editor of *Another University is Possible* (University Readers Press). He is currently at work on two books: *From Civil Rights to Global Justice: Pop*

Culture and the Politics of the Possible, an investigation of pop culture and social movements in the Americas since World War II, and *Border Pitch: A History of the U.S.-Mexico Soccer Rivalry*. His work as an advocate for the arts and humanities includes oversight of 14 different undergraduate programs and research centers; partnerships with museums, libraries, and community organizations across San Diego; and a deep belief that the arts and humanities equip us all with the tools, imagination, and empathy to build a better world.

BEN CHAPPELL is an Associate Professor of American Studies at the University of Kansas and the author of *Lowrider Space: Aesthetics and Politics of Mexican American Custom Cars* (University of Texas Press, 2012). The work on Mexican American fastpitch softball is based on field research he has conducted at annual tournaments in communities between Kansas City and Houston since 2011. This fieldwork is the basis of a forthcoming book. He was part of a team of co-authors to publish the photo-history *Mexican American Baseball in Kansas City* with Arcadia Press (2018). In addition, he has published numerous papers on lowrider car culture, ethnography, and cultural theory, including a contribution to the *Routledge Companion to Latina/o Popular Culture*. An anthropologist by training, he founded the Ethnography Caucus of the American Studies Association and continues to serve as its convener. In public-facing work, he has offered consultation on exhibitions for Kansas Humanities, the Kauffman Museum, the Kansas City Museum, the Chicago Urban Art Society, the Bob Bullock Texas State History Museum, and the Smithsonian Institution. He has served as a Fulbright Guest Professor of American Studies at the University of Regensburg in Germany and has presented the softball research around the United States and in three other countries. In recognition of his efforts to bring academic attention to Mexican American fastpitch, he was presented a sportsmanship award by the Austin Castro Concrete Jokers softball club.

JUAN DAVID CORONADO is an assistant professor of history at Central Connecticut State University. Coronado's research interests include the Mexican American military experience, Chicana/o history, oral history public history, and Latina/o history with an emphasis on class and gender. His recent book, *"I'm Not Gonna Die in this Damn Place": Manliness, Identity, and Survival of the Mexican American Vietnam Prisoner of War* (2018), lies at the intersection of Mexican American, military, oral and

US history while also furthering dialogue on gender. At JSRI, Coronado serves as oral historian in the Oral History of Latinos in Michigan project. Juan David is a native of the Río Grande Valley in South Texas where has dedicated time and efforts to preserve local and public history that has often been omitted by traditional works. Coronado also serves as Co-President of the Southwest Oral History Association.

PAUL CUADROS is an award-winning investigative reporter and author whose work has appeared in the *New York Times*, *The Huffington Post*, *Time* magazine, Salon.com, *The Chicago Reporter*, the Center for Public Integrity, and other national publications. In 1999, Cuadros won a fellowship with the Alicia Patterson Foundation, sponsored by New York Newsday, to report on emerging Latinx communities in rural poultry-processing towns in the South. The Alicia Patterson Fellowship is considered one of the most prestigious fellowships in journalism. The culmination of his reporting was his book, *A Home on the Field, How One Championship Team Inspires Hope for the Revival of Small Town America* (HarperCollins), which tells the story of an all-Latinx high school boys' soccer team as they struggle to find a new home in Siler City, North Carolina. *A Home on the Field* has been selected as summer reading at five universities. In 2014, the television documentary series *Los Jets*, based on his book and produced by Jennifer Lopez, premiered on cable television starring Cuadros. It has since been picked up at Hulu and TubiTV streaming services. Cuadros is an associate professor in the School of Media and Journalism at the University of North Carolina-Chapel Hill. He is also one of the founders of UNC's Carolina Latinx Center. Cuadros continues to write about immigration and is currently working on another book about the Latinx community in the American South.

ARNOLDO DE LEÓN taught at Angelo State University in San Angelo, Texas, for forty-two years. During his tenure at ASU, he authored or co-authored several books, edited or co-edited many collections of essays, and reviewed numerous books. He is most recognized for his classic study *They Called Them Greasers: Anglo Attitudes toward Mexicans in Texas, 1821–1900* (Austin: University of Texas Press, 1983). He retired from teaching in 2015 and holds the title of Distinguished Professor of History Emeritus.

IGNACIO M. GARCÍA is the Lemuel Hardison Redd Professor of Western

& Latino History at Brigham Young University. He is the author of seven books, including *When Mexicans Could Play Ball*, on which his chapter in the current book is based.

CHRISTOPHER GONZÁLEZ is an associate professor of English and director of the Latinx Cultural Center at Utah State University in Logan, Utah. He has published on twenty-first century Latinx literature, film, television, comics, sports, and narrative theory. He is the author of *Reading Junot Díaz* (2015) and *Permissible Narratives: The Promise of Latino/a Literature* (2017), which was awarded Honorable Mention for the 2019 Perkins Prize for the most significant contribution to the study of narrative.

ANDREW T. HARRIS received his BA (History) and MS (Interdisciplinary, focusing on Business, Museum Science, and History) from Texas Tech University. Harris continues to study the history of motor sports and its impact on minorities. Over the past decade, Harris has also studied the mergers and acquisitions among the different automotive manufacturers in a global context. His website, Automotivefamilytree.com, displays all the ownership among different automotive manufacturers, along with their joint ventures, and is used by some of the leading automotive manufacturers and automotive suppliers throughout the world. A leading automotive supplier invited Harris to León, Mexico, to speak about the current affairs of ownerships and joint ventures among the major automotive manufacturers at the Vicente Fox Center of Studies, Library and Museum.

JORGE IBER was born in Havana, Cuba, and raised in the Little Havana neighborhood of Miami, Florida. He taught in the public schools of Miami-Dade County for five years before pursuing a PhD at the University of Utah. He is the author, co-author, editor, or co-editor of 14 books and currently serves as Associate Dean in the Student Division of the College of Arts and Sciences and Professor of History at Texas Tech University in Lubbock. He has been at the institution for 22 years.

JOHN MCKIERNAN-GONZÁLEZ is the Director of the Center for the Study of the Southwest, the Jerome and Catherine Supple Professor of Southwestern Studies, and an Associate Professor of History at Texas State University. His first book, *Fevered Measures: Public Health and Race at the Texas–Mexico Border, 1848–1942* (Duke University Press, 2012), treats the multi-ethnic making of a US medical border in the Mexico-Texas borderlands. He co-edited the volume *Precarious Prescriptions: Contested Histories of Race and Health in North America* (University of Minnesota, 2013) which examines the contradictions and complexities tying medical history and communities of color together. His broad takes on Latina/os in US medical history can be found in *American Latinos in the Making of the United States* and in *Keywords in Latina/o Studies* (New York University Press, 2017). His next project, *Working Conditions: Medical Authority and Latino Civil Rights*, tracks the changing place of medicine in Latina/o/x struggles for equality. Born in the US, he grew up in Colombia, Mexico, and the US south and brings a migrant eye and experience to his projects in public history, medical history, and Latino studies.

ALBERTO RODRIGUEZ currently is an Associate Professor of History and managing editor of *The Journal of South Texas History* at Texas A&M University–Kingsville. Rodriguez has published *Mexican American Baseball in the Alamo Region* (Charleston: Arcadia Publishing, 2015), "Ponte el Guante! Baseball on the US/Mexican Border: The Game and Community Building, 1920s–1970s" in *The Journal of the West* (Fall 2015), "Spanish Southern States Recording Expedition" with Rene Torres in *Journal of Texas Music History* (Fall 2016), and "Africana Aesthetics: Creating a Critical Black Narrative from Photographs in South Texas" in *Africana Theory, Policy, and Leadership: A Social Science Analysis* edited by James L. Conyers Jr. (Transaction Publishers: 2016). His upcoming projects, *Urban Borderlands: Anglos, Mexicans, and African Americans in South Texas 1929–1964* and *Rancho La Union: A Transnational History of the Borderlands* are comparative multiethnic analyses of the Lower Rio Grande Valley, focusing on race relations in American and borderland society with a specialty in Mexican American and African American encounters. Rodriguez holds a PhD from the University of Houston in 20th Century American History with a minor in Women Studies and teaches courses on Latina/o History, Mexican American History, Chicana/o History, Texas History, and African American History.

GREGORY SELBER is a professor of journalism at University of Texas Rio Grande Valley in Edinburg where he has taught since 2001. He is the author of four books on sports in the Rio Grande Valley and has contributed chapters to three books on the NFL published by the Pro Football Researchers Association. Selber is a sportswriter and broadcaster with

35 years of professional experience and who was named the Putt Powell Texas Sports Writer of the Year in 2011. He continues to write and take pictures at Valley sporting events for the *Edinburg Review* newspaper.

ROBERTO SIRVENT is Professor of Political and Social Ethics at Hope International University in Fullerton, California. He also teaches regularly at Claremont School of Theology and Yale University's Summer Bioethics Institute. Sirvent earned an MA from Johns Hopkins University, a JD from the University of Maryland School of Law, and a PhD from the London School of Theology in the UK. He is co-author (with Danny Haiphong) of the new book, *American Exceptionalism and American Innocence: A People's History of Fake News—From the Revolutionary War to the War on Terror*. Roberto edits the *Black Agenda Report* Book Forum and has held appointments as a Visiting Scholar at Yale University, Princeton Theological Seminary, and the University of Copenhagen.

INDEX